Reference and Identity in Jewish, Christian, and Muslim Scriptures

Philosophy of Language: Connections and Perspectives

Series Editors: Margaret Cameron, Lenny Clapp, and Robert Stainton

Advisory Board: Axel Barceló (Instituto de Investigaciones Filosóficas), Chen Bo (Peking University), Robyn Carston (University College London), Leo Cheung (Chinese University of Hong Kong), Eduardo García (Instituto de Investigaciones Filosóficas), Sandy Goldberg (Northwestern University), Robin Jeshion (University of Southern California), Ernie Lepore (Rutgers University), Catrina Dutilh Novaes (Vrije University Amsterdam), Eleonora Orlando (University of Buenos Aires), Claude Panaccio (University of Quebec at Montreal), Bernhard Weiss (University of Cape Town), and Jack Zupko (University of Alberta)

Philosophy of Language: Connections and Perspectives comprises monographs and edited collections that explore connections between the philosophy of language and other academic disciplines, or that approach the core topics of philosophy of language in the Anglo-American analytic tradition from alternative perspectives. The philosophy of language, particularly as practiced in the Anglo-American tradition of analytic philosophy, has established itself as a thriving academic discipline. Because of the centrality of language to the human experience, there are myriad connections between the core topics addressed by philosophers of language and other academic disciplines. The number of researchers who are exploring these connections is growing, but there has not been a corresponding increase in the venues for publication of this research. The central purpose and motivation for this series is to address this shortcoming.

Titles in the Series
Reference and Identity in Jewish, Christian, and Muslim Scriptures: The Same God?
 by D. E. Buckner

Reference and Identity in Jewish, Christian, and Muslim Scriptures

The Same God?

D. E. Buckner

LEXINGTON BOOKS
Lanham • Boulder • New York • London

Published by Lexington Books
An imprint of The Rowman & Littlefield Publishing Group, Inc.
4501 Forbes Boulevard, Suite 200, Lanham, Maryland 20706
www.rowman.com

6 Tinworth Street, London SE11 5AL, United Kingdom

Copyright © 2020 The Rowman & Littlefield Publishing Group, Inc.

All rights reserved. No part of this book may be reproduced in any form or by any electronic or mechanical means, including information storage and retrieval systems, without written permission from the publisher, except by a reviewer who may quote passages in a review.

British Library Cataloguing in Publication Information Available

Library of Congress Cataloging-in-Publication Data Available

ISBN 978-1-4985-8741-9 (cloth)
ISBN 978-1-4985-8743-3 (pbk)
ISBN 978-1-4985-8742-6 (electronic)

Contents

Preface   vii

Introduction   xi

1	Reference Statements	1
2	Rules for Reference	19
3	Story-Relative Reference	39
4	Mentioning	59
5	Identification within History	77
6	Reference and Identity	97
7	Existence	117
8	The God of the Philosophers	131
9	Identification in the Present	149
10	Revelation	171
11	Intentionality	193

Bibliography   207

Index   221

About the Author   227

Preface

Many books, often philosophy books, are a long time in the writing. As an undergraduate in 1974, I was surprised to learn that my tutor, the late Peter Alexander, had been working on his book on Locke for twelve years. The book was published in 1985, twenty-three years after its conception.[1] But this book has been a *very* long time in the writing. It began with an idea in 1984 that I discussed in a rather bad paper I presented at one of the legendary seminars in room K, chaired by the late Christopher Williams at Bristol University. I write this preface in 2019, exactly thirty-five years and nearly half a lifetime later.

The idea was about what philosophers call reference statements, namely statements that (apparently) say of some *word*, let's say the name "Boris," that it refers to some *person*, namely Boris himself. In the 1980s, my example would have been "Margaret" referring to Margaret Thatcher, in the 1990s, "Major" referring to John Major, the 2000s, "Blair" referring to Tony Blair, and so on. The number of British prime ministers testifies to the lengthy gestation of this book.

It had struck me that while a reference statement appears to express a relation between a word and a thing, the appearance is misleading. Perhaps a reference statement is true not because of a word-world relation between language and reality, as the grammar suggests, but an *intralinguistic* or word-word relation. Do not misunderstand: I do not mean that the word "Boris" refers to the word "Boris." On the contrary, what "Boris" refers to is not the word "Boris," but Boris the man. The insight was that what makes the reference statement

"Boris" refers to Boris

true is a relation between the term that is *mentioned*, namely the grammatical subject of the reference statement, the one enclosed in quotation marks, and the term that is *used*, namely, the grammatical accusative of the sentence, the one without quotation marks. The relation is intralinguistic, not a relation between a word and a person. If that sounds strange, you may enjoy this book.

The idea needed a lot of work. I left teaching and research in the late 1980s for a somewhat different career, but stuck at the idea of intralinguistic semantics in my spare time, producing over the years at least three versions of this book. None of them was quite right, and none of them touched on any biblical subject, until my old friend and sparring partner Bill Vallicella published "Do Christians and Muslims Worship the Same God?"[2] exactly four years ago as I write. (For complete disclosure, I must say that Vallicella, a philosophical realist, disagrees with practically everything I write, and endorses absolutely no part of the extreme anti-realist position of this book. He has always been supportive of my work, and strengthened it through his steady and inventive challenges, although he certainly disagrees, as he tells me, with the end result.)

While I had used scriptural texts as examples of reference before, the idea of basing a whole book on these examples had not occurred. But it seemed to me that these texts would be the right frame in which to place the intralinguistic picture of reference. The scriptures are a strong counterexample to contemporary theories of reference, which take demonstrative reference as the starting point for reference in general. Pharaoh's daughter finds a baby in the rushes, then later takes the baby to Pharaoh, pointing to it and saying, "I name this baby 'Moses.'" According to the standard theory, the demonstrative, "this baby" refers to Moses directly, and at the same time establishes a semantic relation between the proper name "Moses" and the baby referred to, a relation which is somehow preserved when the name is passed to other people, even when the baby is no longer present, and pure demonstrative reference is not available. The standard theory starts with demonstrative reference as the paradigm, and moves to non-demonstrative reference as a particular case. The idea advanced in this book, by contrast, is that we start with reference as we find it in the texts. The *people* are no longer before us, all we have now is the words, yet we understand the reference. We know that the second book of Exodus refers to Moses, but we have never been acquainted with Moses himself. Why can't reference start with reference within a text, and move to demonstrative reference as a particular case?

That is the idea of this book, and the book will speak for itself, but there is one confusion that has occurred to practically everyone who has reviewed it, so I shall give due warning at the outset. I say that the truth conditions of a reference statement are *intralinguistic*. I claim that what makes "'Frodo' refers to Frodo" true is the same *kind* of phenomenon that makes "'Donald

Trump' refers to Donald Trump" true, so reference is really not a relation between language and the world, but between language and language. Reference is a word-*word*, not word-*world* relation, as Brandom puts it. Then practically the same objection occurs to everyone at once: surely the name "Donald Trump" does refer to Trump, so the reference relation cannot be intralinguistic? I reply: yes, "Donald Trump" does indeed refer to Trump, because the reference statement "'Donald Trump' refers to Donald Trump" is true. But the relational nature of the statement does not prove the existence of a reference *relation*. My claim is not that the reference statement is false—for it is true—but I claim that what *makes* it true is not a relation between language and reality. You can object on various reasonable grounds that my claim about reference statements is wrong, ill-founded, poorly supported, and so forth, but it is not enough to object that some reference statement involving "Trump," or "Johnson," or "Merkel" is true, for I do not claim it is false. The question of what *makes* it true is the core question of this book.

Many people helped me in various ways. The late Jonathan Lowe pointed me to work on similar lines by Charles Chastain and Robert Brandom. Peter Geach told me I had stumbled upon a very deep problem, referring to a chapter in his *Mental Acts*, but gave no hint of a solution. Although Mark Sainsbury, while editor of *Mind*, turned down a paper of mine on the subject of fictional reference (also bad), he later followed my work with encouragement and support. It was he who suggested Lexington press.

My late parents were incredibly supportive, sometimes through the darkest of times. I am sad they did not live to see the project through. This book is dedicated to their memory. Thanks go to my long-suffering wife Fiona for putting up with the project for so long (thirty years, to be precise), and to my two children, who did not suffer so long but occasionally (only occasionally mind you) missed a bedtime story due to the siren call of the book. It was my daughter who suggested the example of the naked fugitive (chapter 3), the mystery man who fled from the arrest in Gethsemane without a stitch.

I thank the editors and staff at Lexington, particularly Jana Hodges-Kluck who had the vision to take on this project, and Lenny Clapp who with endless fortitude and patience saw through several versions of the manuscript with his sharp and perceptive comments, despite his initial (and so some extent continuing) suspicion of the core idea. I thank Magali Roques, who provided many helpful comments on early versions of the manuscript, and also David Brightly, who is not a philosopher but whose insightful comments added value in so many places. The customary rider applies.

Finally, I record a very special debt of gratitude to the late Michael Welbourne and the late Peter Alexander for persuading me to return to Bristol as a postgraduate in 1979.

D. E. Buckner, London, 2020

NOTES

1. *Ideas, Qualities and Corpuscles*, Cambridge: Cambridge University Press, 1985.
2. William F. Vallicella, "Do Christians and Muslims Worship the Same God?" *Typepad*, Tuesday, December 22, 2015, https://maverickphilosopher.typepad.com/maverick_philosopher/2015/12/do-christians-and-muslims-worship-the-same-god.html.

Introduction

HERESY OR IDOLATRY?

It is recent, yet it is also one of the oldest controversies in the troubled relationship between Christianity and Islam. In December 2015, Wheaton College professor Larycia Hawkins was suspended after pledging to wear a hijab during Advent in support of her Muslim neighbors, and after writing in a Facebook post that Muslims "like me, a Christian, are people of the book, and as Pope Francis stated last week, *we worship the same God.*" On December 22, the college stated that the suspension resulted "from theological convictions that seem inconsistent with Wheaton College's doctrinal convictions," suggesting the action was not due to wearing the hijab. Hawkins was asked to clarify certain "significant theological questions" such as how can Christians worship the same God if Muslims cannot affirm that "God the Father is indeed the Father of our Lord Jesus Christ." On February 6, 2016, the college announced that Hawkins would not be fired, but that she would voluntarily resign in order to close the situation, whereupon she found a new position at the University of Virginia.

The affair reignited a controversy that is as old as Christianity's first engagement with Islam. What do Christians and Muslims mean when they respectively utter the name "God"? Of course, a Muslim might not utter the English name "God," but the English is simply a translation from the name used in ancient Hebrew (*yhwh*)[1] or ancient Greek (*o theos*), and German and French Christians use the names "Gott" and "Dieu" for the same divine being. The question is: Who are they referring to? Are Christians and Muslims referring to the *same* divine being when they utter the name that corresponds to "God" in their own languages?

If the same, the situation is one of mutual charges of heresy. In his book *De Haeresibus*, probably written at Saint Sabas monastic community around 724, John of Damascus says that the Muslims call Christians *Hetaeriasts*, or "Associators," because Christians introduce an associate with God by declaring Christ to be the Son of *God* and *God*.[2] John replies, "you speak untruly when you call us Hetaeriasts; we retort by calling you Mutilators of *God*." On this account, Muslims and Christians accuse each other of being heretics, but this is only possible when both are referring to the *same* being. Neither would have accused the ancient Greeks of heresy for any of their beliefs about Zeus, for the ancient Greeks were idolators: worshippers of a false god. But when John says that Muslims are "mutilators of *God*," it is the Christian God he is referring to. Muslims, according to him, have false beliefs *about* the true God. Peter the Venerable (1092–1156) also saw Islam as a vile form of heresy.[3]

If, on the other hand, Christians and Muslims are referring to different supernatural beings, we have mutual charges of idolatry. In his *Refutatio Mohamedis* (c. 870 AD), a long and frequently abusive polemic about how the "camel driver" Muhammad deceived the Agarenes (Muslims) into worshipping a false god, an apostate demon, who had "appropriated the divine name," Niketas Byzantios accused Muslims of *idolatry*.

> Their god is the devil, who *imitates* God, although, fearing he fails in his purpose, he is cunningly silent about [his] proper name, that is notorious among all men, and rather brings before himself the name of the true God.[4]

Niketas argues on mainly philosophical and linguistic grounds, distinguishing between an empty name, which has no proper object, and a name which has been abstracted from its proper object and applied to something alien, neither of these being a true name, which signifies the true nature [*logos*] of its bearer, and which principally denotes the bearer.

> As the name of one thing [is applied] to the wrong thing, and as a bearer of one name [is applied] to the wrong name, that leads to error.[5]

According to Niketas, it follows from the semantic properties of the name "God" that Christians and Muslims do not worship the same God.

The disagreement is therefore not *just* about different and inconsistent belief systems. Everyone agrees that Christianity and Islam have considerable theological differences. Muslims do not believe in a Trinity ("Praise be to God who has never begotten a son").[6] Christians do believe in such a thing ("For there are three . . . the Father, the *Logos* and the Holy Spirit, and these three are one."[7] Muslims recognize the historical existence of Jesus, but do not believe he was crucified and rose from the dead, whereas belief in the resurrection is an article of faith for Christians. Everyone agrees that the two faiths are in disagreement about these beliefs; the problem is what the beliefs are *about*. When a Christian says "God is triune" and a Muslim says "Allah is not triune," do they *contradict* one another or not? John says they do, for they assert contradictory predicates of the same God. Niketas says they do not, for one asserts of the Christian God that he is triune, the other asserts of the nameless demon that he is not triune.

The difference between John and Niketas has striking parallels with the recent Hawkins controversy. To some, mostly fundamentalist Christians, it seemed obvious that a God who apparently rewards suicide bombers with a place in paradise can't be the God they worship. Others argued that the fundamental conceptions of the deity are too different. The Revd. Dr. Magdy Gendy, lately of the Evangelical Theological Seminary in Cairo, said, "I worship the triune God. The God *they* worship is none of my business," when he was interviewed by *Christianity Today*.[8] This is essentially Niketas's position.

By contrast, the academic philosophers who entered the debate mostly took the side of John of Damascus. Edward Feser argued that we cannot understand the deep theological differences unless we understand "the true nature of Islam as a kind of 'heresy', a transformation of Christianity rather than an entirely novel religion."[9] Other analytic theologians, such as Francis Beckwith and Dale Tuggy, also argued that Christians and Muslims do, in fact, worship the same God. Baylor philosophy professor Francis Beckwith held that incomplete knowledge or a false belief about God doesn't mean Muslims are worshipping a different being. Otherwise they couldn't have false beliefs *about* God. Yale theologian Miroslav Volf thought that "Muslims and Christians who embrace the normative traditions of their faith refer to the same object, to the same Being, when they pray, when they worship, when they talk about God. The referent is the same. The *description* of God is partly different."[10]

Arizona philosopher William F. Vallicella took a different line, which is the starting point for this book. He argued, against Beckwith and Tuggy, that it is not at all obvious which of the following views is correct.

View 1: Christian and Muslim can worship the same God, even though one of them must have a false belief *about*[11] God, whether it be the belief that God is non-triune or the belief that God is triune.

View 2: Christian and Muslim must worship different Gods precisely because they have mutually exclusive conceptions of God. So it is not that one of them has a false belief about the one God they both worship; it is rather that one of them does not worship the true God at all.[12]

The question of which view is correct requires deep investigation into the philosophy of language, Vallicella argued, and it requires an explanation of how *reference* is achieved. How do linguistic expressions attach or apply to extralinguistic entities? How do words grab onto the world? What makes our utterance of "Socrates" signify Socrates rather than someone or something else? What makes my use of "God" (i) have a referent at all and (ii) have the precise referent it has?

The question also exposes a fault line running through the whole of contemporary analytic philosophy, indeed it is older than that. We may hold with Frege, Russell, Searle, and many others that reference is routed through, and determined by, some sort of *descriptive sense*, whereby a singular term identifies or picks out an external object by means of an associated uniquely applying description. If this is how reference operates, "God" refers to whatever entity, if any, that satisfies the description, and hence there are different descriptive senses attaching to the Muslim and Christian conceptions of God.

D1: "the unique x such that x is omnipotent, omniscient, omnibenevolent, created the world ex nihilo and is *non-triune*";

D2: "the unique x such that x is omnipotent, omniscient, omnibenevolent, created the world ex nihilo, and is *triune*."

Clearly no one entity can satisfy both D1 and D2. Although the descriptions overlap, nothing can be both non-triune and triune, hence if reference is determined by description, the Christian and the Muslim cannot be referring to the same being.

Alternatively, we may hold, with John Stuart Mill, and contemporary philosophers of language like Nathan Salmon, that the proper name like "God" refers directly, with no intermediary descriptive content. Mill compared a proper name to a chalk mark on a door, a symbol assigned to the object itself, so that we may understand which thing is spoken of. This will not work if the object is not revealed to us, but Kripke and others have argued that the use of a name can be causally connected to its bearer, so that (for example) the Christian's use of "God" can be traced back though a long causal chain to an initial baptism, as it were, of God by, say, Moses on Mount Sinai. If so, the question of whether Muslims and Christians refer to the same God depends on the existence of the right causal connection, rather than any descriptive content. Anglican bishop Mouneer Hanna Anis of Egypt said, "For us as Christians, and only by his grace, God has *revealed* himself in the person of his son Jesus Christ, whom Muslims do not *know* in this way."[13] If he is right, then Christians and Muslims do not refer to the same being by the names "God" and "Allah," respectively, but not because of the different descriptions they associate with God. Christian Trinitarians and Unitarians have fundamentally different conceptions of the nature of God, yet the causal connection determining their use of the name "God" is the same.

At the time of writing, the debate between descriptive and direct reference theories of proper names is a live one (with direct reference being something like the "orthodox" view). Its immediate roots are in the early twentieth century, but it is older, and it is closely related to the problem of individuation, fiercely disputed in the Middle Ages. The medieval "scholastic" philosophers took as their starting point Porphyry's hierarchical classification of genera and species from the most general genus down to the most specific species and individuals. Thus, Socrates is a living being, an animal, a rational animal, and so on. But what particular feature makes him *Socrates*, and not some other person? Porphyry thought that an individual (ἄτομα) consists of properties (ἰδιοτήτων) "of which the combination will never be the same in any other, for the properties of Socrates can never be the same in any other particular persons."[14] Yet, as Peter Abelard (1079–1142) argued,[15] the accidental properties connected with some description can hardly enter into the imposition of the signification of the name, or the name would change its meaning through time. "Socrates was called Socrates before he became a musician, and will be so called after he ceases to be the son of Sophroniscus [i.e., after Sophroniscus dies]."[16] The philosopher theologian John Duns Scotus (c.1265–1308) developed a complex theory of an *individuating difference*, or "thisness," a feature that makes a person *that* person, and no other. Few philosophers have followed him, but the problem of individuation remains a problem, and it is clearly related to that of reference to individuals. Does the name "Socrates" mean "curly-headed white man, skilled in music and philosophy, son of Sophroniscus"? Or does it signify a purely, that is, non-complex, individuating feature that distinguishes him from all others? It is one of the oldest and most intractable problems in philosophy.

My purpose in this book is to develop a theory of reference that will answer the question of whether the Jewish, Christian, and Muslim scriptures refer to the same God, moreover answer it within a semantic framework that is equally acceptable to both atheists and fideists.[17] It is primarily a work in the core topics of philosophical logic, namely reference, identity, truth, and existence. The main thesis is that all reference is *story-relative*. We cannot tell which historical individual a person is talking or writing about or addressing in prayer without familiarity with the narrative (oral or written), which introduces that individual to us. Thus, we cannot understand reference to God, nor to his prophets, nor to any other character mentioned in the Jewish, Christian, or Muslim scriptures, without reference to those very scriptures. In this context, we must understand God as the person who "walked in the garden in the cool of the day" (Gen. 3:8), and who is continuously referred to in the books of the Old and New Testament, as well as (I argue) the Quran. Singular reference and singular *conception* is empty outside such a context.

No substantive original thesis in biblical hermeneutics or theology is intended, although I will try to use the most recent scholarly views in both topics, and clearly there will be *some* theological implications of what is primarily a philosophical thesis. For example, the "classical" conception of God, namely as uncaused, uncreated, unchanging, and transcendent creator of the universe, can clearly be arrived at by some process of natural reason, unaided by revelation (except the "revelation" of pure reason), and independently of scriptural authority. But if we cannot understand the name "God" without reference to biblical texts, reason on its own cannot reveal God to us.

The method will be, as far as possible, to avoid the technical apparatus and terminology of modern mathematical logic. Technical concepts (singular reference, identity, subject and predicate, proposition, and so on) are unavoidable, but will be presented in the context of biblical narrative in a way that clearly illustrates the concepts, showing rather than explicitly describing them. No position on the existence or non-existence of God, or of his nature, or of the truth or falsity of any of the three scriptures, is intended, nor should any be understood.

NOTES

1. Strictly speaking, the English expression "God" is almost never used to translate the tetragrammaton. It translates *elohim*, a common noun meaning "god" or "gods." "Y hw h" is a proper name that is used much less frequently. The only instances in which "Y hw h" is translated as "God" are passages containing the combination of words "adonai Y hw h," meaning "the lord Y hw h," occurs, conventionally translated as "the lord GOD," the capitals corresponding to the tetragrammaton in the Hebrew text.

2. John of Damascus, Migne, *Patrologia Graeca*, vol. 94, 767.

3. Translated Resnick, 2016.

4. Niketas Byzantios (Niketas of Byzantium), *Confutatio dogmatum Mahomedis*, in Migne, *Patrologia Graeca*, vol. 105, 792, my emphasis.

5. Ibid., 793.

6. *Quran* 17:111.

7. 1 John 5:7.

8. Jayson Casper, "What Arab Christians Think of Wheaton-Hawkins 'Same God' Debate: Controversy echoes what Mideast Christians have wrestled with for centuries," *Christianity Today*, January 13, 2016, my emphasis.

9. Edward Feser, "Liberalism and Islam," 2016, http://edwardfeser.blogspot.co.uk/2016/01/liberalism-and-islam.html.

10. Bob Smietana, "Wheaton College Suspends Hijab-Wearing Professor after 'Same God' Comment," *Christianity Today*, December 15, 2015.

11. My emphasis.

12. William F. Vallicella, "Do Christians and Muslims Worship the Same God?" *Typepad*, December 22, 2015, https://maverickphilosopher.typepad.com/maverick_philosopher/2015/12/do-christians-and-muslims-worship-the-same-god.html.

13. Jayson Casper, *Christianity Today*, January 13, 2016, my emphasis.

14. Porphyry, *Isagoge*, in Busse 1887, 7, trans. Owen, O.F., *The Organon, or Logical Treatises of Aristotle*, 617.

15. Peter Abelard, *Dialectica*, in De 569 (f. 197r–v), see also Ashworth, "Medieval theories of singular terms."

16. Ibid., *Antequam musicus esset, Socrates dictus est, vel postquam filius Sophronisci non erit, Socrates dicetur.*

17. Which would be impossible, for instance, if the semantic theory involved Russellian propositions, supposedly Platonic entities expressed by sentences which "entrap" their components. If the sentence "God is Allah" expressed such a proposition, God (and Allah) would be such an entrapped component. Alston (*Perceiving God: The Epistemology of Religious Experience*, 10) faces a similar difficulty. His book is designed for a general audience, so he avoids terms like "awareness of God," which suggest that God exists, preferring to speak of experiences that are "taken by the subject to be an awareness of God." But this still requires using the term "God," and so requires a semantic theory, acceptable to believers and non-believers alike, that explains the term "God."

Chapter 1

Reference Statements

I have little to say about prayer or worship. The question of this book is about *reference*. If the name "Allah" in the Quran refers to what "The Lord" refers to in the New Testament or to what "YHWH" refers to in the Hebrew Bible, then clearly Jews, Christians, and Muslims are referring to the same god, whatever language they speak. If praying to is a form of address using a name, and if the name refers to the same being, then Jews, Christians, and Muslims are *praying* to the same god.[1] But many deny this, particularly when it comes to the possible identity of God and Allah.

Nor am I *primarily* concerned with the question of the existence of the individuals mentioned in the Bible, including that of the divine being himself. There is independent contemporary evidence for the existence of some of the individuals mentioned in the New Testament, including Herod Archelaus and Herod the Great (whose names are on coins), Pontius Pilate (referenced as "prefect of Judea" on a limestone inscription discovered in 1961), and Quirinius (mentioned on a tomb inscription), but this book is not primarily about the historical truth of the Bible, nor the existence of any or all of the biblical characters. It is about how we are able to *refer to* or *identify* them. If reference is a relation of some kind between language and reality, what is the nature of that relation? How can there be such a relation if some of the characters do not even exist? How is reference successful, given our limited information about the individuals referred to? In particular, how can we succeed in referring to the same person or being, even when we do not know that we are doing so? How can the writers of the New Testament refer to people in the Hebrew Bible, such as Isaiah and Moses? How can the Quran refer to the same people? What being are they talking about when they use the proper names "God," "יְהוָה" or "الله"?

1

The central puzzle is what makes the following reference statement true (or false).

The second word of the Quran refers to God.

If we can answer this, we can answer the question of whether Jews, Christians, and Muslims worship the same God. The reference statement contains a mention*ing* term ("second word of the Quran"), the verb phrase "refers to," and the referring term "God," as well as implying the existence of a mention*ed* term that is not in the statement itself, namely the second word of the Quran, the word we translate as "Allah" or "God," transliterated as "al-lāhi."[2] Clearly the statement is true when the mentioned term (the second word of the Quran) *co*-refers with the referring term ("God"). If the second word of the Quran refers to some divine being X, and if "God" in the aforementioned statement also refers to X, the identity statement "God is Allah" is true.[3]

The thesis of this book is that such co-reference is not an extralinguistic relation between the two terms and an external, extralinguistic object (God), but rather an intralinguistic semantic relation between the terms themselves. Thus, it is true even for atheists that "God" refers to God, and that Jews, Christians, and atheists *worship* the same God. I call this the *intralinguistic thesis*. It follows that a reference statement is illusory: its linguistic form purports to express a relation between a mentioned term and an object, but instead is verified by a relation between the mentioned term and the referring term. In this chapter, I shall (i) outline the standard theory of reference which is the main target of this book; (ii) outline some of the problems with the standard theory; (iii) introduce the key points of my non-standard *intralinguistic* theory of reference; and (iv) set out how the book is organized.

THE STANDARD THEORY OF REFERENCE

"Reference" has many senses, and a common understanding of the word derives from an early mistranslation of the Frege's term *Bedeutung*.[4] A common and pre-theoretical definition is that a term *refers* when it signifies *which* thing we are talking about in making a statement.[5] "Reference" I shall characterize as what happens when we refer, and I shall use the terms "identification" and "designation" as synonymous for the most part with "reference." Reference is what singular or definite terms do, and what common or indefinite terms don't. The name "Socrates" in "Socrates is running" tells us which person is said to be running, or (in philosophical jargon) tells us which individual *satisfies the predicate* "is running." Singular terms contrast with common terms, which do not specify who satisfies the predicate. "Some philosopher is running" is true if at least one of Socrates, or Plato, Aristotle, and so on is running, no matter which one. Thus, "some philosopher" does not refer. Or suppose it did, for example, to Socrates. Then, "it is not the case that some philosopher is running" would be true when Socrates is not running, even if it is the case that some other philosopher, say Plato, is running, which is absurd.

The *standard* theory of reference, sometimes called "direct reference," is primarily a theory about proper names. It involves two assumptions. The first is the *nondescription* assumption, that a proper name has no connotation or descriptive sense that determines its reference. As Abelard argued, the accidental properties connected with some description can hardly enter into the imposition of the signification of the name, or the name would change its meaning through time. "Socrates was called Socrates before he became a musician, and will be so called after he ceases to be the son of Sophroniscus [i.e., after Sophroniscus dies]."[6] More recently, Kripke has said much about this. The second assumption is what Devitt calls the *semantic presupposition*[7] that there are no other possible candidates for a name's meaning other than a descriptive meaning, or the bearer of the name itself. If both assumptions are correct, the meaning of a proper name is none other than the bearer itself, that is, the name is merely a tag or label for its bearer, and has no other significance.

These two assumptions (nondescription and semantic presupposition) are of crucial importance to the theoretical framework of classical (i.e., the twentieth century) semantics, entailing as they do that sentences with empty names cannot express propositions. In that framework, the truth conditions or *proposition* (or *information content*) expressed by a sentence, relative to a context, are compositionally determined by the semantic values or *referents* of the terms in the sentence.[8] The structure and components of the proposition mirror the structure and components of the sentence expressing the proposition. To understand a sentence we have to grasp its truth conditions: the way the world has to be if the sentence is true, but the truth conditions are determined by the *referents* of the words in the sentence, including the referent of any proper name. Hence, we cannot understand what is expressed by the sentence unless the words, including any proper names, have a referent. As Evans, in his exposition of Frege, says:

> The Proper Name "John" has the role of introducing an *object*, which is to be the argument to the function introduced by the concept-expression "ξ is wise"—a function which maps all and only wise objects to the value True. Thereby, and only thereby, is the sentence determined as having a truth-value, and, therefore, as having the significance of a complete sentence—something capable of being used alone to make an assertion.[9]

When a sentence contains an empty name, the name cannot introduce an object as argument to the function, the function has no value, that is, no truth value, and the sentence cannot express a thought or a proposition. Evans again, quoting Frege:

> The sentence "Leo Sachse is a man" is the expression of a thought [*Ausdruck eines Gedankens*] only if "Leo Sachse" designates [*bezeichnet*] something.[10]

The standard theory also entails that the existence of a bearer is presupposed, rather than asserted, by a subject-predicate sentence containing a proper name. As Frege argues, the negation of "Kepler died in misery" is not "Kepler did not die in misery, or the name 'Kepler' has no significance,"[11] that is, "Kepler died in misery" is not a conjunction of the statements that "Kepler" is significant and that Kepler died in misery.[12] According to the standard theory, it is presupposed rather than asserted that that the name "Kepler" is significant, hence (because the name signifies the bearer) it must be presupposed that the bearer exists.

A further corollary of the standard theory is that there can be only one reason for a proper name sentence being false, namely that the predicate does not apply to the subject. Hence, on that theory, there can be only one form of negation for proper name subject-predicate sentences, namely wide scope or sentential negation. If "Moses was a prophet" is false, it is because Moses existed but was not a prophet. This corollary is reflected in the standard notation of the predicate calculus: the negation "Fa" is "~Fa." On the standard theory, proper names are not descriptive, or properly speaking, are not *predicable*, a predicable being an expression that yields a proposition *about* something if we attach it to an expression, that is, a singular term, which *stands for*, that is, designates or refers to, what we are forming the proposition *about*.[13] As Geach says:

> To Frege we owe it that modern logicians almost universally accept an absolute category-difference between names and predicables; this comes out graphically in the choice of letters from different founts of type for the schematic letters of variables answering to these two categories.[14]

A predicable can be empty if nothing has the property it expresses, for example," round square." Frege explains that a common name like "planet" has no direct relation to the Earth. You can understand the concept it signifies without anything falling under the concept, for a predicable is not intrinsically about any object. "If I utter a sentence with the grammatical subject 'all men,' I do not wish to say something *about* some Central African chief wholly unknown to me." But a proper name cannot be empty. "A proper name that designates nothing is illegitimate (*unberechtigt*)."[15]

Thus, on the standard theory, reference is a relation between a linguistic expression, such as a proper name, and an extralinguistic item, the object that an author (or speaker) uses the expression to write (or talk) about, and so is an extralinguistic or word-world relation.[16] The co-reference between the names "God" in the first line of the Quran, and in "The second word of the Quran refers to *God*," is explained by means of an external relation to a third item, namely God himself. We understand that the first token signifies God, that the second token signifies him also, and thereby understand that the two tokens co-refer. The co-reference takes place only because the tokens both "hit" the same object in external reality. According to the standard theory, "reference" is primary, co-reference is secondary.

The standard theory of reference, which begins with Frege,[17] contrasts with the traditional "Aristotelian" semantics, which it supplanted at the end of the nineteenth century. In Aristotelian semantics, there is also a distinction between proper names and common terms. At the beginning of chapter 7 of the *Perihermenias*, Aristotle says that some "things," that is, terms, are universal, others singular. He has in mind the distinction between a common term ("man") and a proper name ("Callias"). A universal or common term is that which *by nature* can be predicated of (κατηγορεῖσθαι) different individuals, such as Socrates and Callias.[18] A proper name is what can be predicated of only one individual. Following Aristotle, scholastic logicians like Peter of Spain claimed that a singular term is suited by nature (*aptus natus*) to be predicated of (i.e., to denote) one thing only.[19] His contemporary William of Sherwood said that "Socrates" is predicable of one person only "with respect to the form signified by the name *Socrates*."[20]

However, in Aristotelian semantics, unlike standard semantics, there is no fundamental distinction between names and predicables. Both proper and common names lie in the same sort of relation to an object, a relation which the medieval semanticists called *suppositio*. But a proper name is proper to just one object, so proper name propositions are universal as well as existential. "Socrates is a philosopher" states that at least one person is (identical with) Socrates, and that every such person is a philosopher. Hence, just as a common name like "planet" can be empty if there are no planets, so a proper name can be empty yet function perfectly well in a proposition. "Bilbo Baggins is a hobbit" states that at least one person is (identical with) Bilbo, and that every such person is a philosopher and so, while it states something perfectly coherent, is false. On the Aristotelian theory of the proposition,[21] a subject-predicate sentence containing a proper name asserts rather than presupposes the existence of the proper name's bearer, and asserts (or denies) that the predicate applies to it. Thus, there are two causes of the sentence being false: (i) the predicate does not apply to the bearer (or does apply, if the sentence is negative), (ii) there is no bearer at all. There are also two forms of negative: wide scope, where the negation applies across the whole sentence, and narrow scope where the negation applies to the predicate only.

Thus, in Aristotelian semantics, sentences with empty names are false, rather than lacking a truth value.

In summary, a singular term signifies by telling us *which* individual satisfies the predicate of a proposition. In the proposition,[22] "Moses is a prophet," the proper name "Moses" tells us which object is said to be a prophet, or which individual satisfies the predicate "is a prophet." Any theory of reference needs to explain how this is possible. According to the standard theory, this is achieved by means of a semantic relation between the term and the object, that is, a semantic relation between a linguistic item, a word such as "Moses," and an extralinguistic item, namely Moses himself. The standard theory is the target of this book.

PROBLEMS WITH THE STANDARD THEORY

There are a number of well-known problems with the standard theory, and an extensive literature has been devoted to engaging with them. I summarize the main difficulties as follows.

(1) The theory leads to the absurdity that objects, including large planetary masses, are actually a part of our thought. We use language to signify our thoughts, with the aim that others can understand or grasp what we have said. What is signified is what is understood, as the medieval philosophers put it,[23] and what is understood is the thought the speaker has expressed. But if a proper name signifies its bearer, the bearer must somehow be a part of the thought expressed. This is absurd. I can express the thought that Jupiter is a planet, but how can Jupiter, with its massive gravitational field and poisonous atmosphere, be literally a part of my thought?[24]

(2) The theory provides no coherent explanation of how we establish a connection between names and their bearers. Mill says (*A System of Logic*, I. ii. 5, see also I. v. 2.) that they are simply marks for objects, giving the example of a chalk mark upon a door, but, perhaps seeing how this fails to explain how a proper name can be a mark of something that is not in front of us, or which has long since ceased to exist, he says that this is by analogy only, and that the mark is upon our *idea* of the object. "A proper name is but an *unmeaning* mark which we connect in our minds with the *idea* of the object, in order that whenever the mark meets our eyes or occurs to our thoughts, we may think of that object" (my emphasis). He does not explain how a mark can be meaningless, yet be connected in our mind with the idea of an object, nor does he explain what the idea of an

individual object is. He says elsewhere that our concept of Caesar is "the presentation in imagination of the individual Caesar as such,"[25] but this does not help much.

(3) The theory has difficulty in explaining how we frequently use names that we know to be empty, for example in fiction, and how it is possible that many names that we believe to have a bearer may possibly not have a bearer, for example "Moses." According to the theory, the meaning of a proper name is the bearer itself, so a sentence containing an empty name cannot have a meaning. But the Torah appears to be meaningful, whether or not Moses existed, as is a work of acknowledged fiction such as *The Lord of the Rings*. Furthermore, it requires that a name must have a bearer, which seems absurd. "Moses is a prophet" says of someone (Moses) that he is a prophet, "Moses is not a prophet" says of the same person that he is not a prophet. One or the other must be true, so on the standard theory, both propositions require us to say something *of* Moses, which we can't do unless he exists. How then do we deal with the possibility that Moses does not exist? Indeed, how do we deal with the possibility that God does not exist? When the atheist denies "God exists," the name "God" must signify precisely what the fideist asserts by the same sentence. On the standard theory, this seems impossible.

(4) The standard theory suggests that different proper names for the same bearer could be substituted without changing the meaning of a sentence. Thus "Cicero is Tully" has the same meaning as "Cicero is Cicero," given that "Cicero" and "Tully" have the same bearer. Yet no one would disbelieve "Cicero is Cicero," for it expresses a logical truth, while someone might not believe "Cicero is Tully." This suggests the two names have a *different* meaning, yet the standard theory says they have the *same* meaning.

Though these are not the only problems, they are recognized as the main ones.

THE INTRALINGUISTIC THESIS

The intralinguistic thesis defended here consists of three connected claims. The first claim, the co-reference thesis, is that there is a phenomenon I call *signified* or *guaranteed* co-reference, where it is clear simply from the meaning of two statements that if one statement asserts (or denies) that some thing is such and such, then the other statement asserts (or denies) that *the same thing* is so and so. The paradigm is pronominal back-reference. It is part of our understanding of pronoun use that if "*Herod* realized that he had been outwitted, and *he* was furious" is true, then the first part of the sentence says that someone had been outwitted, and the second part says that the same person was furious. When I talk about "co-reference," I shall always mean this form of anaphoric co-reference. Pronouns are a paradigm, but clearly different tokens of the same proper name can co-refer in the same way, for example, the first and second occurrences of "God" at the beginning of the book of Genesis.

> In the beginning *God* ('ĕ-lō-hîm, ὁ θεὸς, *Deus*) created the heavens and the earth. Now the earth was formless and empty, darkness was over the surface of the deep, and the Spirit of *God* ('ĕ-lō-hîm, θεοῦ, *Dei*) was hovering over the waters.

I claim that there is nothing *philosophically* difficult about explaining co-reference. That is not to say that the explanation, which is a scientific and technical matter, is not complex and difficult, but rather that it is a task for computational linguistics, not philosophy. It is non-philosophically difficult to explain the exact rules by which we determine co-reference in all cases, which I will discuss in the next chapter, but it seems clear that in the natural and obvious reading of the passage given earlier, the two tokens of "God" have a common referent, if they have a referent at all, and so there is no philosophical difficulty. The philosophical difficulties are whether co-reference implies reference (I argue that it does), whether reference implies reference to something (I argue that it does), and whether, if so, reference to something implies that there is (or there exists) something such that it is referred to (I argue that it does not, but this raises some difficult questions that I defer until chapter 7).

The second claim, the *reference* thesis,[26] is that the semantic value of a proper name consists solely in its anaphoric co-reference with its antecedents in a chain of co-referring terms, and that the truth of a reference statement depends upon such co-reference, even if no referent exists.

As stated earlier, a reference statement contains a mention*ing* term, such as "second word of the Quran," a mention*ed* term, a token available in some antecedent text or utterance, and a *used* term. For example:

- In the beginning *God* created the heavens and the earth.
- *The fourth word of the previous sentence* refers to *him*.

The mentioning term is "The fourth word of the previous sentence," the mentioned term is "God," and the used term is "him." On the standard theory, the truth of a reference statement depends (i) on an external relation between the mentioned term and an external referent, in this case, God, and (ii) on the same relation obtaining between the referent and the term in the reference statement itself. Thus, on the standard theory, the relation must obtain *twice*: between the proper name "God" and the pronoun "him." The reference statement must have an external truthmaker, in this case God.

On the reference thesis, by contrast, no extralinguistic truthmaker is required. The conditions for the reference statement to be true are, first, that the mentioned term ("God") anaphorically co-refers with the used term ("him"). This is clearly so in the above example, hence the reference statement must be true whether or not "God" has an external referent at all, so cannot express a relation between "God" and an external referent. The second condition is that the mentioned term must have some antecedent in a chain of co-referring terms. If a story begins "There was a young man called 'Mark,'" then we can say truly that "Mark" refers to the young man, for the mentioned term "Mark" has the antecedent "a young man," which co-refers with "*the* young man" in our reference statement. But we cannot say that "a young man" refers to Mark, for "a young man" cannot be an anaphor term, given that the whole purpose of an indefinite term is to block any kind of back-reference. An indefinite term *a* cannot locate any previous term *b* such that it is clear simply from the meaning of the statements containing them that if one is true of a thing, the other, if true, is true of the same thing also. Some writers (such as Sommers) have claimed that indefinite terms, such as "a young man," have a sort of non-identifying reference. This is a mistake, which I shall discuss in chapter 3.

Thus, according to the reference thesis, a reference statement is illusory: it purports to express a relation between a mentioned term and an object, but such a relation is not what makes it true. What makes it true is a relation that is *intralinguistic*, although its grammatical form misleadingly suggests the relation is *extralinguistic*. On this hypothesis, co-reference is primary, reference is secondary. The thesis has wide ranging implications (e.g., for received logico-philosophical principles such as the necessity of identity).

I will not argue for the thesis at length now, except to say, and to avoid any confusion, that I am *not* claiming that one term refers to another. I am not, for instance, saying that "God" refers to the *word* "God," or that the name "Moses" refers to the *expression* "the man who led the Israelites out of Egypt." On the contrary, "Moses" refers to a man, not an expression. That is to say, it is true that "Moses" refers to a man. However I claim that what *makes* it true is not some external reference relation between "Moses" and that man, but rather an internal relation between the reference statement and some textual or uttered antecedent. Nor does the name refer to the *concept* of Moses, for the noun phrase "the concept of Moses" does that.[27] Nor do I claim that there are intentional objects or non-existent things. I shall argue (see chapter 7) that the name "Asmodeus" refers to Asmodeus, so the name "Asmodeus" refers to *something*. I shall argue that we can truly think of

Asmodeus hence, in thinking of Asmodeus, be thinking of something. But the grammatical objects of intentional verbs like "refer to," "think of" do not require that there be anything that satisfies them. The fact that "Asmodeus" refers to something does not entail that there is (or exists) something which is the referent of "Asmodeus," nor that "Asmodeus" has a referent, for the non-intentional verb, phrase "has a referent" does not function in the same way as the intentional verb phrase "refers to." I say this to avoid all confusion about my use of that verb phrase in the text that follows.

The third claim, the *dependency* thesis, is that communicating with proper names is dependent on the availability of a common text such as the Hebrew Bible, which *uses* those names ("Moses") within a narrative, rather than a dictionary, which contains mostly general names ("prophet") and which merely makes the names without using them.

Any theory of proper names must explain why names for our relatives, friends and neighbors are generally not in dictionaries, and why learning how to use them is not in any sense a prerequisite for learning the language, whereas common names like "red," "round," "person," "house," and so on are found in all dictionaries, and are in some sense necessary for understanding the language. Somewhere in between, there are proper names, such as "Caesar" and "Moses," which are found in some dictionaries, but are not in any sense necessary for understanding *English*, as opposed to understanding history or theology.

Any theory must also explain why there is a proper name/common name distinction, and a local/national distinction between proper names. Locke explains the first on the assumption that in order to understand a proper name, we must be acquainted with its bearer, so that we have "the idea in my mind" of it, and in order to communicate using the name, the other person must also be acquainted with the bearer.[28] Common terms, by contrast, signify "general ideas," which are separated from the circumstances of time and place, "and any other ideas that may determine them to this or that particular existence." Since we use language to communicate our thought by combining general ideas, language for the most part consists of general terms.

Reid explains the local/national division by a similar reasoning. He says the meaning of a local name is "known" only to the people in the locality, assuming like Locke that we can only know it through acquaintance with the bearer. Such knowledge will be unavailable to the greater part of the community that uses the language. There are a few proper names that are understood by the whole community (he mentions "the Sun" as an example, but presumably "Caesar" and "Moses" would do), but that is because the bearers are known to the whole community.[29]

These explanations are inadequate. In what sense are the very individuals Caesar and Moses "known" to the whole community that understands their names? How exactly are we acquainted with them? How is it we understand names like "Frodo" and "Sherlock Holmes" that have no bearers, so that there is no possibility of knowing or being acquainted with the bearers? I shall argue that our knowledge begins and ends with the *text* that introduces those names. If the texts (*The Gallic wars*, *The Lord of the Rings*, etc.) are available to the whole community, the whole community is able to understand the names. Acquaintance with the text is both sufficient and necessary. No acquaintance with the individual is necessary, nor is it even sufficient. If I am confronted with Caesar, I do not know that this individual conquered Gaul, unless I am know that that *this person* is Caesar.

Hence, if our knowledge begins and ends with the *text* that introduces names such as "Caesar," "Moses" and "God," we cannot understand the proper name "God" without acquaintance with the Hebrew Bible, or some text that co-refers with it, and so cannot have a singular *conception* of God.

ORGANIZATION OF THE BOOK

In the second chapter, I defend the co-reference thesis, arguing that there is a natural reading of a text to which all authors will try to conform, not always successfully, and this natural reading determines the co-reference of the singular terms occurring in the text. There is evidence for systematic rules or heuristics known to both author and reader, and which in principle suggests the possibility of mechanical systems or algorithms for determining co-reference. A common reference is an objective property of the text. No acquaintance or knowledge of a bearer is necessary. I claim that, in principle, a computer could analyze the text of *The Lord of the Rings* to determine the set of terms, which co-refer with "Frodo Baggins," or with "Gandalf," and so forth.

In the third chapter, I introduce the dependency and the reference theses through the puzzling phenomenon (sometimes called the puzzle of *unbound anaphora*) of proper names introduced by indefinite description, such as "a man named Moses" and "a woman named Martha." It can be shown that these proper names co-refer in some sense with their indefinite antecedent, yet the antecedent itself does not refer. I claim this is because the meaning of a singular term is *non-transportable*:[30] it co-refers with some indefinite antecedent, but the whole purpose of an indefinite term is its indifference to what came before in the order of reading, hence no singular term that occurs before the antecedent can refer *forward* to it in the way that a subsequent anaphor can refer *back*. No term prior to the antecedent can have the meaning of an anaphor term subsequent to it.[31] This, and not Locke's conception of acquaintance, is what distinguishes general terms, which are transportable, from singular terms, which are not. Singular anaphor terms are semantically dependent on the chain introduced by some indefinite antecedent, and so dependent on the text itself. They have no general dictionary-defined meaning, which we can understand as part of learning the language. Our understanding begins and ends with some *text*. This is the dependency thesis.

The *reference* thesis is that we can make a reference statement in a text where the referring term of that statement has guaranteed co-reference with the mentioned term, so that the term must itself have a non-transportable meaning. We cannot specify the reference of a term used in a narrative without that specification *itself* being a part of the narrative.

In chapter 4, I address the question of co-reference between texts that are not independent, that is, when a text such as the New Testament mentions or cites the Hebrew Bible, and I distinguish between citation and reference.

Chapter 5 concerns *implied* or *imputed* co-reference between independent texts, where it is not signified that the same person is a character in both texts, but where we can reasonably infer that it is the same person, or where we could write a history using information from both texts, where the co-reference was signified. For example, the identity we assume between the man called "Moses" in Exodus and the man of the same name in Numbers or Deuteronomy is signified. If the men were different, the author would have said so, therefore to understand the text at all, we have to understand the identity. But the identity we assume between the man called "Pilate" in Philo's *De Legatione ad Gaium*, and the man of the same name in the Gospel account, while fairly certain, is merely probable. The identity is not part of the *meaning* of the separate accounts, since they were independently written by different authors. It is not as though Philo would tell us whether the man he calls "Pilate" is or is not the same as the man of the same name in the Gospels. He was almost certainly unaware of the Gospels. Likewise, the author of the Gospels does not mention Philo's text.

I argue that history involves taking separate accounts such as this—perhaps very short accounts contained in baptismal records and other kinds of register—and *imputing* co-reference by converting the probable identity into semantic identity. Thus, in writing "Pilate was ordered by Tiberius to remove the shields from the palace in Jerusalem" and later "*he* handed Christ over to be crucified," the historian converts a probable identity between the man who Philo said removed the shields and the man who the Gospel said handed Jesus over, into a semantic one, via the pronoun "he." I take up the philosophical implications of such probable (i.e., contingent) identity in the following chapter.

Chapters 6 and 7 concern two corollaries of the co-reference thesis that conflict with standard semantics. Chapter 6 considers, and rejects, two contemporary philosophical theories of reference. The first is strong *Millianism* or "direct reference," which holds that the proposition, the bearer of truth and falsity, is not a linguistic item, a sentence capable of truth and falsity, but a *Russellian* proposition: an extralinguistic item expressed by an assertoric sentence. According to this theory, the semantic value of a proper name is the bearer itself: the proposition expressed by "Peter preached in Galilee" contains both Peter and Galilee. I argue that the semantic value of a proper name consists solely in its (intralinguistic) co-reference with its anaphoric antecedents, and that because its meaning is not transportable, it can have no semantic connection to its bearer. Thus, identity statements flanked by proper names can be informative when the proper names do not co-refer. Such an identity is not like "catsup is ketchup," where the *transportable* meaning of the two terms is identical.

The second theory, following from the first, is that identity statements involving proper names, if true, are necessarily true. It was first stated by Ruth Barcan Marcus in 1947, becoming widely known and accepted after Saul Kripke's defense of it in *Naming and Necessity*. I reject the theory by rejecting the principle of substitution on which it depends. Even if "Cicero" refers to Cicero, and Cicero is the same person as Marcus, it need not follow that "Cicero" refers to Marcus.

Chapter 7 is about existence. The co-reference thesis implies that proper names are meaningful even when empty. A proper name acquires its meaning through guaranteed co-reference alone, and so does not need a bearer in order to have a meaning. Hence, the fideist and the atheist can meaningfully disagree, given that "God does not exist" denies a referent, but not a meaning for the name "God." However, the thesis involves two logical problems. First, "God does not exist" implies "something does not exist" in standard logic, and "there is no such thing as God" implies "there is no such thing as something." Second, it follows from the reference thesis that "'God' refers to God" is true, even if "God" has no referent, that is, even if God does not exist. Yet standard logic requires that "a R b" implies "for some x, a R x."

I argue that the grammatical form of a reference statement differs from its logical form. The relation that is suggested by its grammatical structure, that is, between the name "Asmodeus" and some supposed demon of that name, is not the relation that makes it true. "Tobit is referring to a demon" is like "Tobit needs a wife," which is true precisely because Tobit has no wife.

In chapter 8, I consider the objection that "God" may not be a proper name at all, but a disguised description, such as "The omnipotent omniscient being." If so, our conception of God would available to anyone who understands the meaning of "omnipotent," "omniscient," and of other common ordinary language terms, and so would be transportable as I have defined it, not semantically dependent on some part of a commonly available text. The question is whether such as conception of "God" is the *standard* one, which I take up in the next chapter.

Chapter 9 is an extension of the co-reference thesis to names that occur in everyday written or spoken communication. This requires resolving a problem suggested by Kripke, namely that we can understand the meaning of two proper names referring to the same thing, without believing that they refer to (or designate) the same thing. I argue that, while communication media do not form a single physical text, they are constructed as though they were a single text: a virtual text. To understand any name requires a context, which requires, in turn, that the appropriate parts of the narrative, or the virtual narrative, are available. We can move from "S assents to *p*" to "S believes that p" so long as the name that is mentioned in the sentence assented to co-refers with the name used in the "that" clause, and where the test for co-reference involves the rules of disambiguation common to all narratives, not just physical ones.

Chapter 10 is a further extension of the co-reference thesis to demonstrative identification. The forms of reference and identification discussed so far involve an *intra*linguistic semantic connection between propositions that allows us to identify a character within the framework of a narrative by grasping which individual a character is the *same* as. All reference is, as it were, relative to some large narrative about *some* world. How do we know the narrative is about *this* world? This question prompted Strawson to eliminate story-relative identification by grounding it in some form of *demonstrative* identification, so that even if an individual cannot itself be demonstratively identified, "it may be identified by a description which relates it uniquely to another particular which can be demonstratively identified."[32] If we can do this, can't we also identify *God* in this way, by some form of supernatural revelation? The name "God" may co-refer in some trivial way with tokens of that name in the scriptures, but why can't it refer in some stronger, non-trivial way, through prayer or meditation, or through God's direct action in the world? I appeal to Hume's principle that any objects of perception may be numerically different even though they perfectly resemble each other. Perceptual information, unlike linguistic information has only *indefinite* content, and there is nothing in our *perception* of some object that signifies whether it is numerically the same as or different from any other perception. Even if there were some private perception that identified its object (such as direct revelation from God), it would be impossible to communicate the identity using public language.

The final chapter extends the co-reference thesis to thought itself. I turn to the connection between my conception of reference and the concept of worship, in order to discuss a phenomenon that has captured the imagination of philosophers for at least a hundred years: *intentionality*, the supposed relation of "aboutness" between thought and its object. Just as I have claimed that reference statements are illusory, so I claim intentionality is also an illusion. A reference statement like "the name 'God' refers to God" expresses an apparently word to *world* relation (that "God" refers to God), even though what makes it true is a relation between word and *word* (the co-reference of the term "God" as *I* use it, with the same term in the Hebrew Bible). Likewise, "Aashir is praying to *God*" appears to express a real extramental relation between Aashir and God. This is an illusion, similar to the folk belief that eyebeams are emitted from the eye. We cannot understand the name "God" and we cannot have a *singular* conception of God without reference to the biblical texts.

Thus, I answer the question of the book, namely whether Jews, Muslims, and Christians worship the same God. All have the same singular conception of God, because the three texts (the Hebrew Bible, the New Testament, the Quran) are in a sense one. Both the New Testament and the Quran complete (and sometimes aim to correct) the text on which they are based, and it is this fact (alone) that provides a common understanding of the proper name "God," in whatever language it is written.

NOTES

1. Durrant (*The Logical Status of "God"*), 2ff argues that from *actual occurrences* of "God" in religious language, citing examples of prayers, such as "*Almighty God*, the fountain of all goodness, we humbly beseech thee . . .*"* the term "God" is not a proper name. The main examples I shall use in this book are not from prayer, but rather the three scriptures themselves, but even in this prayer, it seems that "Almighty God" co-refers with "thee," suggesting that "Almighty God" is a referring term.

2. The Quran opens "bismi *al-lāhi* al-rrahmāni al-rrahīmi," "In the name of God, the Most Gracious, the Most Merciful." Transliteration by Ali, *The Glorious Qur'an*, 6. Note that in the Arabic itself (not the transliteration), the word "God" is not the second word, given that Arabic script reads right-to-left.

3. That is, assuming that the tokens "God" and "Allah" have the same meaning in the identity statement as the same tokens in the original texts. I shall discuss the question of disquotation in chapter 9.

4. In the 1952 edition of *Translations from the Philosophical Writings of Gottlob Frege*, Max Black and Peter Geach translated "Über Sinn und *Bedeutung*" as "On Sense and *Reference*." The German word *Bedeutung* actually means "signification" or "meaning." Peter Long and Roger White were the first to translate it as "meaning" in the English version of Frege's *Posthumous Writings*. In the third (1980) edition, Geach and Black changed to "meaning" (thus "On sense and meaning"). However, as Dummett pointed out, the term "reference" could not be dislodged by a quarter

of a century of philosophical discussion and commentary on Frege's work, and the original English usage has stuck.

5. "A proper name [is] a word which answers the purpose of *showing what* thing it is that we are talking about, but not of telling anything about it" (Mill, *A System of Logic*, 1. ii. 5, my emphasis). See also Prior, *Objects of Thought*, 155, Strawson, "On referring," (*Logico-Linguistic Papers*), 1–27.

6. Ibid., *Antequam musicus esset, Socrates dictus est, vel postquam filius Sophronisci non erit, Socrates dicetur.*

7. Devitt, "Against direct reference" (*On Sense and Direct Reference: Readings in the Philosophy of Language*), 463.

8. The idea that a sentence expresses its truth value can be found as early as Frege's *Grundgesetze* §32. He says that a significant sentence determines under which (truth) conditions (*Bedingungen*) it signifies the truth value *True*, and that if it does signify the True, it is a sort of name for the True, and the sense of this sentence-name is the thought is that the (truth) conditions are met. Actually the idea can be found much earlier in Buridan's *Treatise on Consequences* (King 1985, Book I chapter 1), but it is doubtful that Buridan had any influence on Frege.

9. Evans, *The Varieties of Reference*, 10.

10. Frege, *Posthumous Writings*, 174, see also p. 130. Frege's position here is somewhat muddled by his attribution of "sense" to empty terms, so that proper names can have at least some kind of meaning, as well as a designation or reference. This is irrelevant to the present discussion, but see Evans, *The Varieties of Reference* chapter 1 for ample Frege exegesis.

11. Geach and Black, *Translations from the Philosophical Writings of Gottlob Frege*, 69, except I am translating Frege's "Bedeutung" as "significance" rather than "reference." This is consistent with the rest of the third edition translation, which aimed to replace "reference" with meaning, with the dictionary translation, where "Bedeutung" is given as signification, meaning, standing for, and so on, and (I believe) with Frege's intention. The passages from Frege's comments on Schroeder are barely intelligible otherwise.

12. Frege clearly presumes that if a sentence is meaningful, then it is meaningful whether true or false. But if the sentence asserts of any of its components that the component is meaningful, and if the meaning of the sentence depends on its components, the sentence would not be meaningful if false.

13. Geach, *Logic Matters*, 52.

14. Ibid., 59.

15. Frege, G. (1895) "A critical elucidation of some points in E. Schroeder's Vorlesungen Über Die Algebra der Logik," *Archiv fur systematische Philosophie*, 1895, 433–56, trans. Geach in Geach & Black, 86–106, p. 454, my emphasis. See also "On concept and object," *G&B*, 42 ff. "A concept . . . is predicative. On the other hand, a name of an object, a proper name, is quite incapable of being used as a grammatical predicate" (p. 43). We can, of course, say that someone is Alexander the Great. But this involves a different use of the word "is," that is, the "is" of predication versus the "is" of identity, which I will discuss later.

16. The term is Brandom's (Brandom, *Making it Explicit*, 301).

17. There is a dispute about whether Frege's account of reference implies the standard theory, but I am not concerned here with matters of Fregean exegesis. Evans, *The Varieties of Reference* chapter 1 is the *locus classicus*.

18. Aristotle, *On Interpretation*, 17b1.

19. *Aptus natus est praedicari de uno solo.* Quine (*Word and Object*, 96, my emphasis) says "a singular term is one that *purports* to refer to just one object."

20. Kretzmann, *William of Sherwood's Introduction to Logic*, 110.

21. In Aristotelian semantics, a proposition is a type of sentence which, unlike a question or a command, is capable of truth or falsity. In Fregean semantics, the sentence expresses a proposition, an extra-mental Platonic truthbearer.

22. Traditionally, the proposition is the bearer of truth and falsity. Aristotle distinguishes (*On Interpretation* 17 a4) a sentence (λόγος, oratio) from a proposition (ἀπόφανσις, propositio) or declarative sentence (λόγος ἀποφαντικός, oratio enuntiativa), for only the proposition is capable of truth and falsity. Thus, a prayer is not a proposition (nor is a question or a command). He dismisses all other types of sentence in order to focus on the proposition, saying that other types of sentence are the domain of rhetoric or poetry. Contemporary philosophers take a different view of the proposition, regarding it not as a type of sentence, but rather as the meaning or thought or "Russellian proposition" expressed by the sentence. Some regard it as a wholly extralinguistic item, which includes as a component the object that the proposition is about, although Russell himself did not seem to have endorsed this. Whenever I use the word, I shall mean an assertoric or declarative sentence, a form of words in which something is propounded, put forward for consideration, and which is thus capable of being true or false, rather than a thought or a meaning. People who don't like "proposition" can replace it mentally with "statement."

23. *Significare sequitur intelligere.*

24. Frege himself acknowledged the problem: "that part of the thought which corresponds to the name 'Etna' cannot be Mount Etna itself.... For each piece of frozen, solidified lava which is part of Mount Etna would then also be part of the thought that Etna is higher than Vesuvius. But it seems to me absurd that pieces of lava, even pieces of which I had no knowledge, should be parts of my thought" (Frege, "Letter to Jourdain" in Moore, 43). See also Frege's letter to Russell, Jena 13 November 1904, in Frege, *Philosophical and Mathematical Correspondence*, 169, where the examplar is Mont Blanc "with its snowfields."

25. Mill, *An Examination of Sir William Hamilton's Philosophy*, 323.

26. This thesis bears a superficial resemblance to the one worked out in Brandom (*Making it Explicit*, 305–327) and *passim*. Brandom argues that a reference statement like "The term 'Leibniz' refers to Leibniz" can be interpreted as "The one referred to by the term 'Leibniz' = Leibniz," where the indirect description "The one referred to etc." is anaphorically dependent on some previously occurring token of "Leibniz." The resemblance is only superficial, in my view. For example, Brandom quotes with apparent approval Chastain's claim that indefinite descriptions can be straightforwardly referential. See my discussion of this point in chapter 3.

27. This is an old argument. Quine (*Methods of Logic*, 199) argues that "Parthenon" names the Parthenon and only the Parthenon, whereas "the Parthenon-idea" names

the Parthenon-idea. Frege ("On sense and reference," 31) says that the sentence "The Moon is smaller than the Earth" is not about the idea of the Moon. "If this is what the speaker wanted, he would use the phrase 'my idea of the Moon'" Earlier than that, Mill (*A System of Logic*, I.v.i) notes that "fire causes heat" does not mean that my idea of fire causes my idea of heat. "When I mean to assert any thing respecting the ideas, I give them their proper name, I call them ideas: as when I say, that a child's idea of a battle is unlike the reality, or that the ideas entertained of the Deity have a great effect on the characters of mankind." In the late thirteenth century, Duns Scotus argued that if "stone" referred to the idea of a stone, then Aristotle's claim in *De anima* III "A stone is not in the soul, but the idea of a stone" would be contradictory, because "being in the soul" is first removed from the idea of a stone, which is signified by the name "stone" by the first part of the proposition, "a stone is not in the soul," and yet in the second part, the same predicate would be attributed to the "same subject" (*Duns Scotus On Time and Existence*, 31, I have changed the translation from "species" to "idea").

28. Locke, *An Essay Concerning Human Understanding*, III. iii. 3.
29. Reid, *The Works of Thomas Reid*, 389.
30. Sainsbury, "Fregean sense," 136.
31. It may be objected that in English, as well as in Greek and Latin, a relative may anticipate a pronoun in such a way that the pronoun refers to a preceding or succeeding relative or vice versa. I deal with this objection in chapter 3.
32. Strawson, *Individuals*, 21.

Chapter 2

Rules for Reference

My first thesis is that co-reference is *signified* or *guaranteed* when it is clear from the meaning of two terms that if they have a referent at all, they have a single referent, that is, that if one is true of a thing, the other, if true, is true of the same thing also. Consider pronouns: if the (definite) antecedent refers, the pronoun refers to the same thing. Since we understand this even when the antecedent term is empty ("As soon as *the demon* smells the odour, *it* will flee"), it follows that the co-reference is signified without any semantic connection between the terms and some external object. The connection is internal or intralinguistic, and must be determined by some rule of use. There can be co-*reference* without a co-*referent*.

I shall argue that the same must be true of proper names and definite descriptions and that, while the rules may be complex and difficult to specify, they must nonetheless exist.

RULES FOR REFERENCE

The question of what authors *wish* to convey through their work *in general* is an old and difficult question,[1] but we cannot doubt their specific ability to successfully convey, *which* individual they are writing about. Our ability to comprehend a narrative involves keeping track of which character is which. There are about 31,000 verses in the whole Bible, and (from Aaron to Zurishaddai) about 2,000 characters. The biblical narrative would make little sense if we were unable to tell whether the same character was the subject of any two of those verses, or not. There are more than 700 occurrences of the proper name "Moses" in the Old Testament, and it is crucial to our ability to comprehend the work that we understand that these are not ambiguous names for 700 different people. Chastain calls such a set of names an *anaphoric chain*, namely "a sequence of expressions such that if one of them refers to something then all of the others refer to it."[2] The chain does not have to consist solely of proper names, but will normally be a mixture of proper names and other singular expressions.[3] The question of how we resolve anaphoric chains is remarkably difficult, but it belongs to the science of computational linguistics, rather than philosophy.

Computational linguists traditionally distinguish co-reference from anaphor. Co-reference is when two terms refer to the same entity "in the world," anaphora is when "a term (anaphor) refers [*sic*] to another term (antecedent) and the interpretation of the anaphor is in some way determined by the interpretation of the antecedent."[4] I reject this distinction, for I regard co-reference and anaphora as essentially the same phenomenon. To start with, we understand complete fiction, where all proper names and pronouns are empty, because we are able to bundle up singular terms into different anaphoric chains. Hence co-reference cannot depend on reference to the same entity "in the world." The claim that an anaphor "refers to" another *term* is misleading for the same reason, as though the relation between a pronoun and its proper name antecedent were intralinguistic, but the relation between two co-referring proper names were not. As for the interpretation of the anaphor being determined by the interpretation of the antecedent, the idea seems to be that pronouns are essentially ambiguous, their sense (or reference?) determined by the immediate context, whereas proper names have a fixed and context independent reference. One dictionary defines anaphor as "an expression that can refer to virtually any referent, the specific referent being defined by context."[5] But this is not true. Proper names also are essentially ambiguous and require a context. Consider the name "Moses" in a book about the Pentateuch as contrasted with a book about Moses Maimonides. Clearly the rules determining proper name co-reference will be different from the rules determining pronoun co-reference, and I shall come to that, but this does not mean that co-reference is essentially a different phenomenon from anaphora.

Pronoun Resolution

The resolution of pronoun anaphora has received much attention in the literature, although the record is dismal. Hobb's algorithm in 1978 was an early attempt.[6] The algorithm starts at the NP (noun phrase) node immediately dominating the pronoun and searches in a specified order for the first match of the correct gender and number.[7] The algorithm is purely syntactic; there has been some progress since the 1970s by using semantic properties of the term. For example, it seems as though a pronoun will not have a distant antecedent, and so *entities* introduced recently are more *salient*, and thus more likely to be the antecedent of back-reference, than those introduced earlier. Lappin and Leass have proposed that salience values should be cut in half each time a new sentence is processed,[8] and that entities mentioned in subject position are typically more salient than those in object position. Centering theory, developed by Barbara J. Grosz, Aravind K. Joshi, and Scott Weinstein in the 1980s, proposes that discourse has a kind of center, which remains the same for a few sentences, then shifts to a new center. It is this center that is typically pronominalized in that there is a tendency for subsequent pronouns to take it as antecedent. Modern algorithms perform better than Hobb, but state of the art accuracy for general co-reference resolution is sadly quite low, in the range of 60 percent.

This is a puzzle, for it means we do not understand something that humans do easily, namely reading a simple story. Children soon learn to do this, yet the most advanced computational techniques fail. Does this mean there are no rules? Surely not. Either co-reference (1) is enabled by a sort of telepathy between author and reader, whereby the author telepathically communicates the intended reference to the reader, (2) involves some semantic relation between language and reality that a computer could not possibly emulate, or (3) is a property of the text, in which case, there must exist some method of decoding it. I rule out the first on the assumption that telepathy is impossible, particularly between an author who probably died in the second millennium BC and a reader in the third millennium AD. I rule out the second both as implausible, and because it is the principle target of this book. That leaves the third. I summarize the reasons supporting it here.

First evidence: rules exist. Ordinary grammar books talk about the error of *faulty* or *vague* pronoun reference, and specify a rule like "A pronoun should refer back to a single *unmistakable* antecedent noun." To be sure, it is difficult to give a criterion or an algorithm for "unmistakable," but as I said earlier, human readers clearly have the ability to keep track of which individual is which, *without* making mistakes, also human writers have the ability to enable this by clearly expressing their meaning. When mistakes occur, this is the fault of the writer, not the reader. Humans would not make rules if humans were unable to apply them.

Second, the difficulty that computers have with some exception cases is not that there is no rule, but rather that the rule requires knowledge of human affairs and customs. For example:

Gen 4:20 Adah gave birth to Jabal; *he* was the father of those who live in tents and raise livestock.
Gen 4:26 Seth also had a son, and *he* named *him* Enosh.[9]
Gen 12:18 So *Pharaoh* summoned Abram. "What have you done to me?" *he* said.

The first example requires knowledge that "Adah" is the name of a woman, not a man, which is provided in 4:19 ("Lamech married two women, one named Adah and the other Zillah"). This knowledge could be given to the computer through a list of all proper names classified by gender, but in any case, there is a further clue given by "gave birth to." The computer would have to understand that only women can give birth. There is another difficulty: the verse could easily have been written "*Lamech had a son*, Jabal; he was the father of those who live in tents and raise livestock," with no clue given by pronoun gender. To understand why "he" still refers back to "Jabal," we would have to understand the purpose of 4:19–22, which is to tell us which occupations the descendants Lameth followed. Jabal was the ancestor of tent dwellers, Jubal of musicians, Tubal Cain of blacksmiths. This, in Chastain's words, is a convention "relevant to the genre."

Gen 4:26 is an example of a double pronoun use: "*he* named *him* Enosh." The assumption is that the verb is not reflexive, otherwise the reflexive pronoun "himself" would have been used.[10] We also know that human biology generally precludes children naming their parents. Gen 12:18 requires understanding of speech conventions. If "he" refers to Pharoah, and Pharoah uttered "What have you done to me?," then "you" refers to Abram and "me" to Pharoah. To understand that "he" refers to Pharoah, we have to understand what Abram is doing, which is explained by 12:17. God is inflicting plagues because Pharaoh has taken Sarai, Abram's wife.

Third, the knowledge required is likely to be timeless and universal (or at least relatively stable over time, and across languages). We can generally understand texts written in ancient languages and by authors from very different cultures. Mark wrote, "Herod feared *John*, knowing that *he* was a just man" with the intention that "he" (αὐτὸν) should refer back to "John." His intention was realized even though he wrote in Greek, and his English translators have followed him by using the appropriate English pronoun, as do Latin translators ("Herodes enim metuebat Iohannem sciens *eum* virum iustum"), French ("Hérode craignait Jean, *le* connaissant pour un homme juste"), German ("Herodes aber fürchtete Johannes; denn er wußte, daß *er* ein frommer und heiliger Mann war"), and so on. They are able to translate the reference because they understand the rules of the language they were translating into, and Mark would have understood the rules of the original Greek in exactly the same way. Imagine he was working from some lost text in Aramaic, which used the same pronominal reference, or that he had some mental sentence which he wanted to translate into Greek. Thus, the rules cannot be arbitrary if the knowledge required to apply them is knowledge of human nature itself, including the nature that drives people to construct such stories.

Fourth, the cases where resolution is impossible are where no appropriate rule exists.

> On the way, at a place where they spent the night, the LORD met *him₁* and tried to kill *him₂*. But Zipporah took a flint and cut off her son's foreskin, and touched *his₃* feet with it, and said, "Truly you are a bridegroom of blood to me!" So *he₄* let *him₅* alone. [Exodus 4:24-26][11]

Rabbinical interpreters have offered a wide range of meanings for this text.[12] The first "him" could refer to Moses, or to his son, either of whom has been struck down by some illness caused by God. The second clearly co-refers with the first. But whether "his feet" refers to Moses' feet, his son's feet or God's feet, is difficult to say. As for the fourth and fifth, logic suggests that the subjects are different, and also that the fifth "he" co-refers with the first and second (the attempt on his life is dropped). But whether it is Moses or his son is not clear. One translation has "it" for the fourth pronoun, meaning the illness that struck down Moses (or his son). The text is most likely corrupt, but that confirms the point that no appropriate rule exists.

Of course, a complete theory governing pronoun resolution is likely to be complex and difficult, and is a problem for computational linguistics, but it is not my purpose to offer a precise theory of co-reference resolution, or any general theory of how people signify and understand co-reference. My assumption is such a theory must be *possible*. There have to be certain well understood rules of communication, which allow both authors and translators to communicate reference by written or spoken signs, in whatever language they choose.

Proper Names

While pronoun resolution is difficult, proper names and definite descriptions are somewhat easier. For proper names, the rule is that tokens of the same name *always* co-refer, except when they have been disambiguated in some way. If there are two or more people called "Mary," the rule is that the name should be further qualified by means of a patronymic or description. For example, Mary Magdalene is qualified as *Magdalene*, as is Mary *the mother of James and Joseph*, who is also called the *other* Mary (Matthew 27:61, 28:1).[13] Likewise, where the reader might think that different individuals had the same name, or where it is not clear, a description may be added. Thus, John 11:2 states, "It was that Mary [the sister of Martha] *who anointed the Lord with ointment*," in case we think she is a different Mary, although Luke does not say whether they are the same or different. Likewise, Acts 13:14

tells us that the Apostles came to Antioch in *Pisidia*, to distinguish it from the Antioch in *Syria*.

The ambiguity can also be resolved by the passage of time. There are two people called "Herod" in the gospels. The first, the infant boy slayer of Matthew 2, was Herod the Great (74 BC – 4 BC), whereas the person to whom Jesus was sent before his crucifixion (and the one who had John the Baptist murdered) was Herod the Great's son Herod Antipas (Matthew 14:1; Luke 3:1). There is no overt disambiguation in Luke. Luke 1:5 says, "In the time of Herod king of Judea," and Luke 3:1 says, "In the fifteenth year of the reign of Tiberius Caesar—when Pontius Pilate was governor of Judea, Herod tetrarch of Galilee." However, the infant killing episode took place at Jesus' birth, whereas Luke 3 explicitly states that Jesus was about thirty.

The convention that non-disambiguated tokens of the same name co-refer gives rise to the following puzzle, Quran 3:33-35:

3:33 Indeed, Allah chose Adam and Noah and the family of Abraham and the family of *Imran* over the worlds—
3:34 Descendants, some of them from others. And Allah is Hearing and Knowing.
3:35 [Mention, O Muhammad], when the *wife of Imran* said, "My Lord, indeed I have pledged to You what is in my womb, consecrated [for Your service], so accept this from me."

The context makes it clear that the "wife of Imran" is the mother of Mary and grandmother of Jesus. But the list in 3:33 implies that Imran is the father of Moses, meaning that Moses is Jesus' uncle! This apparent inconsistency was noticed by John of Damascus as well as Niketas Byzantios,[14] who thought Muhammad had confused Jesus' mother with Moses' sister Miriam the prophetess, who "took a timbrel in her hand, and all the women followed her, with timbrels and dancing."[15]

The fact that there is a natural reading at all, that is, reading both tokens of "Imran" as having the same reference, and reading "wife" as meaning a woman who has undergone a legal marriage ceremony with the person she is wife of, suggests some sort of rule or heuristic for determining reference, and the logical difficulty of the natural reading implies, as Spinoza argues in another context, that the author of the scripture made an error in doctrine, or that he did not know how to express himself properly, both of which undermine the authority of scripture.[16] Perhaps the natural reading is not the *correct* reading, but this requires defining what "correct" means here. For example, the traditional reading, probably following the commentary of Al-Baidawi,[17] avoids the problem of Moses being the uncle of Jesus on the assumption that the first occurrence of "Imran" refers to the father of Moses, the second to the father of Mary. Dawood follows this in an explanatory footnote to his translation.[18] Others have suggested that both tokens of "Imran" do refer to the father of Moses, but since "wife" in Arabic also means "woman," "wife of Imran" must be read as "woman of Imran," that is, a descendant of Imran, just as Luke 1 says that Elizabeth was "of the daughters of Aaron," meaning a descendant of Moses' brother Aaron.[19] A third interpretation is that both tokens of "Imran" refer to the father of Mary.[20]

The difficulty with any alternative reading, as Spinoza persuasively suggests,[21] is it that it implies a *correct* interpretation, that is, a method or rule of interpretation, which we could systematically apply to every passage of the scripture, which other writers could emulate without going astray. Otherwise there is no method or rule for interpreting scripture, and "anyone could make up anything [i.e., any interpretation] he liked." This is the precisely the difficulty with the interpretation of Quran 3.33–35. The first interpretation implies the rule that we may use the same proper name, without qualification or warning, to refer to different individuals. But if this rule were systematically employed, we would everywhere find sudden jumps like the one from Imran the father of Moses in 3:33 to the grandfather of Jesus in 3:35, which we generally don't find, and the principle would hardly be recommended in manuals of style, or courses in clear speaking. The whole point of a proper name is for consistency of reference: unless indicated otherwise, repeated tokens of the same *name* have the same *reference*. The second interpretation implies that "sister of" is systematically ambiguous between a living relation and a descendant, yet there is no evidence of the term "sister" being used in this way in any other part of the Quran.[22] The third, namely that "Imran" in 3:33 refers to the father of Mary, leads to the difficulty that the list does not include the grandfather or father of Noah, so why should it include the grandfather of Jesus? The point of the list is to mention all those individuals (Adam, Noah, Abraham, Imran) as chosen above all others by God. Also, why does the list not include Moses, who the Quran mentions more than any other prophet, if not because the Imran of the list is Moses' father? Sale[23] mentions a further interpretation by some Muhammadan writers who "have imagined that the same individual Mary, the sister of Moses, was miraculously preserved alive from his time till that of Jesus Christ, purposely to become the mother of the latter." Hermeneutically, this is the least problematic reading, although it conflicts with the principle that names of people from wildly different time periods do not co-refer (unless it is explicitly stated that the person had lived to be 1,000 years old).

The fact that different authors can write a single large and complex work is further evidence for a uniform or natural method of interpretation. The author of Psalm 106 who says that Phinehas "stayed the plague," is almost certainly different from the author of Numbers 25:7, who says that Phinehas, "son of

Eleazar," kills an Israelite man and the Midianite woman who he brought into the camp "before the eyes of Moses." But the author of the Psalm is presumably aware that there is a Phinehas "the son of Eli" mentioned in 1 Samuel 1:3, and so adds a description and a background to distinguish them, so that the meaning is not "Phinehas, son of Eli," but rather, "Phinehas, plague stopper." Likewise, the author of Deuteronomy[24] would be aware that it is the fifth book in the series, and that Genesis, Exodus, Leviticus, and Numbers precede it. Even if the books were authored separately, the *editor* would have been aware of this. Thus, Joshua begins "After the death of Moses," Judges begins "after the death of Joshua," and so on. The author of that sentence is glancing over his shoulder back to the text that ends Deuteronomy 34, assuming the reader will have it available also. Each successive chapter or book could thus have different authors without impacting the unity of the narrative, so long as they wrote *as if* they were the same author.[25] There is no reason why multiple authors cannot achieve the same effect as a single author, so long as each author understands the text or texts that will be available to the final audience. They (or the editors) have complete control over *which* characters are introduced, and over the *order* in which this happens. It does not matter whether they are different, so long as each author is aware of the background information available to the audience, and the multiple authors act as though they were a single author. Think of the different people who write the different episodes of a television soap series. Nothing in the story-relative account requires that the same proper name always signifies co-reference, any more than use of the same pronoun signifies this. The "standard" use of a proper name in the same text is one which conforms to unstated but commonly understood rules for resolving ambiguity.

In some exceptional cases, the ambiguity is resolved on the assumption that co-reference would lead to internal contradictions. For example, Acts 1, where the name "Judas" occurs twice.

> Acts 1:13 Coming in, they went up into the upper room where they dwelt, Peter and John, James and Andrew, Philip and Thomas, Bartholomew and Matthew, James the son of Alphaeus and Simon the Zealot, and *Judas the brother of James*.
> [..]
> Acts 1:16 Brethren, he [Peter] said, there is a prophecy in scripture that must needs be fulfilled; that which the Holy Spirit made, by the lips of David, about *Judas, who shewed the way to the men that arrested Jesus*.

This appears to break the rule that successive tokens of the same proper name always co-refer. Clearly in this case they do not. But this is signaled in two ways. First, by a sort of description. One person called "Judas" is described as the brother of James, the other as the betrayer of Christ, just as one person called "Mary" is qualified as *Magdalene*, another person so-called as *the mother of James and Joseph* (see earlier). Second, it is signalled from the context that the first person called "Judas" is still alive, being present at the meeting of the brethren, whereas the second is now dead, as Peter explains in verse 18.

Descriptions

The rule for descriptions seems to be that terms involving the same definite description always co-refer, and that an indefinite description can refers forward to some definite description, but (as will be discussed in the next chapter) never *backward*. Ezekiel 10:7 says that one of the cherubim took a burning coal "and put it into the hands of *the man in linen*." Who is the man in linen? Refer back to 9:2:

> I saw six men coming from the direction of the upper gate, which faces north, each with a deadly weapon in his hand. With them was *a man clothed in linen* who had a writing kit at his side.

The indefinite description "a man clothed in linen" in 9:2 refers forward to 10:7, so to speak, although it cannot refer further back. There might have been another man in linen mentioned prior to 9:2, but it would not be signified that he was the same (or different) from the one in 9:2. By contrast, it is part of the meaning of the text that the man in 9:2 and the man in 10:7 are the same person.

The definite article plus a description generally requires prior mention of an individual fitting that description.[26] There should be no definite article in the first verse of the *Odyssey*.[27] Note that no individual in reality need satisfy the description in order for the definite description to identify its *verbal* antecedent ("a demon"). It is enough that some individual is *said* to satisfy the description.

Although proper demonstratives[28] cannot occur in a historical narrative, they can occur in a relative context, for example, in direct speech, such as Matthew 12:49: "Pointing to his disciples, he said, 'Here are *my* mother and my brothers.'" The rule is that when the person making the speech says "I," the pronoun co-refers with "he," when he says "you," the pronoun co-refers with "he," referring to the person who is being addressed. I shall discuss such cases in the chapter in demonstratives.

Objectivity

That there is a natural interpretation of the reference of any part of a text, and that it is difficult to define alternative ways of interpreting that part in a way that would work systematically across the *whole* text, suggests that co-reference is a real and objective property of a text, rather than a product of unmediated authorial intention, for the author's intention is necessarily unknown unless the author is able to express it unambiguously in writing, and such expression is only possible if there is some method or rule of interpretation understood by both author and reader. We must distinguish what an author or editor wants the text to signify, from what the text itself signifies. The text may have some private significance to the author that it has to no one else, but semantic reference is not private in this sense. Perhaps Mark wrote, "Herod feared *John*, knowing that *he* was a just man" intending that "he" should refer to Herod, rather than John. But this intention is irrelevant, given that, *as expressed*, it refers to John. *Finis sermonis est intellectum constituere*[29]: the purpose of language is to establish understanding, which is only possible when there is a systemic method of doing so. If it were possible to divine the correct meaning from the author's intention alone, spoken and written language would not be necessary at all.[30]

Thus, co-reference is a *real* property of the text. By "real" I mean objective, observable or determinable by others. The letter "A" is objective in that anyone who understands the roman alphabet can recognize a token of the type "A," which is the whole purpose of having an alphabet. There are even mechanical systems for recognizing text, which would not work unless being a token of the letter "A" were not some mental or psychical feature, but rather an objective property that many different people, and some machines, could recognize. It is true that some tokens of the letter are harder to recognize, and that machines have more difficulty with handwritten tokens than printed ones, but that is a matter of economics. We have a system for producing well-written tokens of the letter "A" that allows us to produce tokens that everybody, including machines, can recognize, but it may take time to write neatly. Or we can save time and scribble. Similarly, we can make a precise reference to a character by using a proper name rather than a pronoun, by analogy with writing the letter "A" neatly, or we can use a pronoun, by analogy with scribbling. Passages such as the one about Zipporah, where pronoun resolution is impossible, are actually rare.

Meaning and Understanding

It follows from my definition of co-reference—a semantic relation such that it is clear from the meaning of two terms that if they have a referent at all, they have a single referent—that co-reference is an equivalence relation: it is reflexive, symmetric, and transitive. Every term clearly co-refers with itself, for if it has a referent, it has a single referent, so the relation is reflexive. It is symmetric—if a co-refers with b, then b co-refers with a. And if a, b, and c have a referent, and if a co-refers with b, and b co-refers with c, then a and b have a single referent x, and b and c have a single referent, which must also be x, hence a and c also have x as a referent, and the co-reference relation is transitive.

It also follows from that definition that if any person S understands the meaning of any two co-referring terms, then he or she understands that they co-refer, for if they understand the terms, they understand their meaning, and their meaning, as co-referring terms, is precisely that if they have a referent, they have a single referent. But it does not necessarily follow that understanding an occurrence of a name requires us to comprehend every past occurrence with which the occurrence co-refers. In order to understand the name "Moses," we do not necessarily have to understand every one of the 700 occurrences of that name in the Hebrew Bible. Indeed, a text can easily be constructed so that it is clear from the meaning of a very small number of terms that they co-refer. Suppose that a is a proper name, that b is a pronoun referring back to b, and c is another pronoun referring back to b. To verify that c co-refers with a, we first have to check that c refers back to b, then that b refers back to a, so we have to check three terms in all. But pronouns have a local or *short* range, eventually terminating backward in some *long*-range term such as a proper name or unique description. If there is a rule that tokens of the same long-range term always co-refer (or if not, that there is explicit disambiguation such as with "Phinehas"), and that different long-range terms never co-refer unless stated otherwise, then it will be easy for a reader to quickly identify co-referring terms, wherever they occur in the narrative, without interpreting all the terms in the narrative. For example, if we find a pronoun in one place, and another pronoun of the same gender in another, then trace back the antecedents of each pronoun until we find two corresponding long-range terms. If the long-range terms are the same, then assume they co-refer, if they are different, assume that they do not co-refer.

Thus, we do not have to be a scholar to understand the name "Moses," wherever it occurs. To decide whether the "he" in Ex. 2:15 co-refers with "the servant of the Lord" Deut 34:5, we find what "he" refers back to ("Moses"), and what "the servant of the Lord" refers back to ("Moses" again), and we have the answer. Nor do we have to understand the whole of a book previously written in order to construct a new book with fresh anaphorically co-referring chains, some of which link back to chains in the book written earlier. The Bible had many authors, all of whom were probably scholars, but scholarship is not strictly necessary. We merely use the same rules as the readers use. As long as we know which existing character we want to speak of, we can look for their name or unique description, then use that term to continue the chain, followed by suitable pronouns or descriptions.

This is not to say that readers cannot be mistaken about the co-reference of different terms. This can happen in two ways. First, the author may not have used the rules correctly, and created a term that referred back to two or more chains. This error probably occurred in the "Imran" example given earlier, where it is not clear whether the name refers to Moses' father, or Jesus' uncle. Co-reference is then strictly impossible. Second, the rules may have been clear enough for many readers, but not clear for all readers, some of whom may assign the wrong co-reference. The possibility of such error does *not* invalidate my claim that if any person S understands two co-referring terms, then he or she understands that they co-refer, since it is clear that in such cases, the interpreter has failed to follow the rules, thus has failed to understand the terms. Such a possibility has an important application in my resolution of Kripke's belief puzzle (see chapter 9).

AUTHOR AND READER REFERENCE

It is common to distinguish between speaker and hearer reference (and by extension, author and reader reference). Strawson[31] says that when two people are talking, the speaker may refer to or mention some particular by means of proper names, pronouns, descriptions, and so on, whose function is to *enable* the hearer to identify the particular. This is "speaker reference" or "identifying reference." But the hearer may not in fact identify that particular, according to Strawson, so there can be speaker reference without hearer reference. Kripke discusses a similar example, claiming that the speaker's referent is the object which the speaker *wishes* to talk about.

Now, there may be cases of *spoken* reference where this distinction makes sense, that is, in cases where the speaker communicates their intention by gestures or other forms of demonstrative indication, but such cases have no relevance where the only context is written language. We are concerned with texts, the most recent of which was disclosed around 630 AD, that is, nearly 1,400 years ago, the authors (or transcribers)[32] of which are long since dead, so we are unlikely to know what their wishes or intentions were, except from the texts themselves, which either enable us to identify the reference, or do not, as in the case of Exodus 4:24–26, or Quran 3:35, or any other parts of the three scriptures where the interpretation is in doubt. In the case of texts, there is only reader reference, namely, the reference, which a reader competent in the language and with the conventions of the genre, would understand.[33] There is writer reference, in a sense, but that necessarily coincides with reader reference. For the same reason, there can be no reference failure, strictly speaking. Reference tells us which individual a proposition is about, so if the language fails to tell us this, there is no reference at all. The "failure" in question is an *alienans* predicate, like the *fool's* in *fool's gold*.

THE PROPERNESS OF PROPER NAMES

The anaphoric framework explains the properness of proper names better than Aristotelian or standard semantics, neither of which offers a compelling explanation of why proper names "properly" belong in the same sense to only one individual.

There is a long history of attempts to explain properness within the framework of Aristotelian semantics, of which perhaps the best known is Duns Scotus's fourteenth-century thesis that a specific nature (e.g., man) has a unity that is less than numerical unity, and that a specific nature is made individual (i.e., this man, Socrates) by the addition of a positive individuating factor, which Scotus calls the individuating difference (*differentia individualis*), or *haecitas*—"thisness."[34] The idea has found support more recently from Alvin Plantinga, who has argued that the name "Plato" expresses an individual essence of Plato. The essence is "incommunicable to any other" (explaining its properness); moreover, an individual can have two or more essences, which are logically but not epistemically equivalent, explaining why "Hesperus is the evening star" and "Phosphorus is the evening star" express epistemically different propositions. Haecceity properties explain how negative existential statements could be logically possible, but raise the problem that, if Moses no longer exists, the name "Moses" expresses an *unexemplified* haecceity,[35] which seems implausible. How can the haecceity property exist independently of Moses, floating around in the ether without a bearer? Other philosophers have also found the notion challenging.[36]

The alternative to the standard theory is to suppose that a proper name expresses some kind of property, or combination of properties.[37] But as Mill argued (and Kripke after him), if "Moses" signifies the concept of a certain set of attributes that happen to be uniquely satisfied, one of two things follows. Either, if I meet a person who corresponds exactly to the concept I have formed of Moses, I must suppose that this person actually is Moses, and lived in the second millennium BC, or else I cannot think of Moses as Moses, but only as *a* Moses; and all those that are mistakenly called proper names are common names. "Either theory seems to be sufficiently refuted by stating it."[38]

Moreover, if the name expressed some non-singular property, or set of such properties, we could coherently deny, *using that name*, that its bearer possessed it. It is not, as Wettstein puts it, that a description like "being the man who led the Israelites out of Egypt," or "being the man who was found as a baby by Pharaoh's daughter" and so on, *searches* the world, *finds* its satisfier, and *attaches* the name to it. For the referent itself, the man who really did lead the Israelites from Egypt might well have done something else.[39] Moses *might* have chosen to stay in Egypt working for Pharaoh, and might not have led the Israelites out of Egypt. His mother might have decided to keep him, and so on. Kripke:

> He might never have gone into either politics or religion at all; and in that case maybe no one would have done any of the things that the Bible relates of Moses.[40]

This doesn't mean that in such a possible world, he wouldn't have *existed*, he just wouldn't have *done* those things. Hence, the existence of Moses cannot be reduced to the existence of a man with such attributes.

For similar reasons, Mill argued that a proper name signifies no attributes as belonging to its bearer, that it is more like a mark placed directly on the bearer and so, strictly speaking, has no meaning at all.[41] It merely "answers the purpose of showing what thing it is we are talking about, but not of telling anything about it" (*System* I. ii. 5). This idea did not originate with him—elsewhere Mill cites Reid's claim that a proper name "signifies nothing but the individual whose name it is," and that when we apply it to an individual "we neither affirm nor deny anything concerning him"—which Reid himself probably got from the Greek grammarian Apollonius Dyscolus.[42] But as I noted in the previous chapter, Mill does not explain how a mark can be meaningless, yet be connected in our mind with the idea of an object, nor does he explain what the idea of an individual object is.

The standard theory is a development of Mill's theory, and is attended by the same difficulties. It explains properness by a semantic connection between proper name and bearer whereby the name can only signify that thing, but this leads to all the well-known difficulties mentioned in the last chapter, for example (i) how a large planetary body like Jupiter could be a part of a meaning or a thought, (ii) how identity statements involving different names for the same thing, such as "Hesperus is Phosphorus" can sometimes be informative, and (iii) how negative existential statements, which apparently deny a meaning for the name, are possible at all.

By contrast, the anaphoric hypothesis offers a simpler explanation of properness. On the anaphoric thesis, the semantic function of a proper name is to associate the proposition, which contains it with an antecedent anaphoric chain, such that any two terms in the chain, including the proper name in question, signify that if they have a referent at all, they have a single referent. Other singular terms such as definite descriptions and pronouns have a similar function, but a proper name has no other function, being simply a tag for its chain of antecedent terms. We can clearly see this if we express the content of the following single proposition:

A hobbit called "Bilbo" lives in a hole

by means of two separate "that" clauses, namely, (i) a hobbit is called "Bilbo" and (ii) *Bilbo* (or "he" or "this hobbit") lives in a hole. It would be ridiculous to suppose that the proper name, when used, signifies some individual essence of a hobbit, or that it directly signifies the hobbit himself. If the single proposition does not express Bilbo-ness, which it cannot because it is an indefinite proposition, and if the propositions signified by the two "that" clauses express the same thing as the single proposition, then the two propositions cannot express Bilbo-ness either, despite the use of the proper name in the second "that" clause. But there is no need to run into the sorts of philosophical difficulties generated by individuating differences or direct reference, so long as we see the proper name as a mere tag that allows us to join two propositions into one, as above.

Hence, a proper name cannot have a plural. Or suppose it had. Then we could use the name to signify both that the same thing is such-and-such, and that a different thing is such-and-such. But a proper name cannot signify identity and difference at the same time, so it cannot have a plural. A common name, by contrast, can be used to signify both "the same F" and "another F," because its purpose is not to continue an anaphoric chain. The anaphoric account has no philosophical difficulties at all. We run into such difficulties only if we suppose that a name signifies some essential property of an individual, or the individual itself, rather than a property of the language alone.

SUMMARY

I have argued that co-reference is rule governed, and that it in no way depends upon any semantic relation between a text and extratextual items. The difficulty faced by computers in comprehending human texts does not conflict with this principle. The ability to understand a text like the Hebrew Bible presupposes the ability to keep track of which individual is which by assigning the right token of a singular term to the right subject. This requires not just knowledge of the syntax and semantics of the language, but knowledge of the genre, or of human nature itself. Such knowledge determines the "natural" reading of the text, deviation from which can only be justified if it justifies the same reading systematically across every passage of the scripture, and which other writers could emulate without going astray. For this reason, the proper names "Noah," "Abraham," and "Moses" have the same reference, that is, co-reference, in all the parts of the Hebrew Bible, even when the parts are written by different authors. Co-reference is objective in the sense that there are systematic rules or heuristics that determine sameness of reference. Otherwise there could be no "natural" reading of the scriptures.

The existence of such rules is crucial to determining the truth conditions for reference statements, which I shall discuss in the next chapter. I shall argue that a reference statement is true if and *only* if the term that is mentioned in the statement co-refers with the term that is used, hence if co-reference is an *objective* property of the text, the truth of a reference statement depends on properties of the text, rather than some extralinguistic relation between language and reality.

NOTES

1. Readers interested in the more general question of scriptural interpretation should consult Gracia 1995 and 2001, although Gracia's work is reliant on an outmoded theory of reference derived from Searle.
2. Chastain 1975, 205. Sommers (1982) also proposed the idea that proper names and indeed all definitely referring expressions are anaphors, but the idea precedes both writers. A similar idea was mooted by Prior, "Oratio Obliqua," originally published 1963, and Geach discusses something similar in *Mental Acts*. Strawson introduced the closely connected idea of story-relative reference in 1959, which he may have borrowed from W. E. Johnson (*Logic*, 1921), who distinguishes between what he calls the "Alternative indefinite" article, as in "A man must have been in this room," which should really be interpreted as "Some *or other* man must have been in this room" from what he calls the "Introductory indefinite," which occurs at the beginning of a narrative, for example, "Once upon a time there was *a boy* who bought a beanstalk." Johnson then supposes the narrative to continue: "*This boy* was very lazy," where the phrase "this boy" means "the boy *just mentioned*," that is, "the same boy as was introduced to us by means of the indefinite article." The affinity with Strawson's idea should be obvious. Johnson's work includes an early use of the term "reference" that is close to its contemporary sense. For example, he says "Here the article 'this,' or the analogous article 'the,' is used in what may be called its *referential sense*" (my emphasis). Johnson, *Logic*, I. vi. §4 (p. 85).
3. Chastain ("Reference and context," 216) rightly observes that "the ability to comprehend a novel, a biography, or even a single paragraph presupposes the ability to keep track of who's who by assigning a given singular expression to the right anaphoric chain, where the latter will normally be a mixture of proper names and other singular expressions. This means, for example, knowing when an occurrence of 'she' in Lolita belongs with the occurrences of 'Lolita' and when it belongs with the occurrences of the names of the other female characters in the book. The ability to identify anaphoric chains of this sort is obviously very complex: we employ our knowledge of the syntax and semantics of the language, plus our knowledge of how discourses are constructed, plus our knowledge of whatever special literary or scholarly or other

conventions pertain to the genre in question, plus our knowledge of what the writer is likely to have meant, and so on."

4. From a presentation by Christopher Manning, https://web.stanford.edu/class/archive/cs/cs224n/cs224n.1162/handouts/cs224n-lecture10-coreference.pdf.

5. Wiktionary.

6. Hobbs, "Resolving pronoun references."

7. Dominance is a primitive of syntactic analysis, which interprets sentence structure in terms of "trees," with dominant nodes higher up in the structure than dominated ones.

8. Lappin and Leass, "An algorithm for pronominal anaphora resolution."

9. I checked the first two of these examples with a user of Stanford CoreNLP tagger, a state of the art neural system, who told me it got them both wrong. However, the Hobb algorithm gets the "Seth" one right.

10. For example, Latin *sibi*, Greek ἑαυτοῦ. Hebrew uses a different way of expressing the reflexive.

11. I have used a translation consistent with the Hebrew, which uses pronouns only. Some translations resolve the difficulty of interpretation by use of the proper name, for example, NIV "At a lodging place on the way, the LORD met Moses and was about to kill him."

12. Silverman, *From Abraham to America: A History of Jewish Circumcision*, 86.

13. Other than Mary Magdalene, of course, since there were only two Marys at the tomb. Mary, mother of Jesus, was not present at that point, although confusingly she also had sons called James and Joseph, common names in first-century Galilee.

14. John of Damascus, *De Haeresibus*, 766, Niketas of Byzantium, *Confutatio dogmatum Mahomedis*, 790.

15. Exodus 15:20. If the "Imran" mentioned in Surah 3 is not the father of Moses, how did Muhammad discover the name? The father of Mary is not named in the New Testament, although Christian tradition knows him as "Joachim." If the author was using a name familiar to his readers, they would associate it with Imran the father of Moses. Otherwise it would be meaningless, unless there was a tradition in the Near East about Mary's father, but history is so far silent about that.

16. The Quran (3:7) says that some of its verses are specific, others ambiguous, whose meaning is known only to God. "Those whose hearts are infected with disbelief observe the ambiguous part."

17. Hughes, *Dictionary of Islam*, 206.

18. See also Esposito, *The Oxford Dictionary of Islam*, 136, on the tradition that Mary's father was *also* called Imran.

19. Sahih Muslim (transl. Siddiqi) Book 25, Hadith 5326 "When I came to Najran, they (the Christians of Najran) asked me: You read 'Sister of Harun', (i.e. Mary), in the Qur'an, whereas Moses was born well before Jesus. When I came back to Allah's Messenger I asked him about that, and he said: 'The (people of the old age) used to give names (to their persons) after the names of Apostle and pious persons who had gone before them.'"

20. Ibn Kathir, *Tafsir Ibn Kathir*, Vol. 2, 29–30, "Allah also chose the household of Imran, the father of Maryam bint Imran, the mother of ʿIsa [*Jesus*], peace be upon

them. So `Isa [Jesus] is from the offspring of Ibrahim, as we will mention in the Tafsir of Surah Al-An`am, Allah willing, and our trust is in Him."

21. Spinoza, *Theological-Political Treatise* (trans. Michael Silverthorne, Jonathan Israel), 7, 136.

22. A further difficulty is that in 19:28, Mary is called the sister of Aaron, who was the brother of Moses. Dawood says "sister" here means a virtuous woman. According to Hughes (*Dictionary of Islam*, 328), Al-Baidawi says she was called "sister of Aaron" because she was of Levitical race; but Husain says that the Aaron mentioned in the verse is not the same person as the brother of Moses.

23. Sale, *The Koran, Commonly Called the Alcoran of Mohammed*, 56.

24. Strictly speaking, the author or *authors*, or *editors*.

25. This basic assumption is occasionally violated. Moses is supposed to be the author of the whole of the Pentateuch. But as Spinoza points out (*Theological-Political Treatise*, 8.3, trans. Michael Silverthorne, Jonathan Israel, 119), the words of Deuteronomy 31.9 "and Moses wrote the Law" cannot be the words of Moses, but rather of another writer who has temporarily forgotten that he is writing as if he were Moses. The author of Genesis 12.6 says "the Canaanite *at that time* was in the land," forgetting that if he had been writing at that time, rather than later, the Canaanite would *still* be in the land.

26. An exception being the phenomenon of "bridging": I saw a house. The roof had a hole in it.

27. Basset, "Apollonius between Homeric and Hellenistic Greek: The case of the 'Pre-positive Article'" in Matthaios, ed., 260. A *cold opening* (or: *in medias res*) is a literary device that deliberately flouts this rule. For example, "It was just noon that Sunday morning when *the sheriff* reached the jail with Lucas Beauchamp" (William Faulkner, *Intruder in the Dust*, 1948); "*He* was born with a gift of laughter and a sense that the world was mad" (Raphael Sabatini, *Scaramouche*, 1921); "*She* might have been waiting for her lover" (Graham Greene, *England Made Me*, 1935). Strawson ("On referring," 331) calls it the "spurious" use of the definite article, claiming that sophisticated fiction depends on it, as opposed to the "unsophisticated kind" which begins "once upon a time there was . . ." The technique suggests the earlier part of a text has been lost, as though a page or two is missing, and hence the co-reference is missing. The use of a definite article in the first verse of a work of fiction implies a semantic dependence on some antecedent that is simply not available. The same is true of complete definite descriptions like "tallest girl in the class," or indeed "son of God."

28. That is, demonstratives that involve pointing or gestures or other actions external to the text.

29. *Intellectum constituere*: literally to create or establish understanding.

30. Essentially the same point is made in Kripke "Speaker's reference and semantic reference" (262), who distinguishes what a speaker's words mean, in a specific context, and what he actually meant, or intended, on that occasion.

31. Strawson, *Individuals*, 15–16.

32. Both the Hebrew Bible and the New Testament have human narrators. However, the central narrator of the Quran purports to be Allah himself.

33. Kripke calls this *semantic reference* ("Speaker's reference and semantic reference," *passim*).

34. Scotus used the term *haecitas* only twice: see *Quaestiones super libros Metaphysicorum Aristotelis, Libri VI–IX*, 7.13 n61, p. 240 and 7.13 n176, p. 278, but his followers popularised it under the spelling "haecceitas."

35. Plantinga, "A Boethian compromise," 137.

36. See Vallicella, *A Paradigm Theory of Existence*, 97–104 for other compelling arguments against Plantinga-style haecceity properties.

37. E.g. Searle, "Proper names."

38. Mill, *An Examination of Sir William Hamilton's Philosophy (1979)*, 322–3. Mill's example is "Caesar."

39. Wettstein, "On referents and reference fixing," 112, see also Kripke, *Naming and Necessity*, 31, 61.

40. Kripke, *Naming and Necessity*, 58.

41. Mill, *A System of Logic*, I.ii.5.

42. See Mill, *An Examination of Sir William Hamilton's Philosophy*, 1979, 323, citing Reid, *The Works of Thomas Reid*, 412. See also Reid, ibid., 219–20, where he says that a definition is the explication of the meaning of a word in terms of words whose meaning is already known, for which reason there can be no logical definition of individual things, such as London and Paris. Reid's source was James Harris's book *Hermes*, published in 1773, an outline of Dyscolus' work on grammar. The idea can also be found in Aristotle, who points out in the *Metaphysics* (7.15, 1040 a27) that even when a term, such as "night hidden" denotes only one thing, namely the sun, it is still common because there could be two such objects. He contrasts this with a proper name like "Cleon," which can denote only Cleon.

Chapter 3

Story-Relative Reference

14:51 And a certain young man (νεανίσκος) followed him, with a linen cloth (σινδόνα) cast about his naked body; and they took hold of him.

14:52 And with the linen cloth cast off, he fled from them naked.[1]

INTRODUCTION

Mark mentions the young man just once. Perhaps he is the same man "clothed in a long white robe" that Mary Magdalene, Mary the mother of James, and Salome saw later when they entered the empty tomb (16:5), but Mark does not say. He clearly knows who the man is—he says "a certain" young man (*quidam*, τις), but he chooses not to identify him. Some have speculated that he was Mark himself. Others, that he represents a flight from Jerusalem, and from martyrdom. Yet I can *talk* about him, as many puzzled scholars have done in the past. Correggio and others *painted* him. Given we know so little about him, how is it that we can *refer* to him at all?

The gospels are rich in characters like the naked fugitive. Many, like him, are nameless. In Mark, these include the Gerasene demoniac (5:1–20) who is introduced as "a man with an unclean spirit"; a woman with a flow of blood (5:25–34) who is cured by touching Jesus' clothes, "an executioner" sent by Herod (6:27) to behead John the Baptist; a Syro-Phoenician woman (7:24-30) whose daughter Jesus cures of possession. Although there is extended reference to them by the pronouns "he" or "she," or by descriptions such as "the woman," none of them are named. Others are merely introduced without further mention, such as "one of Jesus' disciples" (εἷς τῶν μαθητῶν – 13:1), who may or may not be the same as any of the disciples referred to elsewhere. Others are named, but mentioned only briefly: for example, "Andrew and

Philip, and Bartholomew and Matthew, and Thomas and James of Alpheus, and Thaddeus [Jude] and Simon the Cananean" (3:18).

Other characters are named, and are the subject of extensive reference within the New Testament, but nowhere else, for example, Simon Peter (called "Simon" in 1:29, 30, 36; "Simon Peter" in 3:16; 14:37; "Peter" in 8:29, 32-33; 9:5; 10:28; 11:21; 14:29; 14:54, 66-72; 16:7; [16:9]). We do not find them in contemporary historical records outside the Bible. Jesus himself, the subject of all four gospels, is referenced frequently in the Acts of the Apostles, as well as occasionally appearing in person, but there is nothing about him in any independent contemporary document. He is mentioned frequently by Paul in his letters, but these are generally thought to have been written *before* the gospels, and the letters are in any case not independent witnesses. The first independent mention of Jesus is in Josephus's *Antiquities of the Jews*, written probably 93–94 AD, books eighteen and twenty, although there are doubts about the authenticity of these passages.[2] The second is by Tacitus, who mentions Jesus' execution by Pilate in a page of his *Annals* (c. AD 116), book fifteen, c.44. All subsequent references to Jesus, to Simon Peter and the other apostles, depend wholly on the information about him provided in the New Testament.

This brings me to the puzzle of *unbound anaphora*, of how singular terms introduced by indefinite description, such as "a man named Moses," "a woman named Martha," and "a man in the crowd," can co-refer in some sense with their indefinite antecedent, even though the antecedent itself does not refer. Mark says that the naked fugitive left the linen cloth, and that *he* fled. I can now say, using the pronoun "he," (Gr. ὁ, Lat. *ille*,), that Mark is able to identify or refer to *the young man*. I have just made a reference statement! The word "he" in *Mark*'s text is the mentioned term, the expression "the young man" in *my* previous sentence is the referring term. I have used the reference statement to tell us who, that is, which individual, the mentioned term refers to. But how can the statement tell us this when we don't know who the man is? His identity, like the identity of many characters in the Bible, is unknown. Mark's text does not tell us who the young man is (nor who is the Gerasene demoniac, the Syro-Phoenician woman, the executioner sent by Herod). But I can make a reference statement, and a reference statement tells us which person a term refers to. So I can say who he is referring to, but Mark can't, apparently. How do we explain this?

STORY-RELATIVE REFERENCE

The puzzle of story-relative reference is central to Strawson's book *Individuals*. He begins with what he calls *story-relative* identification.[3]

A speaker tells a story which he claims to be factual. It begins: "A man and a boy were standing by a fountain," and it continues: "the man had a drink." Shall we say that the hearer knows which or what particular is being referred to by the subject-expression in the second sentence? We might say so.

We know which individual is being referred to by the subject-expression "the man," because it distinguishes the man "by means of a description which applies only to him," but Strawson says this is relative identification only, for we know which particular individual is being referred to *of the two particular creatures being talked about by the speaker*, but we do not, without this qualification, know what particular creature is being referred to.[4] He distinguishes this from identification *within history*, saying that the former is identification only in a weak sense.

His story consists of two sentences, but there is nothing to prevent us from adding new anaphor sentences, which refer back to the initial indefinite antecedent, or from creating new indefinite sentences introducing new characters, indeed this is how the Biblical stories can be told at all. For example, Mary is introduced (Luke 1:27) by the indefinite description "*a virgin* engaged to a man whose name was Joseph, of the house of David." The narrative continues with the definite description "*the virgin's* name was 'Mary,'" after which Luke refers to her by a pronoun or her proper name. For example: "When Elizabeth heard *Mary's* greeting, the child leaped in *her* womb" (Luke 1:41). Likewise, Elizabeth is introduced by the indefinite description "a descendant of Aaron [whose] name was 'Elizabeth.'" Nearly all the characters in the gospels are identified in this story-relative way, being mentioned in no other *contemporary* historical source. These include all the twelve disciples, and other disciples, such as Bartimaeus, Jairus, his daughter and wife, Joseph of Arimathea, and Mary Magdalene. Other references, such as to Isaiah, Moses and Elijah, are to individuals in the Hebrew Bible, but they, like the majority of individuals mentioned there, are mentioned nowhere else.

Story relativity was a puzzle for Strawson. The focus of his work, and of the work of his student, Gareth Evans, was a criterion for a form of *absolute* reference, which he believed would be stringent enough to eliminate relative identification.[5] He claimed to have found it in the spatio-temporal network in which we as speakers are located, which gives us—because of our place in that network—a point of reference that individuates the network itself, and so helps us to individuate the other particulars within the network by means of dating and placing systems. He sought to ground identification in terms of *demonstrative* identification, arguing that even if an individual cannot itself be demonstratively identified, "It may be identified by a description which relates it uniquely to another particular which can be demonstratively identified."[6] Much of this book is an examination—and rejection—of that claim.

In this chapter, I shall address the problem of how a story can introduce characters indefinitely, for example as "a" young man, or "a" woman with a flow of blood, yet go on to refer to these characters using *anaphoric* chains of co-referring definite or singular terms.

How can a definite term co-refer with an indefinite term? A definite term can refer *back*[7] to an indefinite one.

There was *a* young man. *The* man was wearing a linen cloth.

But what about that initial description or name? What *term* does it *refer back* to, and what *individual* does it *refer* to, *simpliciter*? In the previous chapter, I provisionally defined co-referring terms as those whose meaning requires that, if they have a referent at all, they have a common referent. So it seems that the terms "a young man" and "the man" have a common reference, assuming the young man existed at all. But can an indefinite term like "a young man" refer?

TRANSPORTABILITY

I shall show that singular terms in a story-relative context, even proper names, do not have a meaning that is *transportable*.[8] By a transportable meaning, I mean one that can belong to any token, regardless of context or order. Consider

There was a young man. *He* was wearing a linen cloth.

The two sentences imply that some young man was wearing a linen cloth. Can any other term in the narrative have the same meaning as the pronoun "he"? Certainly, if the term occurs later in the natural order of reading. It will co-refer in some sense, and is anaphorically connected with the antecedent indefinite description "a young man." But no term that comes before the antecedent can have that meaning, for the whole purpose of an indefinite term is its indifference to what comes before: "a young man" means any young man, not necessarily a specific man already mentioned. That is:

He was wearing a linen cloth. . . . There was a young man.

does not imply that some young man was wearing a linen cloth. Perhaps "he" was an old, or a middle-aged man, or just some *other* man. But the inference depends on the meaning of the pronoun, any term with that meaning will validate the inference, yet no term prior in the order of reading can have such a meaning. Pronouns cannot refer forward to an antecedent term in the way that they refer back: the back reference is a part of their meaning, therefore the meaning is not transportable as I have defined it.

It may be objected that in English, as well as Latin and other languages, a pronoun can anticipate a postcedent that occurs later in the text. For example: "In his *Enquiry Concerning Human Understanding*, Hume raises doubts about our knowledge of necessary connection," where "his" anticipates "Hume." Or in Latin: *Is qui bene se exprimit hoc scripsit*, where "is" anticipates "qui." In reply, in such *cataphoric* co-reference, the semantics of the definite cataphoric term is in suspension, rather like a musical suspension, until the postcedent is identified, at which point the co-reference is understood, and the meaning of the cataphor is clear. Thus, the *meaning* of the cataphor is not transportable to a position before the postcedent, even if the term itself is transportable.[9]

Such non-transportability is obvious in the case of the pronoun, but the same is true of proper names. The sentences

There was a young man called "Mark." *Mark* was wearing a linen cloth.

together, and in that order, also imply that some young man was wearing a linen cloth. The proper name has some semantic connection to the indefinite antecedent "a man called 'Mark'" that licenses the inference. But this is no longer valid if the name occurs before the antecedent. For example

Mark was wearing a linen cloth. . . . There was a young man called "Mark."

Tokens of the same proper name may have different meanings, and the indefinite "a man called 'Mark'" could be introducing us to another person with the same name. For example, Acts 12:12:

He went to the house of Mary the mother of John, *also called Mark*

Is this the same as Mark the evangelist? This idea is suggested by 1 Peter 5:13, where Peter says "She who is in Babylon, chosen together with you, sends you her greetings, and so does my son *Mark*," but this is not a logical inference, but a probable or possible one. Proper names are essentially ambiguous, unless their meaning is resolved by context. In the case given earlier, the context is the indefinite antecedent, which can only occur before in the sequence of reading, never afterwards. In a story-relative context, not even proper names have a transportable meaning.

It could be objected that the singular anaphor term could be replaced by an indefinite noun phrase that included the content of the antecedent.[10] Then we could translate the two sentences

(1) A young man was wearing a linen cloth. He ran away.

as something like

(2) A young man was wearing a linen cloth. A young man who was wearing a linen cloth ran away.

The definite noun phrase "he" is replaced by the indefinite noun phrase "a young man who was wearing a linen cloth." This yields the required inference: the content of the conclusion is identical to the content of the second premiss. But this is problematic for a number of reasons. First, we have to suppose that every singular term in the anaphoric chain means the same as an indefinite term containing everything that was previously asserted in the chain. So the term "Moses" in "Moses was a hundred and twenty years old when he died" is equivalent to "a man who was born into the tribe of Levi, who was abandoned by his mother, taken in by Pharaoh's daughter, killed an Egyptian etc." This is wholly implausible. The term "Moses" does not mean that, and the sentence *itself* does not contain that information.

Second, what if there is another such man?

(3) A young man was wearing a linen cloth. *Another* young man who was wearing a linen cloth ran away.

The second sentence of (3) includes the content of the second sentence of (2), which is supposed to signify that the man, that is, *he*, is the same man, but the term "another" says that the man is different. It would be like saying "another the same man"!

The same line of reasoning shows that the meaning of unique definite descriptions cannot be captured by a unique indefinite description. Consider:

(4) A uniquely omnipotent being is creating. That same being is loving.

We want to describe the content of the second sentence in way that captures how the being that is loving is the same as the omnipotent being that is creating. No analysis based on Russell's theory of descriptions will do the trick.[11] Suppose we analyze the second sentence as follows.

(5) A uniquely omnipotent being who is creating, is loving.

But we could equally say

(6) *Another* uniquely omnipotent being who is creating, is loving.

which includes the content of (5), so (5) cannot possibly mean that the being is the same one as mentioned in the first sentence of (4). Of course, (6) contradicts the first part of (4). Both cannot be true, for there cannot be two uniquely omnipotent beings. But it does not contradict itself, as it would do if "the same as X" meant "possessing the same unique attribute as X." If it did, it would assert that someone who is both the only omnipotent being, and not the only omnipotent being, is loving. But it does not. It simply asserts that someone who is loving is the only omnipotent being, and implies that some other being (the object of the first sentence) is not. The theory of descriptions is inadequate to capture the sense of "sameness" that is asserted or implied to hold between the subjects of different propositions. Of course, if we talk on different occasions about the Prime Minister of the Great Britain, we normally imply that the same person is in question. But that just relies on the assumption that we are talking about the same individual. Assertion of some unique attribute implies or suggests sameness, it does not assert it. Otherwise we would not be able to say that any *other* individual possessed the attribute.[12]

REFERENCE STATEMENTS

The second thesis of this book, the *reference* thesis, is that the truth of a reference statement depends entirely upon *co-reference*, as I have defined it. I claim that the reference statement is true *if* and only if (i) the term mentioned *by* the statement co-refers with the term used *in* the statement, and (ii) the mentioned term is an anaphor, that is, has some antecedent in the chain of co-referring terms to which it belongs. Therefore, since co-reference (as I have defined it) is a purely semantic relation between the terms, and obtains whether or not there is an external object they are related to, its truth is independent of any such external relation. It is true that "Asmodeus" refers to the demon Asmodeus, whether or not there is such a thing as Asmodeus.

I argue as follows. If a story-relative meaning is not transportable, it follows that the meaning of the corresponding *reference statement* is not transportable either.

1. There was a young man called "Mark."
2. Mark was wearing a linen cloth.
3. The name "Mark" refers to *him*.

The third sentence is a reference statement as I have defined it. The mentioning term is "The name 'Mark' above," the mentioned term is the first token of the second sentence, that is, "Mark." The used or referring term is the pronoun "him." Clearly, the statement is true if and only if the used term and the mentioned term co-refer, as they do here. But both the mentioned and the used term refer back to the indefinite antecedent "a young man," back-reference is not transportable, hence the meaning of the reference statement is *also* not transportable, and the standard theory of reference statements seems to be false.

Note the first "if" in "*if* and only if." I claim that a reference statement is true *if* the term that is mentioned co-refers with the term that is used, and if the mentioned term is an anaphor, so that the statement can be true even if there was never any such person as the naked fugitive (e.g., if the author of the gospel invented the character). That is a strong claim, but it is a corollary of the co-reference thesis, as follows.

Both the anaphoric theory of reference and the standard theory of reference start with the pre-theoretical conception of reference, namely the "which-ness" signified by singular terms. A singular term such as a proper name signifies *which* particular thing (as opposed to which *kind* of thing) the speaker or writer is talking about. The sentence "Moses led the people out of Egypt" tells us which person it was who led the people out of Egypt. Singular terms such as proper names, definite descriptions, and pronouns can perform this task of "signifying which," and a proper name performs this function without signifying anything else. To paraphrase Mill, a proper name *shows* us, that is, signifies, which thing it is that we are talking about (or purport to talk about), without telling us anything else about it.

Under this pre-theoretical conception, a singular term can tell us which individual is being talked about without there being any such individual. For example, I discussed the name "Imran" in Quran 3:33 in the previous chapter, where it is unclear whether the name refers to the father of Moses, or to Jesus' uncle. But whether it refers to one or the other is a question for hermeneutics, not for any theory of reference. Depending on what the author of the text was trying to say, it could be true that "Imran" refers to the father of Moses, even if there were no such person as Imran. Sentences like "'M' refers to N" are used in textual analysis as a means of resolving ambiguity, that is, resolving the question of whether the mentioned term "M," typically an ambiguous pronoun, refers to the what the used term "N" means. But we can use such sentences whether or not the terms correspond to anything in reality. Consider the following:

Caliban is *referring to* Prospero when he says, "I am subject to a tyrant, a sorcerer that by his cunning hath cheated me of the island."
Austen *is referring to* Caroline Bingley when she writes "Not a syllable had ever reached *her* of Miss Darcy's meditated elopement."
When Tolkien *refers to* the same Orc as Snaga, he is exercising his role as translator.

The title of *The Lord of the Rings refers to* the story's main antagonist, the Dark Lord Sauron.

We can use the preposition "about" to say much the same thing. For example, we can say that a story like *War and Peace* is about, or refers to, Prince Andrei (among others), or that it is about, or refers to, Napoleon (among others). As Sainsbury has cogently argued,[13] we may be tempted to say that the first statement is not relational whereas the second is, because Prince Andrei is a fictional character, that is, doesn't exist, whereas Napoleon exists, so the second statement expresses a relation between *War and Peace* and Napoleon. Then we puzzle about how the very same form of words ("*War and Peace* is about" or "*War and Peace* refers to") can introduce a relation in the one case but not the other. But there is no puzzle, as he says. A verb phrase like "refers to" or "is about" doesn't express a relation in *either* case. We are tempted to infer the existence of a relation between the story and Napoleon merely on the extraneous fact that Napoleon exists, but the semantics of "refers to" do not require any *relation*. Both a fideist and an atheist may want to agree that the author of Exodus is referring to God to when he writes "Zipporah took a flint and cut off her son's foreskin, and touched *his* feet." Pre-theoretically, we can signify which thing a sentence purports to be about, without there being any such thing. A proper name merely signifies *whichness*.

By contrast, according to the theoretical framework of contemporary semantics, whereby the truth conditions of a sentence are compositionally determined by the semantic values or *referents* of the terms in the sentence, the truth conditions of "Moses was a prophet," are determined by the referents of the words in the sentence, including the referent of any proper name. Within this framework, it would be impossible for any sentence to express the proposition that "Prince Andrei" refers to Prince Andrei, for the proper name "Prince Andrei" is used in the reference statement itself, so its referent must be a constituent of the proposition expressed. But there is no referent, and there can be no such proposition. (There is a similar problem connected with the use of apparently true sentences containing fictional names, such as "there is no such person as Prince Andrei" or "Prince Andrei is a fictional character," which I shall discuss in chapter 7).

But we do not have to accept "traditional" semantics? For a start, there is no long tradition standing behind it. It begins with Frege, who supposed that a singular term has a *Bedeutung* or signification, and that this *Bedeutung* is the signified object itself. It soon occurred to him that this theory did not explain how sentences containing fictional names ("Odysseus was set ashore while asleep") could be significant, which prompted his well-known but muddled idea that names have a sense (*Sinn*) as well as a signification. The idea of "direct reference" is an even more recent innovation, which I shall discuss further in chapter 7. As discussed in chapter 1, the real "traditional" semantics is the one originally proposed by Aristotle, which featured prominently in the philosophy of language of the medieval period.

I have proposed, by contrast, that proper names, and singular terms generally, signify *anaphorically*, and that the anaphoric connections within a chain of singular terms is such that if we understand them at all, then we understand that they must have a common referent, if the referent exists. That is how we are able to comprehend works of complete fiction, such as *The Lord of the Rings*, where even the world itself (Middle Earth) is fictional. We would not be able to make any sense of such a work unless we grasped that if *any* occurrence of "Frodo" had a referent, every occurrence would have that referent (a certain hobbit). Likewise for "Gandalf," "Sauron," and the rest.

The pre-theoretical conception of reference does not involve any explanation of why a statement like "The title of *The Lord of the Rings* refers to the story's main antagonist, the Dark Lord Sauron" should be true, although everyone who knows the story accepts it as true. What I am adding, by way of a theory, is an explanation. Assuming we understand "anaphoric connection" as basic, I claim that what *makes* the statement true is the anaphoric connection between the term that is mentioned, namely the title of the book, and the proper name "Sauron" as it is used in the book.

This theory raises other questions, such as the nature of truth conditions, of what makes negative existentials, such as "there is no such person as Sauron" true, which I shall defer for now (but see chapter 7 for a fuller discussion). The point here is that fictional reference statements are obviously and pre-theoretically true or false, and I offer an explanation, via the idea of an anaphoric connection that I explore throughout this book.

Given that my use of the term "refers" may cause confusion to readers who are wedded to a particular theory of reference, I shall adhere to the following convention. If I use the term "refers" with or without a grammatical object, I am using it in the pre-theoretical sense in which "Sauron" refers, and in which it is true to say that "Sauron" refers to Sauron. I am doing this in order to reclaim the word from any particular theory of reference. By contrast, when I use the verb "has a referent," I use that verb in a way that is consistent with the standard theory, whereby it is false to state that "Sauron" has a referent. Note, however, that I hold that it is merely false to state that "Sauron" *has Sauron* as a referent, whereas according to the standard theory that statement, without a truth condition, is nonsensical.

"INDEFINITE REFERENCE"

Indefinite terms cannot refer. Their indifference to what has gone before is essential to their meaning. However, some philosophers, noting the co-reference between singular terms and their indefinite antecedents, have thought otherwise. Chastain wonders whether sentences containing indefinite descriptions are ambiguous. Sometimes "A mosquito is in here" can be taken as asserting the place is not without mosquitoes, but sometimes can involve an "intended reference" to one particular mosquito.[14] According to Fred Sommers:

> In most cases where "some S is P" is followed by "it is also Q" the pronoun "it" is equivalent to "the S that is P" which indicates that what was *referred to* in the antecedent proposition is an S that is P.[15] (my emphasis)

Heusinger claims that "An indefinite NP refers to a physical or *indefinite object.*"[16]

Geach, by contrast, has vigorously argued that a referring term signifies *which* thing we are talking about in making a statement,[17] so how can we say that the indefinite "a young man" *refers* to any one, if it does not tell us who the young man is? "One of the disciples is standing" is true when any disciple is standing, whether Simon or Thomas or Matthew or any other. It does not tell us *which* disciple this is. So we cannot say that "a young man" refers to some man. As Geach says, the question at once arises: *Who can be the man or men referred to?*[18]

Yet the anaphor of an indefinite antecedent does have a definite reference. We can use an indefinite description that introduces a person by name, then use that name to refer back to the antecedent: "A young man called 'Mark' was in the crowd: *Mark* was wearing a linen cloth." If the name does not refer to Mark when we first used it, at what point *does* it start referring, given that all proper names in a historical text are essentially introduced this way?[19] If it does refer, how are we to understand its relation to the indefinite and hence non-referring term that introduces the name?

There is an extensive literature on this question (i.e., the problem of unbound anaphora) beginning in 1962 with Geach's *Reference and Generality*, and later Evans' "Pronouns, quantifiers, and relative clauses," which generated a new field of research in the 1980s.[20] The dichotomy implied by Geach's title is between a *general* term, as in the "some man" or "a donkey" in "some man owns a donkey," and a *referring* term, identifying a particular individual that the proposition in which it occurs states of or about or concerning that individual that it is F, or G or other, and so picks out or identifies some previously known individual to the hearer, or recalls some individual that the hearer has in mind. Geach has strenuously argued that pronouns are bound to their antecedents rather like the bound variables of quantification theory, and therefore cannot refer. It makes no sense to ask about the "reference" of the variable "x" in "for some x, Fx and Gx," and for the same reason it makes no sense to ask about the "reference" of pronouns. Evans (1977), by contrast, proposed an "E-type analysis" of certain pronouns, whereby they are referring expressions that have their references fixed by description, where the description is extracted (largely) from the linguistic context. But as I have argued, no indefinite description on its own, not even a unique description, can capture the content of a definite description. Nor is Russell's theory of descriptions (which interprets a definite proposition as an indefinite one) adequate to capture the sense of "sameness" that is asserted or implied to hold between the subjects of different propositions.

The puzzle is that an anaphor seems to refer, even though its antecedent clearly does not, but it is only a puzzle on the assumption that a reference statement expresses an external "reference relation" between language and reality. Sommers is clearly tempted by the idea that we can make a reference statement to the object "referred to" by the indefinite term. One can say perhaps "I stepped on *a snail*," then say "I did not see *the snail*," then truly say that the definite description "the snail" refers to *it*. But if we assume that this reference statement, that is, "*the snail*" *refers to it*, expresses an external relation, it follows that "a snail" refers too, because of the co-reference. But an indefinite term cannot refer, as Geach has argued. He is correct that we cannot ask *which* animal "a snail" refers to, in the sense that the answer involves some external relation to an animal independent of the story. But that shows precisely that the reference statement does not express such a relation. The pronoun "it" in the reference statement co-refers with the definite description "the snail," which is an intralinguistic relation, and the reference statement is true for that reason. The anaphor does refer, but only in a story-relative sense, the indefinite antecedent does not. Geach is right that the antecedent does not refer, and Sommers is wrong; Sommers is right that the anaphor refers and Geach is wrong. The error of both positions lies in the assumption of some external reference relation. We can show that "'the snail' refers to *it*" is true without there being any snail, hence without there being any such reference relation.

Sommers has argued that indefinite reference is a kind of *non-identifying* reference,[21] but it is unclear what such reference could be. I have argued that a referring term operates by identifying some previous term in some anaphoric chain in some text, and that this function exhausts its semantics. What could be left over? Moses is introduced by the indefinite term "a son" born of a Levite woman.[22] As I have argued, the purpose of the indefinite term is specifically *not* to identify or co-refer with any previous term in the text, and its whole purpose is to introduce, rather than continue, an anaphoric chain. Moreover, I have argued that both definite and indefinite terms have the same semantics whether or not a bearer exists. Suppose that Moses never existed. Then in such a case the name "Moses" (in the context of the text of the

Hebrew Bible) still refers, because such reference is grounded in an intralinguistic (or intratextual) semantic relation to some antecedent, a relation that exists whether or not the man existed, but the indefinite term "a son," which begins the anaphoric chain corresponding to Moses, has no such antecedent, so does not refer. How does the existence or non-existence of Moses affect the meaning of "a son born of a Levite woman"? What is the semantic property that obtains in the case of Moses' historical existence, and which does not obtain if he never existed? Surely nothing. As Sainsbury says, it is not the job of the logician to effect a segregation between those terms that have a referent and those which do not. Logic is supposed to be a priori, and not to involve the kind of astronomical or literary knowledge required to determine into which category a name like "Vulcan," "Homer," or "Patanjali" falls.[23]

"Indefinite reference" is also problematic in the case of *minimally sourced* descriptions, that is, where evidence for a person fitting the description is scant, typically involving some other sense than sight. It seems that such descriptions cannot refer to an individual, yet they can co-refer with a subsequent description. Geach gives the example: "A philosopher of my time was a heavy pipe-smoker," asserted solely on the basis of the Faculty Board room reeking of pipe smoke.[24] Sainsbury mentions a headmistress who says "a girl, *I don't yet know who*, has been smoking in the lavatories,"[25] based on the smell of cigarette smoke.[26] Elbourne suggests, "A man murdered Smith. The police have reason to think he injured himself in the process," where the reason is the blood at the crime scene that does not belong to the victim.[27] These examples present serious difficulties for any reading that invokes an external semantic relation. As Geach argues, the man who smelled pipe smoke in the Faculty Board room does not need to have *had in mind* or *meant to refer* to some particular faculty member, nor does he make reference to any definite person *concerning whom* we could ask whether *that person* also drank alcohol.[28] However, this means only that the man is not using "a philosophy lecturer" *to refer* to any one philosophy lecturer by name or by some other description. If there were ten members of the philosophy faculty in Geach's story, we could always ask whether *the pipe smoker* was Brown, or Higgins, or Prior or Smith, and so forth. The term "the pipe smoker" does not refer to Brown or Higgins, or anyone else, yet it *does* refer to the pipe smoker, the philosopher the speaker was talking about.

Likewise, we can ask whether *the girl* who the head thought had been smoking was Jessica or Laura or Melanie or Josie. "The girl" does refer, namely to the girl the headmistress *says* might have been smoking in the lavatories, but it does not refer Jessica, or Laura, or Melanie or Josie, just as "the disciple whom Jesus loved," who is never identified as Peter, or Andrew, Thomas, and so forth, does not refer to Peter, or to Andrew, Thomas, and so forth. It is part of the meaning of "the girl the head was talking about" that "the girl" co-refers with the head's utterance that morning, and "Jessica" (e.g.) as used at the school is part of a narrative involving girls, teachers, classrooms, smoking, rule infringements, and so on. But it is not part of the meaning of "Jessica" that it co-refers with "the girl the head was talking about," thus "the girl the head was talking about was Jessica" is contingently true or false, just like "the disciple whom Jesus loved was John."

"Having in mind" is of course irrelevant.[29] As Geach notes, someone might have some girl in their mind when they utter "some girl is loved by every boy," but this does not matter.

> Suppose he has Mary in mind whereas in fact not Mary but Jane is loved by every boy; then "some girl is loved by every boy" will be true although "Mary is loved by every boy" would be false, and hence "some girl" cannot, even for the nonce, be being used to refer to Mary.[30]

As noted earlier, Mark knows who "a certain young man is," for it is the function of the word "certain" to suggest that he knows, but he does not pass on this knowledge, so the indefinite noun phrase does not refer. However (though Geach would disagree), when we add "that disciple was wearing a linen cloth," the definite term "that disciple" refers, by telling us which disciple (namely the one said previously to be standing) was wearing a linen cloth. The reference is relative only, and involves no extralinguistic relation—otherwise the relation would be symmetric, and the introductory indefinite term *would* refer, as Sommers, Chastain, and others have believed.

DEPENDENCY

The third thesis of this book is that singular terms are semantically dependent on a common narrative, written *or* spoken, such as the Hebrew Bible or some oral tradition. A term is semantically dependent on some item, or type of item, when it depends for its meaning upon the existence of that item, so that a proposition depending on that term would not be available to be entertained or expressed if that item did not exist.[31] Contemporary theories of meaning assume that the only form of semantic dependence is object dependence or property dependence. As Devitt suggests, they assume without question the false dichotomy that every term is either "descriptive" (semantically dependent on some property) or "directly referential" (i.e., semantically dependent upon some individual).[32] Locke assumes that we are either acquainted with "common agreements of shape, and several other qualities," to which we assign common names, or we are acquainted with all those "very particular things," that is, individuals.[33] Plantinga contrasts Fregeanism, the doctrine that proper names have descriptive content, with anti-Fregeanism, the doctrine that the semantic function of a proper name is *exhausted* in specifying a referent.

> The crucial contrast, then, between Fregean and anti-Fregean views is that on the former proper names express properties; on the latter they do not.[34]

He follows Boethius, who thought that Plato has a certain property called "Plato-ness" (*Platonitas*), which is a property unique to him, signified by the name "Plato." Plato-ness belongs just to Plato.[35] I shall not discuss his position here, as it is sufficiently refuted by what I have said earlier. The point is that the dichotomy between dependence on objects and dependence on properties is a false one.

A proper name cannot express a property, otherwise its meaning would be transportable. In virtue of how a property term acquires its meaning, there should be nothing to prevent its having the meaning it does, at any point. But proper names in a story-relative context do not have a transportable meaning, therefore such proper names cannot express properties. For the very same reason, their meaning cannot depend on the existence of an object. If a proper name merely signifies its bearer, its signification should also be transportable, but this is impossible. Names are semantically dependent neither on a property nor on an object.

This also means that we cannot in principle describe the *content* of a definite proposition independently of the content of a proposition, which it co-refers with. We have to replicate the same device used in the proposition described, thus:

(7) It says in (1) above that a young man was wearing a linen cloth, and that *the same man* ran away.

We cannot grasp the content of the second that-clause without grasping the first, and cannot therefore say what the second sentence of (1) expresses *without presupposing what is expressed by the first*. To express the content of the second sentence independently, we must somehow say of the man who was wearing a linen cloth that he is no different from the one who ran away, that he is that very man. But this is impossible for the reason given earlier. Suppose the second sentence of (1), that is, "he ran away," is in, or can be re-written in a form that is *semantically independent*; so that its component words are either common words of English, or contained in a special dictionary accessible to everyone, and so that anyone can put together another sentence (Sx) that has exactly the same meaning as the second sentence of (1), but which does not derive its meaning from its contiguity to the first sentence.

(Sx) <common or dictionary term> ran away.

But suppose we read (Sx) before the two sentences of (1). Then, since (Sx) and the second proposition of (1) are supposed to have the same meaning, and because the meaning of (Sx) is that a man ran way, who *was the very same man as the one who was wearing a linen cloth*, we would immediately grasp that (Sx) and (1) are about the same person. But that is impossible: the two propositions of (1) together say that *a man* was wearing a linen cloth and ran away, they do not tell us *which* man is in question, that is, they do not tell us who the man is *the same as*. But if we had grasped (Sx) before grasping (1) we would grasp which man he is the same as. There cannot therefore be such a sentence (Sx), with the same meaning as "he ran away."[36]

This tells us as much about the meaning of "a man" as about the meaning of "the man" or "he." Suppose there were a dictionary containing predicates, each unique to an individual, so that if n such predicates were asserted of subjects, then n individuals would be asserted to exist. Then we could always construct a sentence of the form "some individual is so-and-so," without this sentence having to be true of any of the n individuals. And we could go on to say "that individual is such-and-such," that is, make a definite assertion about an individual who is not necessarily one of those n. The second assertion would be semantically dependent upon the first in a way that it would not be to the dictionary predicates. It is therefore impossible to analyse the second proposition of (1) in a way that is semantically independent of the first. We cannot explain it in terms of the fixed dictionary meanings of the words like "he," "is," "man," "omnipotent," etc. Its meaning is tied not to an expression-type, as could occur in a copy of a dictionary, but to a particular token of an expression. This is despite the fact that the two propositions *taken together* are semantically independent. Anyone who understands English understands what the two sentences mean: that one man (we aren't told who) both wore a linen cloth and ran away. It is their content. But that part of their content that corresponds to the second proposition is irreducible. There is no particular difficulty about this. It is problematic only if we buy a certain semantic theory, which says that singular propositions are either analyzable into quantified statements, or "referential," in the sense that they contain an object in some mysterious way.

SUMMARY

And there followed him a certain young man. Mark suggests he knows who the man is, but he does not pass his knowledge to us. His indefinite article referentially isolates the man from history, or at least it appears so. Yet he says next that *he, the man*, fled from the scene naked. The pronoun "he" (Gr. ό, Lat. *ille*) does tell us which person it was who fled, tells us which person Mark is referring to, within the frame provided by the story, but does not place him, without the frame, within our general picture of history. The man is *referentially isolated*, like nearly all the characters in the gospels: the characters who "leap like salmon" in and out of the pages of the gospels, unnamed and unknown: the Gerasene demoniac, the woman with a flow of blood, the executioner sent by Herod, or those who are named but mentioned briefly, such as Andrew and Philip, and Bartholomew and Matthew, and Thomas and James of Alpheus. None of them have any identity outside the gospels, yet we can identify them within the story.

I have argued that this puzzling story-relative reference is explained by co-reference to an indefinite antecedent. An anaphoric chain is an ordered set of terms where each term in the chain, except the first, co-refers with the previous one. But the first link in the chain has no previous co-reference, for its indefinite nature prohibits any reference further back. Hence all reference within the chain is relative. If not, that is, if it were absolute, the meaning would be *transportable*, so that a term could have the same meaning even if it occurred before the indefinite antecedent. We can form a reference statement that mentions a term in the chain, then use a term to extend the same chain, but this cannot specify the reference in any absolute Strawsonian sense.

The purpose of this book is to show how this form of intralinguistic reference underlies *all* reference: reference to the main characters of all three scriptural traditions, such as Abraham, Moses, and Jesus, to historical characters outside those traditions, such as Pharaoh, Nebuchadnezzar, and Caesar, reference to people living now, including those whom we have known and met as well as those we haven't, and of course reference to *God*.

NOTES

1. My translation from the Vulgate.
2. The doubts exist because in *Antiquities* Book 18, Chapter 3, 3, the text reads, "About this time there lived Jesus, a wise man, *if indeed one ought to call him a man*." It seems unlikely that Josephus, an orthodox Jew, would consider Jesus as someone more than a man, or that he would claim he was the Messiah. This has led many to believe that the passage is a Christian interpolation.
3. Chapter 1. Strawson, *Individuals*, 18. See also the story considered by W. E. Johnson mentioned in our previous chapter: "Once upon a time there was a boy who bought a beanstalk. . . . This boy was very lazy." This is what he calls the *referential* sense of the demonstrative "this" (meaning that the demonstrative refers back to a phrase that introduces the object talked about). He says that "other variations of the

'Referential Definite' are such phrases as 'the former' and 'the latter,' which may be required to secure definite reference." Johnson, *Logic*, I. vi. §4, p. 85.

4. This is one of those plausible accounts that dissolve into incoherence at a closer look. Strawson says that the term "the man" distinguishes by means of a description, which *applies* only to *him*. Yet we can distinguish the character of the man from that of the boy whether the story is true or not, just as we can distinguish the man and the woman in the story of Genesis 2–3, even if the story is allegorical: the description does not have to "apply" to any extralinguistic item in order for the story to make a distinction between two characters. Nor, as I noted earlier, does it have to *uniquely* apply. Nowhere is it asserted or presumed that exactly one man was wearing a linen cloth in Mark's story of the naked fugitive. Nor does the notion of "relative to a range of particulars" make much sense. If the narrative is allegory or fiction, there is no "range of particulars" at all. Moreover, even if there are such particulars, how does identifying in this *relative* way differ from identifying in some *absolute* way, given that either way we have a relation to the particulars themselves? Strawson goes on to compare the characters portrayed in the story to figures in a picture, which we can place in our own general picture of the world because of the placement of the picture itself, although we cannot so place them, without the frame. This is more helpful, but ultimately misleading. The relation between unknown characters depicted in a picture is no less obscure than if they had been portrayed in a story.

5. Strawson, *Individuals*, 18.

6. Ibid., 21.

7. Note the "back." The term "he" refers back to another term, for example, "Mark," but it refers *simpliciter* to Mark himself.

8. I borrow the term from Sainsbury ("Fregean sense," in *Departing from Frege*, 125–36, 136), who points out that in inference we need "transportable" conclusions. For example, the inference (my example) "a is F, therefore it is F" is valid, but the conclusion is not "transportable," that is, cannot be placed in other contexts where the antecedent is missing.

9. Note the extreme form of cataphor in the opening of this book, which begins "*It* is recent, yet it is also one of the oldest controversies in the troubled relationship between Christianity and Islam." What is "it"? The ambiguity is not resolved until the second paragraph, which begins "The affair reignited *a controversy that is as old as Christianity's first engagement with Islam*," that is, "it" is *the* controversy that is as old etc. My point remains. The *term* "it" is transportable to a point in the text that precedes the term upon which its semantics is dependent, but its *semantics* is not thus transportable. We do not understand cataphor until we reach its postcedent, but we always understand anaphor at the point we reach it in the text (assuming the text is coherent in the first place).

10. See Rickless, "The semantic function of chained pronouns" for such a proposal. Sommers (*The Logic of Natural Language*, 332) says that the second sentence of "A French king is at the Ritz. He is quite bald" is equivalent to "the king of France who is staying at the Ritz is bald." Sommers has come the closest of anyone to putting his finger on the truth, but he is badly mistaken here. The first sentence says *that* a French king is at the Ritz, the second sentence *that* he is quite bald, and nothing else.

One could go on to say, for example, that he is not a king, and not staying at the Ritz. This would contradict the first sentence, but it does not contradict *itself*. It does not say, for example, "the king of France who is staying at the Ritz is not a king."

11. There is, of course, an extensive literature on what I have called the *expected completion* approach to descriptions which do not satisfy a unique individual, (as Russell's theory requires if his analysis is not to assert falsely that, only one individual satisfies the description). Neale summarizes this literature in Chapter 3 of *Descriptions* and himself argues for such an approach. Neale also argues, in support of his thesis that definite descriptions reduce to a quantified form, that quantified statements can be similarly incomplete. For example "Everyone was sick" does not assert that everyone in existence was sick, but that everyone *at the party I had last night was sick* (Ibid., 95). But this is the same problem. If I say that some people came to my party last night and go on to say that all *of them* were sick, I go on to say that all of the people mentioned in my original statement, that is, those very same people, were sick. We have the same problem, of explaining what "all of *those people*" means, without deferring to some previous assertion, or piece of information.

12. A character may be described in a work of fiction, who agrees in all points with an existing individual. Yet we should still say that there is no such person X (being a fictional character), and that X cannot therefore be the *same person* as some existing individual, the real-life model Y. In the book *Labels*, Evelyn Waugh attributes all the events that actually happened to him to another character (Geoffrey). The adventures attributed to the narrator are, on the other hand, a mixture of fact and fiction (the US title of the book was *A Batchelor Abroad*, though Waugh, like Geoffrey, was married). Was Geoffrey a real individual, the narrator a fictional character? No: *Labels* is a travel book, work of nonfiction. The narrator was a real person—Waugh—though some of the things attributed to him are made up. Geoffrey, on the other hand, was a complete invention. There was no such person, since there was no person who resembled Waugh *in all respects*, yet who was *numerically different* from him.

13. Sainsbury, *Thinking about Thing*s, 27–8.

14. Chastain, "Reference and context," 212. See also Sommers, *The Logic of Natural Language*, 49.

15. Sommers, *The Logic of Natural Language*, 53.

16. Heusinger, *Reference and Anaphoric Relations*, 249, my emphasis.

17. Geach, *Reference and Generality*, 31.

18. Ibid., 30.

19. As Geach himself notes (*Mental Acts*, 73) "in a series of statements about Smith, I hold, 'Smith' could be replaced the first time by 'a man,' and in later occurrences by 'the same man' or 'the man' or 'he.' Now from a logical point of view the string of statements thus obtained, with the name 'Smith' eliminated, are just one long existentially quantified statement; 'for some x, x was a man, and x committed a murder, and x was hanged.' But this would clearly not do as an account of how judgments are actually formed—especially if the one long statement would have to be very long, as may easily happen when I keep on learning things about somebody." My claim is precisely that this *will* do as an account of how judgments are actually formed, correctly formulated. The complex predication "A man wearing a linen cloth

was in the crowd" states (i) *that* a man was in the crowd and (ii) *that* he was wearing a linen cloth. The two "that" clauses specify the content of two separate propositions (or "judgments") embedded in a complex predication.

20. Evans, "Pronouns, quantifiers, and relative clauses (I)." For a summary of the literature, see Essay III of Klima, *Ars Artium*.

21. Sommers, *The Logic of Natural Language*, 65 and *passim*.

22. Ex. 2:1–2: "Now a man of the tribe of Levi married a Levite woman, and she became pregnant and gave birth to *a son*."

23. Sainsbury, *Reference without Referents*, 65.

24. Geach, "Back reference," 31–2.

25. My emphasis.

26. Sainsbury, *Reference without Referents*, 96.

27. Elbourne, *Situations and Individuals*, 16.

28. Geach, "Back reference," 33, emphasis mine.

29. Sommers' idea (*The Logic of Natural Language*, 59) that definite reference "begins with and is semantically dependent on an indefinite epistemic reference to that individual" is troublesome for the same reason.

30. Sommers, *The Logic of Natural Language*, 6. See also Geach's argument (*Reference and Generality*, 32), "If Smith did have a definite man in mind, there is, as we just saw, a common use of 'refer' in which we can say Smith referred to that man; but it does not follow that the actual phrase 'some man' referred then and there to the man in question." See also Sainsbury, *Reference without Referents*, 96.

31. See Neale, *Descriptions*, 19 in the context of so-called *object-dependent* propositions.

32. Devitt, "Against direct reference," 463.

33. Essay III. iii. 3.

34. Plantinga, "A Boethian compromise," 129, my emphasis.

35. "For if I may coin a new word I would call the particular quality which cannot be shared with any other substance by an invented name of its own to make clearer exactly what I mean. Let us call that characteristic of Plato that cannot be shared Platonity" (*In Periherm*. II, lib. II, c.7; Meiser 136.28–137.7, trans. Smith 2010, 89). *Major Commentary*, Book II, Meiser 1880, 137. See also Porphyry's *Isagoge* (Busse 1887, 7) where he claims that each individual consists of properties of which the combination can never be the same in any other.

36. Thus, we cannot dissolve well-known philosophical puzzles about proper names on the assumption that proper names do not occur as a rule in dictionaries, as Napoli ("Names, indexicals and identity statements," 194) tries to do. It is the very nature of a non-transportable sense that it cannot be captured by any dictionary. A dictionary may contain a definition for "Faversham" as "a market town in Kent," and "Kent" as "a county of England," and so on. Very well, but *which* town in Kent of that name, and *which* county of England, and which country called "England" and so forth. Even a definition such as "the capital city of England" is non-transportable, as I shall argue in chapter 8 ("The God of the Philosophers").

Chapter 4

Mentioning

I have argued that co-reference within the same *scripture* is a trivial matter. The first reference to God in the Hebrew Bible is Genesis 1:1 ("In the beginning *God* created the heavens and the earth"), the last is 2 Chronicles 36:23 ("may *the Lord their God* be with them"). It is as absurd to ask how we know that the two terms co-refer as it is to ask whether "John" and "he" co-refer in "Herod feared *John*, knowing that *he* was a just man." The co-reference between Genesis and Chronicles boils down to the assumption that the editor will strive to make the whole text from Genesis to Chronicles as clear as possible to the reader, with the reader working under the same assumption. One of these assumptions is that if "God" or "the Lord" were an ambiguous name, the text would have said so; but it doesn't, so the two tokens have the same reference. Thus, we don't ask the question of whether the God of Genesis is the same as the God of Chronicles, and there is no "same God?" question for the Hebrew Bible.

I turn now to the question of whether the terms for the divine being can co-refer in different scriptures, and there are two objections to consider. The first is that both the Christian and Muslim scriptures conflict at a fundamental level with the Hebrew scriptures and with each other. According to the standard interpretation of the Christian scriptures, God is a trinity, three *persons* who are one *god*. According to both Hebrew and Muslim scriptures, God is not triune, but is one God alone. According to the Muslim scripture, Adam and Eve were forgiven by God after tasting from the tree,[1] which clearly is not the account in Genesis,[2] where Adam's sin is the basis for the entire cosmology and understanding of salvation in Christianity. These are all fundamental disagreements, at a level so deep it seems difficult or impossible to hold that they are speaking of the same divine being. We cannot conclude, simply from the fact that Muslims and Christians *claim* they are referring to the same God as the Hebrew Bible, that their claim is true, and so appeal to the claim of reference, according to the objection, does not move the debate forward one bit.

The second objection is that, while the Christian version of the Hebrew scriptures agrees closely with the Hebrew one, the Muslim version does not, moreover the Quran supposedly claims that the Hebrew Bible that God handed to the Jews was corrupted, and the original no longer exists. While it is plausible to maintain that there is co-reference between the Christian and the Hebrew texts, there is nothing corresponding to the Hebrew text in Islam, so for the same reason there cannot be co-reference.

Underlying both objections is the problem of how we successfully refer to something, what counts as success, and how success is achieved.

CONTRADICTION

We should first examine whether *contradiction* implies anything about *reference*. It is uncontroversial that there are passages in all three scriptures, which appear to be versions of the same story, but which are different, or which contradict one another. Quran 5 has a version of the Cain and Abel story, which states (5:31) that God (Allah) sent a crow scratching the ground to show Cain how to cover the dead body of his brother (Abel). There is no equivalent in the Hebrew Bible. The Gospel of Matthew (1:1–17) and the Gospel of Luke (3:23–38) have genealogies of Jesus which are difficult to reconcile either with each other or with the Hebrew Bible. Generally, the divergences are greater in the Quran than in the New Testament, which contains mostly direct quotations from the Hebrew Bible, probably from the Greek translation of the Hebrew Bible, the Septuagint.

However, we need to distinguish mere differences of detail, or additions or omissions, from differences with a significant theological impact, as follows.

(i) Between the Quran and the New Testament.

And [for] their saying, "Indeed, we have killed the Messiah, Jesus, the son of Mary, the messenger of Allah." And they did not kill him, nor did they crucify him; *but [another] was made to resemble him to them.* And indeed, those who differ over it are in doubt about it. They have no knowledge of it except the following of assumption. *And they did not kill him, for certain.*[3]

So Jesus did not die, although someone apparently died in *his* place, whereas Christ's death on the cross, as substitutionary atonement for the sin of Adam, is fundamental to Christian theology.

(ii) Between the Quran and the Hebrew Bible:

> Then Adam received from his Lord words (of revelation), and *He relented* toward him. Lo! He is the relenting, the Merciful.[4]

God forgives Adam (and Eve), whereas according to Genesis 3:17, God places a curse upon them, and all their descendants.[5]

(iii) Between the New Testament and the Hebrew Bible:

> For there are three that bear record in heaven, the Father, the Word, and the Holy Ghost: and these three are one.[6]

These doctrines are explicit in the relevant scriptures and are difficult or impossible to make consistent. If God forgave Adam, there is no original sin, but the idea of original sin runs deep throughout the Hebrew and Christian scriptures, particularly the latter.[7] The idea that God is a trinity of three persons is not found in the Hebrew scriptures, and is explicitly denied in the Quran (5:72 and *passim*). That Christ was crucified as atonement for the sin of Adam is the basis of all Christianity. Given disagreements of scripture and teaching so deep, how can we possibly speak of the same God?

As I maintained in the introduction, it is perfectly possible for statements about the same individual to contradict. Consider where the disagreement could hardly be stronger. The fideist says, "God exists," the atheist "God does not exist." Are we to suppose that the fideist is asserting the existence of one being, the atheist denying the existence of another? Absolutely not. The atheist is denying the existence of precisely that which the fideist asserts, indeed it is only possible for them to disagree by assuming a common *reference* (although the atheist denies there is a common *referent*). The claim in the Hebrew Bible that Adam was not forgiven[8] only contradicts the claim in the Quran if they are referring to Adam in both cases. The Christian claim "Christ is the Messiah" only contradicts the Hebraic and Islamic belief expressed as "Christ is not the Messiah" if the referent of "Christ" is the same. Likewise, the claim that Allah forgave Adam contradicts Hebrew and Christian doctrine only if "Allah" *and* "Adam" have the same reference in all scriptures. Again, the claim in Quran 5:17, "They have certainly disbelieved who say that *Allah* is *Christ*, the son of Mary," is about what Christians believe, and wrongly so according to Islam, but this only makes sense if "Allah" refers to God, and "Christ" to Jesus, and the claim only contradicts Christian belief because that is what Christians believe.[9] Contradiction between different claims is not evidence of reference conflict, but rather the other way round. Conflict and contradiction between statements with definite subjects is only *possible* when there is a common reference.

CITATION

Contradiction is clearly no impediment to co-reference between different texts. But what makes co-reference possible at all? I propose the following rule. The anaphor text must identify or *cite* the antecedent text in some way, so that the reader can treat the two texts as though they were one, with the antecedent first in the order of reading, and apply the same rules that would apply *if they were a single text*. This brings us to the subject of *citation*, a way of identifying a particular text, and if necessary a specific part of a text.

There is no need for the last chapter of Revelations to identify the first chapter of Matthew, because the parts of the New Testament are physically bound together, and probably always have been, in a book or *codex*. The codex (Latin *caudex*, "trunk of a tree") appeared around the first century AD. It had many practical advantages over the scroll. It could be opened flat at a single point for easier reading, with any other point randomly and quickly accessible, unlike a scroll as long as thirty feet. Pages could be written on both front and back, the binding allowing the contents of several scrolls to be incorporated into one volume. It is associated with the growth of Christianity, which adopted it early on. In the Christian world, the codex completely replaced the use of the scroll by about the sixth century, although Judaism was slower to adopt it. The earliest evidence of the codex among the Jews is from the eighth century, although it was probably in use before that. Hebrew Bibles in codex form were in widespread use by the tenth century, some of them, like the Leningrad codex, surviving to this day. However, according to Jewish religious law, the codex Bible is unacceptable for reading in the synagogue. The modern synagogue ark contains a *scroll*, not a book. The Greek word "pentateuch" means "five scrolls," or strictly the five boxes ("teuchos") that hold the scrolls, by extension the scrolls themselves.[10]

It is not clear how the scrolls were originally ordered. According to the Babylonian Talmud, the order of the Major Prophets is Jeremiah, Ezekiel, *Isaiah*, whereas in the Leningrad codex, it is *Isaiah*, Jeremiah, and Ezekiel.[11] In some medieval manuscripts, Chronicles comes at the beginning of the Writings, whereas the standard position is at the end. The ordering was probably determined by local tradition.

The location of *parts* of the text was more difficult before the arrival of printing, and of standard editions with standard pagination and organization. All three scriptures now have a referencing system that allows us to identify parts of the text to within a few words. Chapter divisions for the Christian Bible were developed by Stephen Langton in the early thirteenth century. Robert Estienne was the first to number the verses within each chapter, his system entering printed editions in 1551. The Hebrew Bible was divided into verses as early as the sixth century AD,[12] although not into chapters, which were introduced in the time of Rabbi Salomon ben Ishmael (ca. AD 1550),[13] apparently following the success of the Christian chapter divisions. The Quran consists of 114 chapters or *surahs*, of which 86 were traditionally revealed in Mecca, the other 28 in Medina. The suras are not in the chronological order of revelation, the precise nature of which is unknown, although some medieval Islamic writers attempted to determine it, with uncertain results.[14] Some surahs mention particular events that help date them. For example, Muhammad's first revelation was Chapter 96 (probably in the year 609).[15] The canonical ordering is by length, thus the Quran begins with the longest surah, and ends with the shortest. The standard printed edition was first published in 1925 in Cairo, whose numbering is now standard.[16]

Methods of citation have become increasingly sophisticated, with such systems as the Harvard method, which attempts uniquely to identify a work by its author, name and date, place of publication, and any part of the text by page number of the relevant edition. The text will thus be available to the reader in a library, which will also have its own unique way of identifying the text, such as a shelfmark. The International Standard Book Number (ISBN) identifies a "group" or country, a publisher, and a title so that to every book there is a unique ISBN code.

The idea of a standard edition or canonical version is earlier. The Hebrew Bible is written mainly in Biblical Hebrew, with some passages in Biblical Aramaic (such as the books of Daniel and Ezra). The traditional Hebrew text is known as the *Masoretic* Text. There is no consensus as to when precisely the Hebrew Bible canon was fixed, but it was probably no earlier than the second century BC, although may have been as late as the second century AD.[17] By the time the canon was established, and thus by the Christian era, ancient Hebrew was not the universal language of Jewish people, but rather Aramaic, the common language of the Eastern Mediterranean in the first century AD. For this reason, Onkelos (fl. 110) translated/interpreted the Torah into Aramaic.[18] Early printed editions of the Hebrew Bible date back to 1488, but the canonical printed edition of 1524–1525, the so-called second rabbinic bible, is the basis for all subsequent editions, and may have been used as a source for the King James Bible of 1611. Accurate citation requires identifying the edition, as well as the work. An edition should not be confused with a reprint. The latter is just a word for word copy, an edition involves revision, or at least renewed scrutiny, of the text, where the page numbers may differ.

Citation differs from reference in a number of ways. First, while we can refer to a text that no longer exists, we cannot *cite* a text that does not exist. Lost texts are those whose previous existence is known by citations from existing works, for example The Book of Jasher, mentioned in 2 Samuel 1:18, which I am referring to now. But I cannot cite it. To cite is literally "to summon, call upon officially," which is precisely what we cannot do in this case.[19] Second, citation presumes a way of uniquely identifying the text. This is clear in the case of the three scriptures, and is pretty much guaranteed by modern systems of citation. Citation also presumes that all of the cited text is available. Not all of a work may exist—manuscripts frequently have parts of the text missing due to decay, scribal error, or unreadable handwriting. But we cannot cite those missing parts. In the case of citation, the goods are in the shop window. Words, and signs generally, have no substance, consisting of form alone. By contrast, we can never simultaneously observe all the parts of an object. At a microscopic or atomic level, they are mostly unknown to us. Yet we do not require a microscope to investigate the written word, nor do words have a back or front, or any hidden features.

It follows that we cannot claim to cite some part of a text, for a citation is something that we show. A citation is not capable of truth or falsity, any more than pointing is, and the citation is either understood or not. It is simply a matter of pattern matching. This contrasts with reference proper, which is used only when the object referred to is not available to us at all. As Aristotle says, we use names as symbols for objects when it is not possible to "bring in" the actual object before us,[20] whereas the whole point of citation is to make the object, the text, directly available to us. To cite is not to make any statement, capable of truth or falsity. Just as we do not *say* or *assert* who the pronoun "he" co-refers with when we use it, for example, in "Herod feared John, knowing that *he* was a just man," so we do not assert that the cited text exists.

Nor should citation be confused with quotation. Quotation is when the text is copied *verbatim*, that is, in exactly the same words as were used originally. Passages from the Hebrew Bible (possibly from the Septuagint translation) are frequently quoted in the New Testament, nearly always to show that "the scriptures" had been fulfilled in Jesus' ministry. Matt 5:17: "Do not think that I have come to abolish the Law or the Prophets; I have not come to abolish them but to fulfill them." Famously, John 1:23 "I am the voice of one calling in the wilderness, 'Make straight the way for the Lord,'" although modern punctuation schemes incorrectly resolve the ambiguity of Isaiah 40:3–5, which can also be interpreted as "The voice of one crying 'In the wilderness, make straight the way for the Lord.'"

SUCCESSFUL REFERENCE

As I argued in chapter 2, the distinction between failed and successful (co-) reference is a false one. Fool's gold is not gold, nor is a dead man a man. Reference failure is when the reader is unable to tell *which* individual the author is writing about, but the sole function of reference *is* to tell us which individual this is. Of course, the author may have *wished* to do so, and may have had some individual "in mind," but that does not mean he *told* us who this was. Reference, that is, co-reference, either works or it is not reference at all.[21]

How then do we know that reference has taken place? Two things are necessary. First, the cit*ing* text must successfully locate the cit*ed* text. Second, the author must successfully apply the informal rules of co-reference that would apply if both texts were the same text. I have already discussed the *second* condition. In the Herod example, the author intends to use the pronoun "he" to co-refer with "John." If he and the reader understand the correct use of the pronoun, the reader will grasp the co-reference too. There are other rules for proper names and definite descriptions, as I have argued. The *first* condition is satisfied when it is clear to the readers which the cited text is. But how do they know that, when no referencing system is available? There were no methods of standard citation available when the three texts of the three religious traditions were revealed.

One way to approach the question is to engage with the readers themselves, and to consider how the one religion reports what another says, using indirect speech. The Jewish encyclopedia says that of Christianity, "it claims *that* Jesus, its Christ, was and is *a son of God* in a higher and an essentially different sense than any other human being."[22] A Jewish source is reporting, using a "that" clause, what it supposes the Christian sources say. But indirect speech of this kind aims to report what the author meant, or the content of their speech, as opposed to the speech itself, the utterance. The Jewish encyclopedia is reporting what Christians aim to say, and since Christians agree that this is what they are saying, namely, that Christ was and is the son of God, the Christian reference is a genuine reference. Of course, the encyclopedia is not agreeing with what the Christians are saying. It is not agreeing that Jesus is the son of God. But in order to disagree at all, it must interpret what they are saying in the same way. It must interpret "Jesus is the son of God" as a statement about Jesus and the God of the Hebrews, the Jewish God. That is, in reporting the central claim of Christianity says, the encyclopedia must use the name "God" in the same sense that Christians use it. It disagrees that Jesus *is* the son of God, but this is just like the fideist disagreeing with the atheist. So the Christian doctrine aims to refer to the Hebrew God, and Jewish sources accept that it does.

Similarly, non-Muslims tend to report the claims of Islamic scripture in a way that implies successful reference. For example, *Jesus the Messiah in Muslim Thought* has a chapter called "Christ in the Quran," which clearly indicates that the term "Christ" as used in the Quran has the same reference as in the New Testament. The author of the chapter is clearly referring to Christ, but Christ cannot be "in" the Quran without the author accepting that the Quran is referring to him. Indeed, the very title of the book suggests that Jesus can be "in" Muslim thought. I could give many examples of this. I am aware of no scholarly work that treats any of the biblical characters mentioned in the Quran as distinct from those mentioned in the Hebrew and Christian scriptures.

Scriptural commentators are also able to co-refer with the texts they are commenting on. The hermeneutical texts of Augustine, Maimonides, Aquinas, and Spinoza contain terms like "Moses," "Abraham," "Adam," and, of course, "God." Their authors aim to speak of the characters referred to in the Hebrew scriptures, and that is who we take them to be referring to. Otherwise, the whole project of scriptural commentary would be impossible. To make a claim about what the scriptures say about Moses, you have to use the term "Moses" in the same way as the scriptures. Commentators typically cite the passages they have in mind. Spinoza writes:

> As for the fact that God [*Deus*] was angry with him [Balak] while he was on his journey, that happened also to *Moses* when he was setting out for Egypt at the command of God [*Dei*].[23]

Spinoza's own use of the name "Moses" has the same reference as it does in Exodus 4:24-26 because (in effect) he *indicates* that it does, namely by citing that book, chapter and verse. By contrast, Duns Scotus writes:

> Which they show first by the authority of Rabbi Moses, chapter 73, saying "the unity of God is received from the Law."[24]

The name "Moses" here refers to the commentator Moses Maimonides, with Scotus citing Book I chapter 73 of *Guide of the Perplexed*. As long as the author indicates which independent text is relevant, we can apply the same rules as if the text were not independent. Thus the reference to "Moses" in both Spinoza and Scotus is successful. Whether they both succeed in referring to *God* in both cases, particularly given Spinoza's idiosyncratic theory about the meaning of "God," I shall set aside for now.

Often the work is not cited, on the principle that familiarity with the external text can be indicated or signified to the reader in some way. This can be achieved merely by the use of a definite, that is, singular term. As Christophersen suggests,[25] the use of a definite term is *enough indication* that the subject term is familiar to the *reader*.

> In order to show that all bodies were created immediately by God, *Moses* said: "In the beginning God created heaven and earth."[26]

It does not matter that Aquinas does not cite Genesis 1:1. It is a work of theology, and the passage (the opening of the Hebrew Bible) is well known.

He knows the reader will understand the reference, and the reader knows that Aquinas knows this. Likewise, when the Levites ask John the Baptist whether he is Elijah (John 1:21), the writer knows who Elijah is, but he also assumes that his readers will have the same knowledge, that is, that they have the same text in the background, that "Elijah" is a unique name in that text, and thus the reference is unambiguous. It is part of the meaning of the "Elijah" in John 1:21 and the "Elijah" of 1 and 2 Kings, that they co-refer. According to Jeffery, the proper names in the Quran would have been chosen on the basis of the names that would be known to its readers. Christians in the world of the early Quran would have known the Bible not in Greek but in the Syriac translation of the Bible (the *Peshitta*). Since Arabic at that time had no corresponding theological terms for the ideas expressed in the Bible, they (and nearly all proper names of biblical characters) were imports not directly from Hebrew or Greek, but via Syriac Aramaic, spoken across much of the Near East through the fourth to the eighth centuries. Indeed, Rippin[27] believes that the Arabs did not even realize the Hebrew Bible was written in Hebrew, thinking that the language spoken by the Jews in seventh-century Near East was the language they had always spoken.[28]

Context is equally important. Aquinas says:

> For certain people say, for example Avicenna and *Rabbi Moses*, that the thing which God is, is a sort of subsistent being, nor is there anything other than being in God. Hence they say that he is being without essence.[29]

"Rabbi Moses" could mean the author of the Torah (Moses is sometimes known by the Hebrew *Moshe Rabbeinu*, "Moses our teacher"), but given the context is more likely to refer to Moses Maimonides, otherwise known as *Rabbi* Moses ben Maimon.

By contrast, no there is no indication in Philo's text of the existence of the New Testament, or conversely.

> Mark 15:1—So they bound Jesus, led him away and handed him over to Pilate.

> Philo—Pilate was one of the emperor's lieutenants, having been appointed governor of Judaea.[30]

The tokens of "Pilate" in the gospel of Mark have the same reference because Mark knows that his readers know they are all part of the same text. But he is not referring to, that is, not *signifying* the same person as Philo, even though Philo uses the same name, and even though it is fairly certain that the man Philo is talking about is the one Mark is talking about.

An apparent exception is the contrary view of Niketas the Byzantine, which I mentioned in the introduction. He argues that some demon has usurped the name of the true God, and therefore that name, as used in the Quran, does not refer to the true God. He has a theory of proper name reference, which is difficult to understand, but which is roughly as follows. Everything that truly exists is cognized from the name and its bearer at the same time. But sometimes the name can be separated from its bearer, so it becomes a *name only*,[31] which is difficult to translate, although he explains that a name-only can be either an empty name when it signifies nothing, or a name which has the wrong bearer, that is, when it is taken from its proper bearer and attributed to another. A true name, by contrast, signifies the nature of its bearer. Thus, he argues that the Muslim people ("the Agarenes") have been deceived. For "It is easy to persuade this barbarian people, who thoughtlessly cause themselves to be tricked by the name of the God of Abraham."[32]

But in that case, how can Niketas say that this is a *deception*? He says that Muslims have been misled into believing that they are the people of the God of Abraham. But what is that belief? How would we report it? Surely as I have done so earlier, using indirect speech, where the reference of "the God of Abraham" is the same as in the Hebrew Bible. But this reports the content of their belief, so it is a false belief *about* the Hebrew God. That is, Niketas can only report their false belief on the assumption that the term "the God of Abraham," which is a constituent of their belief, refers to the true God. Otherwise they would have a true belief about some false God or demon, namely that they were his people, as opposed to a false belief about the true God. What if they are lying, rather than deceived? In that case, they *say* they are worshipping the true God, but in their hearts acknowledge that they are not, and are really worshipping a demon. But then when they utter the term "the God of Abraham" or even "the true God," it must refer to the true God, not the demon. Otherwise they are not lying: they are *saying* that they worship a demon, and they *think* they are worshipping a demon.

Furthermore, God in the Quran often speaks using the first-person pronoun "I" or "we." If the narrator is a demon, it could be argued that "I" refers to the demon. Then the claim "I am the God of Abraham," uttered by the demon, would be false, but only because "God" refers to the true God. Otherwise it is saying that the demon = the demon. It is similar to the case where Jews deny Jesus' claim that he was God (or strictly speaking that God was his father), but can only do so if both sides agreed on the reference of "God." Otherwise the Jews could not deny what the Christians affirm.

Again, like any commentator, Niketas reports Quranic claims about non-supernatural biblical characters. He says, for example, that the Quran does not state that Miriam was the sister of Aaron and Moses, but of Aaron alone.[33] In reporting what is said, he is assuming that the Quranic names "Aaron," "Moses," "Miriam," and so on have the same reference as in his own text. Otherwise he would be unable to report this at all.

Further evidence of successful reference is when the translator interprets the text for us. Quran 33:7, as translated by Pickthall, reads:

And [mention] when We exacted a covenant from the prophets, and from thee (O Muhammad) and from *Noah* and *Abraham* and *Moses* and *Jesus* son of *Mary*. *We* took from them a solemn covenant.

The five proper names "Noah," "Abraham," "Moses," "Jesus," and "Mary" *look* like names that appear in English in the Old and New Testament, but they would, being translations of names that occur in ancient Hebrew, in Greek, and in classical Arabic in the original texts of the three scriptures. Neither the name "Noah" in Arabic script or its transliteration (Nūḥ) are the same as the English "Noah." Nor does the corresponding Hebrew name resemble the Arabic or the English name. But, just as translators understand the Arabic for "covenant" and render it as the corresponding English word, so they "understand" how to translate the Arabic for "Noah," "Abraham," and so on.

THE PROBLEM OF THE QURAN

It may still be objected that Muslims may not be *citing* the Hebrew Bible correctly. If they are not, are they mistaken at a level so deep they are no longer speaking of the same God?

According to tradition, in year 610, the angel Gabriel (*Jibrail*) appeared to Muhammad in the cave Hira near Mecca when he was forty, reciting to him the first verses of Sura 96 (al-'Alaq), beginning the revelation of the Quran, which had existed from eternity. Over the next twenty-three years he received more revelations until the Quran was completely delivered to him in 632 AD.

Mohammed is described (7:157) as "unlettered" although the word in Arabic also means "gentile." It is uncertain whether each revelation was written down after he recited it to his companions, or whether they memorized it and wrote it down after his death. Shia scholars believe that Ali ibn Abu Talib (cousin and son-in-law of Muhammad, 601–661) received the first transcript of the Quran, dating from six months after Muhammad's death. According to Sunni tradition, the Quran was handed down by contemporaries of Muhammad such as Ibn 'Abbas (d. 73/692 AD) and early authorities, such as Anas Ibn Malik (d. 91/709 AD), who are also said to have contributed to the fixing of the text,[34] although this is contradicted by a report that caliph Uthman (576–656) received the "sheets" from Hafsa, the Prophet's widow, and used them for his version.[35] The existence of different versions prompted Uthman to create a standard version now known as Uthman's codex, and to destroy all variants. By tradition, this is the *textus receptus* of the Quran we have today. The oldest surviving manuscript is the Sana'a palimpsest, found in Yemen in 1972 during restoration of the Great Mosque of Sana'a. The parchment (but possibly not the calligraphy) is dated to before 671.

Note that the Quran contains no copy of the Hebrew Bible, as does the Christian scripture, which contains the so-called the *Old* Testament, although Jewish people would not call it that, as they do not have a "new" Testament. The English "testament" translates the Latin *testamentum* and the Greek *diatheke* (testament, will or covenant), both translations of the Hebrew *berith*, all of which strictly imply some agreement or contract or covenant. The "new" testament means the new agreement established by Jesus between God and people, as opposed to the "old" testament established by Moses. The Christian Old Testament contains nearly all the books, although in a somewhat different arrangement, from the Hebrew Bible. Hence, there is no need to *mention* the scriptures that the New Testament cites, since both are already bound together into a single volume.

While the scripture of Islam is in effect a third Testament, it is not bound together with copies of the Hebrew Bible and New Testament, translated into Arabic. However, the Quran frequently mentions both. Quran 5:14 tells Christians that Allah made a covenant with them, although they had "forgotten" a part of it. It is not explained how Christians could have forgotten the Old Testament when they apparently had copies of it.

Unlike the New Testament the Quran has no precise quotes from the Hebrew Bible. Many of the biblical stories are retold (such as Adam and Eve, Cain and Abel, Sodom and Gomorrah) but they tend to be summaries, often repeated or split over different parts and with less of the detail found in the biblical narratives. Only the story of Joseph is revealed in a single surah (12), with many of the important points omitted, and with many additions. Some important theological points are attributed to Hebrews and Christians although the sources appear to be missing. For example, Quran 5:64, "The Jews say: 'Allah's Hand is tied up,'" meaning that God doesn't provide for his people, yet no such statement is found in the Hebrew Bible. Quran 61:6 claims that Jesus brought tidings of a prophet to come after him "whose name is Ahmad (aḥmadu)," commonly supposed to be Muhammad. But there is no such passage in the New Testament. Some claims seem to be completely inaccurate, such as the sister of Aaron being the mother of Jesus.

There are also names in the Quran that do not appear to correspond to anything in the other two scriptures. For example, "Idris," mentioned in Quran 19:56, 21:85, or "Dhul-Kifl" (21:85–6, 38:48). By tradition the former is Enoch, ancestor of Noah, although Jeffery, following Noldeke, suggests it is the Greek *Andreas* via Syriac. The latter is supposed to be Ezekiel, but it is difficult to interpret such a fleeting mention. Quran 38:48 simply reads "And of Ishmael, Elisha and Dhul-Kifl, who were all just men." The names are not similar to anything found in the Hebrew Bible, and no other context is given. The men themselves are long dead, and even if we found their graves, we could not connect them with the Quran unless there were some sort of label on them. But this would be merely the sort of descriptive identification that I shall discuss in the next chapter.

These textual differences between the Quran and the other scriptures suggest another objection to my claim that Muslims can cite both the New Testament and the Hebrew Bible. While Jews generally accept that Christians are citing the Hebrew Bible and hence referring to the God of the Hebrew Bible, even though the Christian view of God is profoundly heretical to them, the case of the Quran is different. It may be objected that the reason why Jews and Christians did not accept Muhammad's message from the very beginning is that the Qur'an presents versions of stories of the Hebrew and Christian Bible that are incompatible with what these communities determined to be accurate through the formation of the biblical canon. Furthermore, the Quran suggests that the texts of both the Hebrew and Christian Bible have been corrupted in some way. But if there was no accurate text of the Hebrew Bible available to the Quran, no text can be cited. If co-reference depends on the possibility of citation, no co-reference is possible. This is the problem of the Quran.

In reply, the Quran in many places mentions the *Taurat* (Torah) given to *Musa* (Moses), the *Zabur* (Psalms) given to *Daud* (David), and the *Injil* (Gospel) given to *Isa* (Jesus). For example, 5:110, "I [Allah] taught you [Jesus] writing and wisdom and the Torah and the Gospel." Quran 5:44 says that the rabbis and priests were entrusted with the protection of "Allah's book," meaning the Torah, and so on. Some Muslims believe that the Quran teaches that the biblical canon is distorted or corrupt. There are a few verses where the charge seems specific, namely 3:78 ("They distort the Scripture with their tongues"), 5:13 ("The Israelites have broken the covenant, and have 'altered the words from their places'"), 2:79 ("Woe to them for what their hands have written and woe to them for what they earn"), and so on.[36]

Furthermore, some of these passages refer to spoken interpretations of the Hebrew Bible ("with their *tongues*"), and others, for example, 2:79, seem to refer to the Rabbinical *commentaries* on the Bible. In many other passages, the Quran clearly implies that uncorrupted texts exist. For example, 5:47, "And let the People of the Gospel judge by what Allah has revealed *therein*." The people of the Gospel could make no such judgment unless the text still existed intact. In 3:55, God speaks to Jesus, referring to Christians as "those who followed you." This does not depict them as following a corrupt scripture.

Moreover, even if the Quran does claim that the Hebrew and Christian texts are corrupted, it implicitly *mentions* them, for it implies a comparison between the uncorrupted version and the uncorrupted one is possible. If the

Israelites have "altered the words from their places," then there must be two sets of words to compare. The Quran also implies that the uncorrupted texts are available (3:93 "So bring the Torah and recite it"). So, while the Quran does not quote the Bible or cite any particular passage, clearly it mentions it.

Furthermore, Christian discussions of the subject[37] seem to accept that it is the Old and New Testament that the Quran is talking about, in order to counter the suggestion that the Christian scriptures have been corrupted.

> Muslims cannot consistently maintain that the Scriptures delivered previously have been corrupted or lost, since the Qur'an appears to assume that *these Scriptures* are still with the "people of the book" (Christians and Jews).[38]

Note the "that" clause reporting what the Quran is supposed to mean. Clearly the meaning was successfully communicated. The discussion also cites 2:91 ("And they [the infidels] disbelieve in what came after it [the Quran], while it is the truth confirming that which is with them [the Hebrew Bible and New Testament]"), saying that if Jews and Christians didn't have access to these scriptures, *the verse makes no sense*. This appeals to the hermeneutic principle of interpreting a text in a way that maximizes its rationality or sense, on the grounds that the author was trying to do the same. That is, if we understand the Quran correctly, it is the Hebrew and Christian scriptures that it mentions, not some other version that is now lost.

So in overall answer to the objection that Muslims may not be *mentioning* the Hebrew Bible and the Old Testament, and so not referring to the same God, it seems that the best way of making sense of what the Quran says is on the supposition that it is mentioning those scriptures, and so the name "Allah" indeed co-refers with "Yhwh," "God," "Elohim," and so on.

SUMMARY

I have argued that while the Christian and Muslim scriptures conflict at a fundamental level with the Hebrew scriptures, and with each other, these contradictions are not a good reason for supposing that "Allah" and "God" have a different reference. On the contrary, the contradictions presuppose the same reference. For example, the claim that Allah forgave Adam contradicts Hebrew and Christian doctrine only if "Allah" *and* "Adam" co-refer.

When a name appears in a different text *and* the author indicates in some way to the reader that this text is being referenced, then it is also signified that any occurrence of the proper name in the *citation* text co-refers with the name in the *cited* text, that is, we should apply the same rules as if the two texts were one. For example, Quran 3:3 says that Allah revealed "the Torah

(*Tawrat*) and the Gospel (*Injil*),"[39] meaning that when we see names used in either of those scriptures—such as "Moses" or "Abraham" or "Jesus"—then they are to be understood in the same sense, that is, as co-referring tokens.

Replying to the objection that locating an appropriate co-reference between one text and another requires the ability to identify the right text, which is impossible of the true text was corrupted or destroyed, I have argued that there is ample evidence that the texts mentioned by Quran are the Hebrew Bible and the New Testament, and that Christian commentators seem to agree that the only way of making sense of the Quran is to accept this.

This demonstrates that "God" and "Allah" co-refer, as those names are used in the scriptures. However, this does not answer the central question of the book. It does not establish that "Allah" refers to *God*, because the token of "God" I am using here occurs *in my text*, not in any of the three scriptures. How am *I* using the name "God" in *this* text, and how can you tell which terms it co-refers with? That is the next question.

NOTES

1. 2:37, although see 7:24, which does not mention forgiveness, and is closer to the account in the Hebrew Bible.
2. 3:14.
3. 4:157, my emphasis.
4. 2:37, my emphasis.
5. That is, reading "you" as signifying all humanity. See also Psalm 51:5 "Indeed, I was born guilty, *a sinner when my mother conceived me.*"
6. 1 John 5:7, King James Version, see also John 1, John 14, and so forth.
7. At least for Christian apologists. While the notion of collective guilt, that is, that there can be guilt for collective, but not individual agency, is fundamental to many parts of the Hebrew Bible ("For I the LORD your God am a jealous God, visiting the iniquity of the fathers upon the sons to the third and fourth generation of those that hate me" Ex 20:4), and is arguably fundamental to the theology of the New Testament (e.g., in the idea of Christ dying for "our" sins, 1 Corinthians 15:3,15:22, Romans 5:12), the sin of Adam is not prominent in the Hebrew Bible or in the Gospels.
8. The curse is not a fundamental part of Judaism as it is in Christianity. Judaism holds that Adam sinned once, his descendants *many* times, and the concept of original sin, as opposed to collective guilt, is not fundamental to Judaism.
9. See also 5:18. "And the Jews and the Christians say: 'We are the children of *Allah* and His loved ones,'" 5:73 "They have certainly disbelieved who say, [that] Allah is the third of three" [I removed quotation marks].
10. Ska, *Introduction to Reading the Pentateuch*, 1.
11. See, for example, Ginsburg, *Introduction of the Massoretico-Critical Edition of the Hebrew Bible*, 1.

12. Wurthwein, *Text of the Old Testament*, 21; cf. also Bentzen, *Introduction to the Old Testament*, 1:49.

13. Wurthwein, *Text of the Old Testament*, 1:21.

14. Nöldeke (*Geschichte des Qorâns*) also attempted a re-ordering.

15. According to Ibn al-Rawandi. Warraq, "Origins of Islam: A critical look at the sources," in (*The Quest for the Historical Muhammad*, 89–124, p.110) suggests that this is no more than an assumption, based on the command "Recite" at the beginning of the Sura. "The truth is that nobody knew anything about the circumstances of the first revelations, or any of the other revelations."

16. Rippin "Syriac in the Qur'ān: Classical Muslim theories," in Reynolds 2008:2. Variations exist, such as by Gustav Flugel (1834), based on his reading of the rhyming endings of phrases. While it does not correspond to with any known Muslim tradition, it has been the basis of many European translations and other works on the Qur'an. See Saeed, *The Qur'an: An Introduction*, Routledge, 3, also "The Qur'an as scripture, Evolution of the script of the Qur'an and its presentation," pages 51–52.

17. See, for example, McDonald and Sanders, *The Canon Debate*, 5.

18. The hypothesis favored by scholars today is that the translation originated in the second or third century AD, but shows evidence of transmission in the Babylonian academies of the East. See Cook, *A Glossary of Targum Onkelos According to Alexander Sperber's Edition*, xi.

19. Genette, *Paratexts: Thresholds of Interpretation*, 3 about paratexts without texts—works about which we know nothing except their titles. For example, *La Bataille des Thermopyles* of which we know only that the word cnémide [greave] was not to have appeared in it.

20. Aristotle, *Sophistical Refutations*, 165 a4.

21. Writers such as Crane, Evans, and others have compared reference to a sort of target practice, *aiming* to think about or to refer to specific objects, but occasionally failing to hit the target object, and thus failing to have singular thoughts or singular meaning. See, for example, Crane, "The singularity of singular thought," 23; Evans, *The Varieties of Reference*, 317. The co-reference of the two names "Peter" in "*Peter* preached at Jerusalem and *Peter* preached in Galilee" is thus explained means of a relation—the *direct reference relation*—to a third item, namely Peter himself. We understand the second token only because we understand that it bears the same relation to the same extralinguistic entity as the first, as if we succeed in referring to the same object by different tokens because they both "hit" the same object in external reality. This, for the reasons given, is a mistake.

22. "Christianity in its relation to Judaism," Kohler, *The Jewish Encyclopedia*.

23. *Tractatus* ch. 3, p. 51, citing Exodus 4:24–26.

24. *Lectura* I D2 P1Q3. Actually he is referring to Maimonides *Guide of the Perplexed* I ch.75, not 73, and so probably citing a much earlier edition with a different chapter arrangement. See also Aquinas I Sent, d2 q1 art 3: Quidam enim dicunt, ut Avicenna et Rabbi Moyses, quod res illa quae Deus est, est quoddam esse subsistens, nec aliquid aliud nisi esse, in Deo est: unde dicunt, quod est esse sine essentia. Here "Rabbi Moyses" is not the Moses of the Pentateuch, but rather Moses Maimonides (1135–1204), a prominent twelfth-century scholar of the Torah.

25. Christophersen, *The Articles: A Study of Their Theory and Use in English*, 28.

26. *Ut Moyses ostenderet corpora omnia immediate a Deo creata, dixit, in principio creavit Deus caelum et terram.* Summa Theologiae I^a q. 65 a. 3 co.

27. Rippin, "Syriac in the Qur'ān: Classical Muslim theories," in Reynolds, 257.

28. Hebrew probably became a dead language by about 200 BC, supplanted by Aramaic.

29. I *Sent*, d2 q1 art 3, my translation: *Quidam enim dicunt, ut Avicenna et Rabbi Moyses, quod res illa quae Deus est, est quoddam esse subsistens, nec aliquid aliud nisi esse, in Deo est: unde dicunt, quod est esse sine essentia.*

30. *On the Embassy to Gaius*, trans. Yonge, XXXVIII, 299.

31. Nomen solum, ὄνομα μόνον. Niketas of Byzantium, *Confutatio dogmatum Mahomedis*, Migne, 794.

32. My translation of Migne's Latin *(facile est barbarum hunc coarguere populum, qui temere Dei Abrahami appellatione sibi fucum facit)*. Migne, 795

33. *Non enim is dicit (Sur. XIX, 27) Mariam sororem Aaronis et Moysis, sed Aaronis tantummodo.* Ibid., Migne, 727.

34. Blachère, *Extraits des principaux géographes arabes du moyen âge*, 102 ff.

35. Nöldeke, *Geschichte des Qorâns* II.21, cited in Luxenberg, *The Syro-Aramaic reading of the Koran: a contribution to the decoding of the language of the Koran*, 34. Tabari also reports of a sheet on which Umar had written down the notes collected by the companions of the Prophet, cf. *Jami 'al-bayan 'an ta'wil al-Qur'an* I.26 f, Luxenberg, op. cit.

36. See also 2:40–44, 2:85 , 2:89–90, 2:97,2:101, 2:140, 2:146, 2:159, 2:174, 3:69–71, 3:75, 3:199 6:89–92, 10:93, 11:110.

37. Jonathan McLatchie, "A simple reason why the Qur'an cannot be the word of God" 2014, https://crossexamined.org/simple-reason-quran-word-god.

38. Ibid.

39. See also 5:43–44, 5:110 and others. "*We sent down the Torah* containing guidance and light."

Chapter 5

Identification within History

I discussed story-relative identification in chapter 3. If we are told a story, we "know which" person is referred to in the story because we can distinguish one individual from other characters in the story. But there is another sense in which we may be unable to know which person is referred to. We can understand the story of Christ on the road to Emmaus (Luke 24) without knowing that the stranger was actually Christ. As Strawson says, as well as identifying or distinguishing figures in a picture from each other, we need also to place them, without the frame, within our general picture of the world. We can identify the stranger within the story, but the story on its own does not tell us who this man is: we cannot identify him "within history."

Now we *can* identify Christ in history, but that is because of the presence of other "historical" characters (or places). For example, Matthew 2:1 says that Jesus was born in *Bethlehem* in *Judaea* in the days of *Herod the king*.[1] Luke[2] says that the word of God came to John in the fifteenth year of the reign of *Tiberius Caesar*, mentioning also two of Herod's sons[3] and other characters.

How is it that the three scriptures can refer to individuals who are in some sense outside the narrative, such as Pharoah, Caesar, and Muhammad?

REFERENCE IN HISTORY

I shall say that a term in a narrative has historical reference if its understanding requires an anaphoric connection with a term outside that narrative. When Matthew (2:1) says that Jesus was born in Bethlehem in Judaea in the days of *Herod the king*, he is not saying that there was some king in the story called "Herod," and that Jesus was born in the time of that king. On the contrary, he is writing "Herod" on the assumption that the reader has already been introduced to that name, outside the text.

There are two types of historical reference in all three scriptural traditions. First, in the New Testament and the Quran, reference to individuals mentioned in the Hebrew Bible, but nowhere else. For example, Matthew 17:3, "Just then there appeared before them *Moses* and *Elijah*, talking with Jesus"; Quran 19:51, "And mention in the Book, *Moses*. Indeed, he was chosen, and he was a messenger and a prophet"; Quran 37:123, "And indeed, *Elias* [Elijah] was from among the messengers." However, as argued in the previous chapter, these can be considered to be internal references if the books are understood to be a single work, compiled by a single editor.

Second, there are references in all three texts to individuals whose names are in texts outside the scriptures. Examples include Nebuchadnezzar (Nebuchadnezzar II of Babylon, mentioned frequently in the Book of Daniel), Pilate and Caesar in the New Testament, and Fir'aun (Pharoah, mentioned over seventy times), and Zayd ibn Harithah, allegedly the adoptive son of Muhammad (33:37), in the Quran.

With the second type of historical reference, the external text is, as it were, unaware of the existence of the referring text, so there is no cross reference, and so there is the problem of determining when two tokens of the same name are really names for the same person. In 2007, Michael Jursa, an assyriologist at the British Museum discovered a name on a clay tablet with a Babylonian inscription,[4] recording a gift of gold to the sun temple in Sippar. Jursa's English translation is as follows.

> (Regarding) 1.5 minas (0.75 kg) of gold, the property of *Nabu-sharrussu-ukin, the chief eunuch*, which he sent via Arad-Banitu the eunuch to [the temple] Esangila: Arad-Banitu has delivered [it] to Esangila. In the presence of Bel-usat, son of Alpaya, the royal bodyguard, [and of] Nadin, son of Marduk-zer-ibni. Month XI, day 18, year 10 [of] Nebuchadnezzar, king of Babylon.

Jursa concluded that Nabu-sharrussu-ukin was the same as the person referred to as "Nebo-sarsekim" in Jeremiah 39:3, which was important if true, given such historical references in the Hebrew Bible, apart from the mention of kings, are rare. The New International Version translation of Jeremiah is

> Then all the officials of the king of Babylon came and took seats in the Middle Gate: Nergal-sharezer of Samgar, *Nebo-sarsekim a chief officer*, Nergal-sharezer a high official and all the other officials of the king of Babylon.[5]

Jursa's conclusion rests on a complex chain of inference. The date on the tablet refers to the tenth year of Nebuchadnezzar, which would be around 595

BC. The event recorded by Jeremiah is the culmination of Nebuchadnezzar's second siege of Jerusalem in the summer of 587 BC. The texts record events nearly ten years apart, so we have to assume that there could not have been two people, one present at the siege of Jerusalem, and another person with a similar name and similar title who donated gold to the temple a decade earlier. We must also infer that the *names* are actually the same. Jeremiah is written in ancient Hebrew, the clay tablet is written cuneiform *script*, in the Akkadian *language*. The Hebrew written name corresponding to *Nebo Sarsekim* does not remotely resemble the corresponding name in cuneiform script. The sameness of name refers to the name as uttered, requiring an accurate idea of how the cuneiform script was pronounced. According to the British Museum,[6] the tablet proved that the name given by Jeremiah "was *really* pronounced" Nabu-sharrussu-ukin. Perhaps the name wasn't really pronounced that way, because they were different names? A further difficulty with the "name" given by Jeremiah is that there may not be such a name. The NRSV translation is

Nergal-sharezer, *Samgar-nebo*, *Sarsechim* the Rab-saris, Nergal-sharezer the Rab-mag, with all the rest of the officials of the king of Babylon.[7]

That is, it is not clear whether "nebo" qualifies the name "Samgar," so that there are three names (Nergal-sharezer, Samgar-nebo and Sarsechim), or whether there are just two, as the NIV translation suggests. Given that the name "Nergal-sharezer" occurs twice, the NIV translators clearly inferred that that there must be some qualifier attached to the first occurrence to distinguish it from the second, and that "Samgar" is some kind of place name: Nergal-sharezer *of* Samgar. But this is an inference.

Furthermore, if there were two people called "Nergal-sharezer" present at the siege of Jerusalem, might there not have been two people called "Nebo-sarsekim"? Of course the person named in Jeremiah is qualified as a *Rab-saris*, a prince or a eunuch, but the translation of the Hebrew is uncertain. As Christopher Heard comments, "Suppose you somehow stumbled across a fragmentary list of people invited to some event in Southern California, and that list read, in part, '... Harris Kenny Adrian Paul Jim Samuel George Michael Jordan Kennedy Steve Austin James Curtis ...' You also have a receipt for a contribution to a Chicago-area charity, made out to 'Michael Jordan.' Is it reasonable to conclude that the sequence 'Michael Jordan' in the SoCal event list refers to the same person? Not at all, since you don't have any other reason to think that the charitable 'Michael Jordan' was at the SoCal event. It's just as plausible that the string 'George Michael' refers to the pop singer, or that 'Steve Austin' refers to the Six-Million-Dollar Man, or that the whole list consists only of first names, rather than given name + family name pairs."[8]

Historical reference in the Quran is less common, as nearly all the names are of prophets or other individuals in the Hebrew and Christian Bibles, such as Abraham (69 references), Isa/Jesus (nearly 200), and Solomon. Pharoah (Fir'aun) is mentioned frequently in the Quran, nearly all in the context of the Pharoah of the Exodus, but we don't know *which* Pharoah he was, that is, whether he was the person known in Egyptian records as "Rameses II," or "Thutmose II," or someone else. Most attempts at identification involve establishing a date for the exodus from biblical genealogies, then matching this unambiguously with a similar event related in another chronology. It is analogous to historians in 3,000 years' time trying to identify a person known as "the English king" in some text narrating events, which could have taken place between 1750 and 1850, where the king could have been any of the four Georges or William.

Identifying Zayd ibn Harithah is difficult for another reason. While the Pharaohs unquestionably existed, there is little evidence for the existence of Zayd. He is significant as the only Muslim mentioned in the Quran, apart from Muhammad himself, but historians such as Powers have suggested that Zayd's death on a battlefield and Muḥammad's repudiation of his adopted son and heir were "after-the-fact constructions driven by political and theological imperatives." "Zayd may have been a real historical person," says Powers, "but there is little or no correlation between the historical person and the spectacular figure we read about in the Islamic sources."[9]

Muhammad himself is also difficult to locate outside the Quran, where he is mentioned by name only four times, more frequently by the indexical "you."[10] There are only a handful of contemporary references to a man of that name. One was found by William Wright scribbled on a Syriac manuscript of the Gospel according to Matthew and the Gospel according to Mark.

> In January {the people of} Hims took the word for their lives[11] and many villages were ravaged by the killing of {the Arabs of} Muhammad (*Muhmd*) and many people were slain and {taken} prisoner from Galilee as far as Beth[12]

Another is in the *History of Heraclius*, a chronicle of events from the end of the fifth century to 661 AD by Sebeos, a seventh-century Armenian bishop, mentioning "a man of the sons of Ishmael named *Mahmed*"; "*Mahmed* taught them [the Arabs] to recognize the God of Abraham, especially since he was informed and knowledgeable about Mosaic history."[13] There are a handful of other references to a man who has a similar (i.e. *phonologically* similar) name[14] to Muhammad, but we are heavily reliant on a single biography written long after his death, compiled from oral traditions.[15] Pontius Pilate is familiar to everyone who knows the New Testament, but the only historical and contemporary reference to him[16] is by the Hellenistic

Jewish writer Philo of Alexandria (25 c. BC to c. 50 AD). He relates how someone called Pilate (Πιλᾶτος) offended the populace by dedicating some gilt shields in Herod's palace in Jerusalem.[17] There was a complaint to the emperor Tiberius, who ordered Pilate to remove the shields. "And he [Tiberius], when he had read it, what did he say of *Pilate*, and what threats did he utter against him!"

Here we do not have the difficulty of transcription: both Philo's text and the New Testament have the same name written in Greek. It is also reasonably certain that the person mentioned in the gospels and the person mentioned by Philo are one and the same. Although they describe entirely different events, the events are probably from the same period, and the rank ascribed to Pilate by both is similar—Philo says that he is an administrator (ἐπίτροπος),[18] Matthew (27:2) and Luke (3:1) that he is a commander or provincial governor (ἡγεμών).

IMPLIED CO-REFERENCE

I shall define *implied* co-reference as a form of co-reference, which is not *signified* by a text in its current state, but which is implied by properties attributed through different anaphoric chains, and which can subsequently be asserted through an identity statement. Such properties might be that of being governor of Judea in the early first century AD, being a *Rab-mag* or senior official, being the ravager of villages in the third decade of the seventh century, and also being *so-called*, or *so-named*. "So-called" strictly refers to spoken names, that is, as spoken in the language of the person who was called by that name, and so strictly applies only in the lifetime of the person. "So named" refers to both spoken and written names, and applies for as long as a text naming the person survives. I shall call these co-referential and descriptive identification, respectively. These contrast in almost every way.

(1) Descriptive identification involves some real property of an individual, including being so named or so called. A legal name identifies a person for official purposes, and so is usually the written name which appears on a birth certificate. This can only be changed by a legal process. A person can *call* themselves whatever they like, but "being so-called" is still a real relation between the person and the community of people who know them, for the name by which they are called is the reply to the question "what is the name of this person?" asked in their presence, and in the presence of anyone who knows them. Thus, being called "John" is a real property of John, just like having dark hair, being aged thirty-two, being 5' 8" tall, and so on. Think of John with a card around his neck, bearing

his written name, just as a car has a number plate at front and back. Vegetius describes how Roman soldiers were branded (*victuris in cute punctis scripti*), probably with the name or ensign of their general, or the emblem of their unit.[19] Augustine noted that just as Roman soldiers who had deserted were not branded again, so Christians should not be baptized again.[20] The old rumrunners would write details of the cargo on both halves of a torn dollar bill, and the shore agent would present the one half to the captain, who had the other half. If the serial numbers agreed and the torn edges matched, the shipment would be transferred.[21] Each half of the dollar bill identified the other half in a way that was purely physical, that is, it was a real property of each half that it matched the other half. The creation of such indelible marks upon a person or thing is no different in principle from the unique appearance of a face, or the unique sound of a voice, peculiar to only one person, which I shall discuss later.[22] By contrast, co-referential identification does not involve any real property. If we say "Peter preached at Jerusalem and Peter preached in Galilee," there is no property corresponding to the second "Peter" that identifies the second predicate as belonging to the same person as the first. It means nothing different from "Peter preached at Jerusalem and preached in Galilee." Again, some biblical scholars think the Philistine called "Goliath" was killed by Elhanan of Bethlehem, as stated in 2 Samuel 21:19, and that David actually killed another Philistine, the man referred to in 1 Samuel 17. If so, the Philistine called "Goliath" 2 Samuel 21:19 was not known as "Goliath" to those who knew him, or by repute. He would have had another name, say "Benob." Then being called "Benob" would have been a real property of his, while being called "Goliath" is only a sort of Cambridge property, meaningful only through co-reference within the text of Samuel.

(2) Descriptive identification involves inherently repeatable features, co-referential identification does not. Repeatable features are or *can* be possessed by more than one person. There are a hundred people called "John," hence the practice of applying a surname or other additional qualifier to limit the number (although there are still a hundred people called "John Smith"). They can be made less repeatable, by using numbers or other unique identifiers (think of license plates), which in practice apply to one individual only. But any such identifier can be artificially replicated or forged. It is merely repeatable-with-difficulty, as in the case of a brand or a tattoo, or the use of large prime numbers for computer encryption. Co-referential identifiers, on the other hand, cannot be satisfied by more than one subject. In "Herod feared *John*, knowing that *he* was a just man," the pronoun "he"—used in that sense—cannot co-refer with anything apart from "John." There cannot be another *he*.

(3) Descriptive identification provides information of interest to historians. The question of whether the person called "Nabu-sharrussu-ukin" in the Babylonian tablet was the same as the person called "Nebo-sarsekim" in Jeremiah 39:3, and one of considerable historical interest, given that the historical identification of one person in the Bible makes it more likely that other incidental characters are historical. Whether the person called "Muhammad" in the Quran is the same is the person called "Mahmet" in Sebeos' text is of critical importance, given the extreme view held by some that the Muhammad of the Quran never existed, and that Sebeos may have mentioned someone different. The discovery that the rising sun is not new every morning, but always the same, was one of the most fertile astronomical discoveries. Frege noted that descriptive identity statements are *a posteriori*, i.e. known solely on the basis of experience,[23] or rather, on the basis of the *witnesses* available to historians or archeologists, such as the text of Jeremiah and the clay tablet. But when the identification is co-referential, the question is of no historical interest at all. Historians are not interested in the question of whether "he" co-refers with John, given that it obviously does, unless there is a question of textual interpretation. As noted earlier, co-reference is story relative only, and does not identify individuals in the world in any real or practical sense. The philosophically interesting question of whether such historical identification is *contingent*, that is, not necessary, I shall address later.

(4) Descriptive information needs to be maximal, that is, it must contain as much information as necessary to identify an individual with any certainty. "Man" is no good, nor is "governor of Judea" if the period of governance is unknown. Proper names are often of little use because of their inherent repeatability, unless they are unusual enough to be considered unique. By contrast, co-referential information can be as minimal as you please. A name like "John" can be used many times in a text to identify the same person, even though many characters in the world have the same name. As noted in the previous chapter, a non-unique description like "the man," and even a description that is probably unsatisfiable ("the demon") can be used to identify a character. If there never was such a being as Asmodeus, there never was a demon called "Asmodeus," that is, there was never was a being such that the answer to the question "what is *this* demon called?" was "Asmodeus." Jesus is frequently referred to as "the son of God" (e.g. 1 John 3:8). The reader does not have to accept that God has a son, or even that God exists, in order to understand the reference.[24]

Strawson says that the man by the fountain[25] is distinguished "by means of a description *which applies only to him*" but that is manifestly false if "applies" is construed as a word-world relation. There could be many men standing by a fountain at any time, so the description must be construed as co-referential, that is, story relative hence intralinguistic. "The man" does not co-refer with "a man" in virtue of any real relation between language and the world.

REDACTION

Co-referential meaning may disappear (or reappear, or be created) depending on how a text is physically bound together, or ordered. The Mesha Stele, dating from around 840 BC, contains two references to Omri, the sixth king of Israel:[26] "*Omri* was king of Israel, and oppressed Moab during many days . . . *Omri* took the land of Madeba, and occupied it in his day, and in the days of his son, forty years."[27] The repetition of the proper name signifies co-reference, that is, it is part of the meaning of the text that there was a person was king of Israel, and the *same* person took the land of Madeba. In 1869, the stele was broken by a local Bedouin tribe, who heated it in a bonfire, threw cold water upon it and smashed it to pieces with boulders. The stele was later restored and is now in the Louvre museum, Paris, but suppose that it had not, that the fragments had been scattered to the winds, and that the two sentences containing the name "Omri" had been on different fragments. Then the identity would no longer be signified, but would rather be inferred. One sentence would say that someone called "Omri" was king of Israel, the other that someone called "Omri" took the land of Madeba. Based on the fact that one of them was a king of Israel, and given other historical evidence that only one person ever conquered Madeba, or any other information separately available, we could conclude that these were one and the same person, but the identity would not be part of the meaning of the two fragments. Only when there was proof that the fragments were once physically connected as part of the same text,[28] could the stone signify its full meaning, that is, the meaning intended by the person who inscribed the whole text upon the basalt.[29] Likewise, the personal pronouns of "*I* have built this sanctuary for Chemosh in Karchah" and "*I* built Baal-meon" co-refer when the text is not fragmented. But when it is broken up, "I" simply means "whoever is uttering or pronouncing this text," and it is not any more a part of the meaning that this person is the same or different from the subject of other texts. Its meaning does not belong to it of itself, otherwise it would have been the same whether or not the text was in fragments, or reconstituted.

The meaning of a text therefore depends on how its parts are bound together. This may by physical, as when the Mesha Stele was cemented back into one piece, or when the different pages of a codex are stitched or bound together into a single volume, or in a scroll, where there are many separate columns of writing inscribed upon a single long sheet. It may be logical, such as when separately bound works are connected by a list which identifies and orders them. In Babylonia, the Torah was stitched together into a long scroll that was so heavy that it needed more than one wooden roller. Originally each book was a separate scroll. Later works were added, until there were sixteen scrolls in all comprising the Tanakh. The Tanakh itself therefore consists in both the separate scrolls, *plus* the list (or oral tradition) identifying which scrolls are canonical. For example, Tobit, Judith, Maccabees, and some other books included in the text of the Old Testament are not included in the Tanakh.

Reference may also be created by the process of redaction, where different texts created independently of each other are copied, edited, and bound into a single text. This almost certainly happened in the case of the New Testament where the letters of Paul, written not long after the death of Jesus, were collected together with *four* versions of the gospels, probably written much later, after the destruction of the temple in 70 AD. Such redaction may introduce references that weren't there in the original text, or remove references that were. Both Luke and John mention sisters called Mary and Martha. Luke (10:38–42) does not mention the village where they lived, and contrasts Martha who is distracted by serving food, with Mary who sits at Jesus' feet. Both relate the story of a woman who takes a jar of expensive perfume and anoints Jesus' feet (Luke 7:36–50, John 12:1–8). But Luke does not connect the two events, nor does he identify Mary with the woman with the perfume. By contrast, John says they are the same woman.

> Now a certain man was ill, Lazarus of Bethany, the village of *Mary* and her sister Martha. *It was Mary* who anointed the Lord with ointment and wiped his feet with her hair (11:1–2)

The sources may not have stated the identity, in which case Luke correctly reflects their meaning, and John has added something which was not there, or perhaps it was the other way round.

Again, the Hebrew words transliterated as *Elohim* and *Yahweh*, and which are often translated as into English as "God" or "the Lord God," may once have been two different names. As is well known, in Genesis chapter 1, God is exclusively referred by the name "Elohim," but from Genesis 2:4, he is called "Yahweh." The context makes the co-reference clear: whatever is predicated of Elohim is predicated of Yahweh, the being *we* refer to as "God." According to the so-called *documentary hypothesis*, these passages came from different sources, one using the name "Elohim," the other "Yahweh." So it is possible (if the hypothesis is correct) that there were originally two separate narratives, one about "Elohim," the other about "Yahweh," with neither author glancing at the narrative of the other, and hence no identity *signified* between the bearers of the names. Perhaps Elohim was the Canaanite *El*, who is referenced in tablets discovered in 1929 in the ancient city of Ugarit on the northern coast of Syria.[30] See, for example, Deuteronomy 32:8–9, suggestive of an older tradition by which each deity in the divine pantheon, was assigned a separate nation. Israel was the nation that Yahweh received.

> When the Most High gave to the nations their inheritance, when he separated humanity, he fixed the boundaries of the peoples according to the number of divine beings. For Yahweh's portion is his people, Jacob his allotted heritage.

On this hypothesis, the identity of Elohim and Yahweh is simply the result of later editorializing when the sources were collected together, similar to the identity that the author of John asserts between the sister of Martha and the woman who anoints Jesus. The Christian Bible itself results from a binding of the so-called Old Testament to the New Testament. A modern edition of the Bible, containing both Old and New Testament, is a single text, although its parts may exist separately in other editions or textual traditions. As discussed in the previous chapter, the Christian Old Testament is a redaction of different Hebrew texts, containing texts that are the same as those in the Tanakh, sometimes in a different order, but also containing texts (such as Tobit) that are not in the Hebrew canon.

Again, in the gospel of John (19:25), a man called "Clopas" (Κλωπᾶ) is mentioned as one of the people who stood by at the crucifixion. In the gospel of Luke, in Luke (24:13–27), a man called Cleopas (Κλεοπᾶς) is said to be one of the two disciples who met Christ on the road to Emmaus. So according to John, Clopas was present at the crucifixion, but even if they are the same person, is it also true that, according to Luke, Clopas, that is, that same man, met Jesus on the road to Emmaus? Surely not, for Luke only says that *Cleopas* met Christ on the road. He does not say whether any man of that name was at the crucifixion, nor does he mention the gospel of John or any other gospel. The King James version of John 19 spells the name "Cleophas," which is close to the name as spelled in Luke, but this is not an accurate transliteration of the Greek,[31] and is a further example of how an editor or translator can add meaning which may not have been in the original sources. The gospels do not contain the *information* that Clopas was Cleopas, even if they were the same person.

THE DOCUMENTARY HYPOTHESIS

By the end of the nineteenth century a broad scholarly consensus emerged that the Pentateuch was the work of many authors, not one, writing from the time of David to the time of Ezra in about 500 BC. According to the "Documentary" or "Wellhausen" Hypothesis, proposed by Julius Wellhausen (1844 – 1918), the Pentateuch was originally four separate and independent narratives written by four different authors: the Yahwist or "J," writing c. 950 BC in the southern Kingdom of Judah, the Elohist or "E," writing c. 850 BC in the northern Kingdom of Israel, the Deuteronomist or "D," writing c. 600 BC in Jerusalem, and the Priestly source "P," c. 500 BC in Babylon. Supposedly, these were later combined into the current form by different unknown editors.

Thus, in the *first* creation story, a god called "Elohim" (a plural noun for gods or Deity in Biblical Hebrew) takes six days to create the universe—the light and the darkness (1:4), the sky, waters, and land (1:8–10), plants (1:11), the sun moon and stars (1:14–18), fishes, birds, and land animals (1:20-25), and man and woman in his image (1:26–28). In the *second* creation story in Genesis (2:4-19), an anthropomorphic God, called "Yahweh-Elohim," creates the world in a slightly different order, first creating the earth, then watering it (2:6), making man from clay with his own hands (2:7), a garden (2:8) with plants (2:9), and birds and animals (2:19). Yahweh-Elohim walks in the garden in cool of the evening, makes clothes for Adam and Eve, enjoys food Abram offers Him, speaks face-to-face with humans. He can sometimes be bargained with, as in the story of Sodom and Gomorrah, and occasionally relents when dissuaded by Moses. In one strange passage (Exodus 4:24–26), he attempts to kill Moses at an inn, despite having just chosen him as his prophet. According to the Documentary Hypothesis, this is evidence of two different authors—the Priestly and the Jahwist—whose work has been mechanically combined. Niels Peter Lemche identifies the Persian and Hellenistic period (fifth century to fourth century BC) as the likely setting for the composition of most biblical texts, which he claims best explains the "mental matrix" of the literature: a framework of political and religious ideology through which the writers constructed their past.[32]

It is therefore possible (though unlikely) that the four sources originally referred to four different supernatural beings, and that the apparent reference to a unitary being is an illusion caused by combining them into a single text, so that the names appear to have a single reference. Note that the name for the God of the Northern Kingdom, *Yhwh*, is given in the majority of English translations as LORD, following the late Judaic oral tradition of substituting "adonai" (LORD) for "yhwh."

The documentary hypothesis now has less support than when it was originated. It has come under challenge for the weakness of its assumption that the original author of a text would *not* tolerate inconsistency and repetition, and would aim at narrative unity, whereas an editor *would* tolerate the very same thing. If other religious texts use a variety of names for God, why should we have to explain the change of name in Genesis from "Yahweh" to "Elohim" as a change of source? Perhaps the change was for theological reasons. Perhaps what we regard today as infelicity of style was thought appropriate by the original author, or was for emphasis, or rhetorical effect.[33] However, it still dominates textual theory. The current form retains the central idea of the theory, that the sources of the Pentateuch are *recognizable* as independently composed sources, subsequently combined and interwoven by a single almost mechanical editor into a single narrative with rare minor adjustments and insertions.

Whether the hypothesis is true or not, my point remains the same. Co-reference can be created by the process of creating a document from different sources, and such co-reference adds information that was not there in the original sources, by converting descriptive information about identity to co-referential information.

BIOGRAPHY

As a further illustration of the difference between co-referential and descriptive identification, consider the example of how biographers have pieced together information "about" the thirteenth-century theologian John Duns Scotus. We have scant information about Scotus's life, and nothing at all about his early life. What little we have is from a variety of sources, including apocryphal stories and at least one blatant forgery, which biographers have attempted to piece together into a narrative. Here are three such descriptive references:

- Description I: A man called "Ioannes Duns" who was born in Maxton near Roxburgh, son of Ninian Duns, nephew of Elias Duns, Vicar General in the Kingdom of Scotland.[34]
- Description II: A man called "Fr. Johannes Dons" who was ordained priest on 17 March 1291 at the church of St. Andrew at Northampton by Oliver Sutton, bishop of Lincoln.
- Description III: A man called "Iohannes Douns" who was one of twenty-two Oxford Franciscans presented to Bishop Dalderby on July 26, 1300, for permission to hear confession.

Description I is allegedly from a transcript (the "Codex Tueedianus") of the Register of the Franciscan Conventual house at Haddington, East Lothian, by William Tweedie, a *scriba primarius*—clerk or notary—of Haddington toward the end of the sixteenth century, copied verbatim by Fr. Marianus Brockie (1687–1755) in his *Monasticon Scoticanum*, discovered in 1929 by Ephrem Longpré at Saint Mary's College, Blairs, near Aberdeen. The citations from the Codex Tueedianus were later discovered to be forgeries, and the existence of William Tweedie and Elias Duns is doubtful. Yet the fiction is the still the basis for many contemporary accounts of Scotus's early life.[35] Kenny repeats the story, using then unpublished research by Vos as a source. Vos's claim was based on A. G. Little's biographical account, itself entirely sourced from Callebaut 1931,[36] which is, in turn, borrowed from Longpré.[37]

Description II is from Longpré "Nouveaux documents franciscains d' Écosse,"[38] quoting the ordination list from Sutton's register. See also "L'ordination sacerdotale du Bx Jean Duns Scot., Document du 17 mars 1291," *Archivum Franciscanum Historicum* 22 (1929) 54–62. Note the difference in spelling between the names, just as with "Nabu-sharrussu-ukin." The names that historians engage with do not fit the tidy model assumed by philosophers of language.

Description III is from Little, who in 1892, identified the name "Iohannes Douns" in a list of Oxford Franciscans presented to Bishop Dalderby.[39] From these fragments, we could construct the following narrative:

> *John Duns* was born at Maxton near Roxburgh not later than 1265, being the son of Ninian Duns of Littledean. On 17 March 1291 *Duns*[40] was ordained priest in the church of St. Andrew at Northampton by Oliver Sutton, bishop of Lincoln. *He* is found at Oxford on 26 July 1300, when *he* was among the 22 friars of the Oxford convent presented by the minister, Hugh of Hartlepool, to John Dalderby, bishop of Lincoln, for licence to hear confession.

This adds a layer of meaning that was not present in the three fragments. The consecutive use of the same proper name signifies a common reference just like a pronoun, so in the conjunction "John Duns was born at Maxton and Duns was ordained priest at Northampton," it is signified, that is, it is part of the meaning, that some person who was born at Maxton was ordained priest at Northampton. But the two descriptive fragments do not signify this, given that we have to infer that the two descriptions, containing potentially ambiguous proper names, are true of the same individual. In other words, it is part of the meaning of the narrative that a single person was born at Maxton in 1265, was ordained priest in 1291, and was found at Oxford in July 1300, but it is not part of the meaning of the fragments. Furthermore, while "John Duns" identifies co-referentially, the forged document from which it was sourced has no descriptive identification at all. There simply never was a man called "Ioannes Duns," born in Maxton near Roxburgh, son of Ninian Duns, nephew of Elias Duns etc.

Other sources of descriptive identification are the lengthy works that we attribute to Scotus, such as the *Ordinatio* (final revised text) of the Oxford lectures on Peter Lombard's *Sentences* (the main genre of theological writing in the later Middle Ages). The attribution may rest on the name given by the scribe at the beginning, or usually the end of the work, known as a colophon, or on "internal evidence" such as the style and content of the work, or upon (usually infrequent) references to the author's work by contemporaries. In medieval times, it was common not to give the name of the author at all, or to attribute or misattribute authorship in later copies. For example, eight of the thirteen manuscripts of *Questions on the Perihermenias, Opus I* and five of the six manuscripts of *Opus II* attribute the works to Scotus. However, most of these manuscripts date from the fifteenth century, and it is impossible to know whether the attribution was copied from an earlier manuscript, or added at that date. As I have noted elsewhere,[41] the earliest Scotus manuscript is Bruxelles Bibl. Royale 2908, tentatively dated around 1325, seventeen years after his early and unexpected death in 1308. Due to his early death, few of his works had any official circulation during his lifetime, and a number works by other authors were mistakenly attributed to him, in a period where manuscripts were often circulated without the author's name, and where it was not uncommon for an editor, on finding a work whose teaching agreed with or resembled that of a master, to attribute it to him.[42] This could conceivably have happened between 1308 and the earliest dating of the Brussels manuscript. Likewise, Merton Coll. MS. 59, containing Scotus's *Reportatio* or student notes, ends with the comment "Here endeth the lecture of *John Duns*, called the subtle Doctor in the university of Paris, who was born in a certain hamlet of the parish of Emylton, called Dunstan in the county of Northumberland, belonging to the house of the scholars of Merton Hall in Oxford,"[43] but the addition is suspect. For one thing, the statutes of the college excluded monks, and the MS was copied in 1455, nearly 150 years after Scotus's death.

As well as confusing existing with non-existent people (Elias Duns's nephew), details about different identities can be confused. Daniel de Purziliis (or Pergulio) reported a sermon supposedly given by St. Bernardine in Padua in 1423,[44] saying that Scotus often went into a trance-like state, taking himself from the world of sensible things and into a world of non-sensual things (*extractus de sensualibus ad insensualia*). But his brothers in Cologne did not know this, and thinking him dead, hastily buried him. When his Parisian disciples returned, knowing of this tendency, they found he had been buried alive.[45] Gilbert Génébrard (1535–1597) later added a fanciful detail about Scotus being found on the steps of the vaulted mausoleum, with his hands gnawed off.[46] Paul Jovius repeated the story[47] with the claim that, with pitiful moaning (*miserabili mugitu*), Scotus repeatedly smashed his head against the stone door of the vault, which when opened revealed his body, with the head smashed open (*eliso capite*). This seems to confuse the story of Scotus with an apocryphal tale about Pope Boniface VIII, who when imprisoned in his apartments, fell into a violent rage, invoked Beelzebub, though nobody was in the room to hear him, bolted the door, and after gnawing his staff ("a good long one"), bashed his head against the wall and strangled himself with the bed-clothes.[48]

Thus, we start with source documents containing proper names, which are equivalent to the *indefinite* description "someone called such and such." These are like the pile of stones that Arthur Evans discovered at Knossos, from which we then construct a superstructure based on inferences, guesswork, and frequently romantic ideas about the past. For example, from Manelli's life of Scotus:

> The arrival of Friar John was a signal event for the College and for the University of Oxford. The presence of such extraordinary intelligence, coupled with a piety and goodness no less eminent, greatly enriched both the College and the University, helping to bring the highest esteem to both . . . . From his arrival, the young Friar John began to amaze both professors and students by his intelligence and astuteness.

Some of Manelli's inferences are impeccable. We know that Scotus possessed a keen and subtle intellect, at least his contemporaries said so. Great was the weight of arguments with which he was assailed: 200 syllogisms which he listened to with a quiet and attentive mind, and wonderful memory, as he untied the knottiest of them as easily as Samson snapped the bands of Delilah. Clearly the arrival of such a person at Oxford would enrich the university, and bring esteem to it, at least at some point in the future, and probably such an intelligent person would "amaze" his professors.[49] But they are inferences for all that. They more resemble Evans's "reconstruction" of the palace at Knossos, or Mantel's fictionalized biography of Cromwell than anything that might actually have happened.

HISTORY

As well as primary artifacts, such as registers of birth, ordination lists, and monumental inscriptions, histories are often also based on *other* histories. Our main source for the life of Augustus Caesar is *The Annals* (Latin: *Annales*) by Roman historian and senator Tacitus (AD 56–after 117), a history of the Roman Empire from the reign of Tiberius to that of Nero, the years AD 14–68, written around AD 109. Some scholars think that as a Roman senator, Tacitus had access to *Acta Senatus*—the Roman senate's records, but it is difficult to judge. Nissen's law, named for the nineteenth-century scholar Heinrich Nissen, states that ancient historians usually worked from just one main source, not using critical judgment in choosing between sources, but sticking to the one chosen.[50]

The history on which a history is based may itself be sourced from another history, now lost. Edward Gibbon was one of the first historians to provide a biography for Western readers, in his monumental *The History of the Decline and Fall of the Roman Empire*, chapter 50. There were a limited number of primary sources for European writers of that period, and Gibbon, who professed his "total ignorance of the Oriental tongues" relied extensively on Jean Gagnier's 1723 Latin translation of a biography by the Syrian Abu'l-Fida (1273–1331), writing more than 600 years after Muhammad's death.[51] This work is little more than a transcript of Ibn Al-Athir's biography, which, in turn, relies almost entirely on that of al-Tabari (d. 923), which, in turn, relies on Ibn Sa'd (d. 843) who relied on his master al-Waqidi (d. 823), and Ibn Hisham's edition of the biography by Ibn Ishaq (d. 768), now lost. Thus, there is only a single chain of transmission back to the *Sirat al-nabi* of Ibn Ishaq, although the *Kitab al-maghazi* of al-Waqidi is considered by some scholars to include independent sources.[52] As for Ibn Ishaq, writing more than a century after the Muhammad's death, he relied on hadiths, the oral tradition of the Prophet's sayings, the authenticity of which have been disputed.[53]

It is not my purpose here to make any judgment about the authenticity or reliability of early Islamic history. The point is that with regard to the origins of Islam, we are in substantially the same position as with the New Testament and much of the Hebrew Bible, so that co-referential identity is often imposed upon descriptive identity in ways that are subtle and hard to spot. The move from a series of indefinite references involving "a person called N" to a series of references that *use* the name N, and which impute more information than strictly existed in the original sources, is buried in the sources of historical works, so that history in some sense is a covert reconstruction of reality, like the palace that Evans "recreated" at Knossos. The information contained in a history or biography is almost always more than the information contained in the fragmentary evidence on which it is based.

SUMMARY

There are two distinct ways in which we may identify an individual "within history." The first is a form of signified co-reference between one text (the anaphor text) to another (the antecedent text), where the anaphor text indicates or suggests the identity of the antecedent text to the reader in some way. It is really a form of story relative identification where the narrative comprehends more than one text. Examples of this are the references in the New Testament and in the Quran to Moses ("And remember We gave Moses the Scripture"). In the second way, that is, implied co-reference, a probable identity is inferred from similarity of name or description in independent texts, such as when the name "Pilate" (Πιλᾶτος) appears in the New Testament and in the writing of Philo, or when the Arabs of "Muhmd" are claimed to have ravaged many villages near Hims. Here, the identity is not signified, is merely probable, *and is not part of the meaning of the source texts.*

Using the second means of identification, writers are able to construct "historical" texts using the first means of identification, such as *The History of the Decline and Fall of the Roman Empire,* which combine different *descriptive* sources into a single narrative. Thus, the identity of the man who was ordered by Tiberius to remove the shields from Herod's palace in Jerusalem, and the man who washed his hands before the crowd, can be signified by the historian, even though the sources may only suggest it. The meaning of the whole is greater than the meaning of the parts. There is no *essential* difference between reference in a story, and reference in history. Think of history as a *very* long story.

NOTES

1. I.e. Herod the Great.
2. Luke 3:1–2.
3. Herod tetrarch of Galilee and his brother Philip.
4. British Museum collection ID 114789. See http://www.britishmuseum.org/research/collection_online/collection_object_details.aspx?objectId=1571630&partId=1.
5. Jer 39:3, NIV.
6. British Museum press announcement, July 10, 2007.
7. Jer 39:3, NRSV.
8. https://web.archive.org/web/20070927194301/http://www.heardworld.com/higgaion/?p=680. Philip Davies points out (by email) "As for the problem of Hebraizaing of Akkadian (Assyrian, Babylonian) names, there is occasionally some doubt. For example, we have 'Osnappar' in Ezra 4:10, which looks most like *Ashurbanipal*, but the historical reference seems unlikely: the probable candidate is Sargon II, who effected the deportations into Samaria in the late 8th century. Thus we have Tiglath-Pileser, of whom there were a few, referred to sometimes as 'Pul.' It is likely that the biblical writers were not too well informed about Assyrian kings - hence Daniel's 'Darius the Mede' (the Dariuses were Persian), and other confusions between Babylonian and Assyrian rulers."
9. Quoted in Glaser, "Quran figure Zayd is a literary construct, says scholar," see also Powers, *Zayd,* 96.
10. For example, 9:58, "And among them are some who criticize *you* concerning the [distribution of] charities," 11:7. "But if *you* say, 'Indeed, you are resurrected after death', those who disbelieve will surely say, 'This is not but obvious magic,'" cf. 12:102, 16:82, and so on.

11. That is, pledged submission in return for their lives.

12. *Fragment on the Arab Conquests*, ll. 8–11, 14–16, 17–23, quoted in Hoyland, *Seeing Islam as Others Saw It*, 117, noting that "whatever appears in curly brackets is unreadable, so any letters/words given are conjectured."

13. Sebeos, trans. Thomson, *The Armenian History Attributed to Sebeos*, 95, from the critical edition by Abgaryan (*Patmut'iwn Sebēosi*, 135, see also Macler, *Histoire d'Héraclius : par l'évêque Sebeôs*, 95).

14. According to Robert Thomson (email June 8, 2016), in Armenian script Mahmed, Mahmad would be: Մահմէդ, Մահմադ. The later writers would spell these names: Մահմէտ, Մահմատ. *Muhammad* would be: Մուհամմատ.

15. The *Sirat al-nabi* of Ibn Ishaq. See section 5.

16. There is also the "Pilate stone," a damaged limestone block discovered at the site of Caesarea in 1961 inscribed with Pilate's name.

17. *De Legatione ad Gaium*, Περι αρετων και πρεσβειας προς Γαιον XXXVIII/299–305.

18. Ibid.

19. *De re militari* ii.5, in Reeve, ed., 2004:39.

20. *De Baptismo contra Donatistas,* I.4.5.

21. Metcalfe, *Whispering Wires: The Tragic Tale of an American Bootlegger*, 59.

22. Elbourne, *Situations and Individuals*, 6.1.2, following Burge, also mentions "the social and psychological practice of naming, forestalling the Kripkean objection (Kripke, *Naming and Necessity*, 68–70) that it is trifling to say that sages are called 'sages.'" However, this fails to distinguish the referential and descriptive features of proper names.

23. In Kant's sense of a posteriori, see *Critique* A2. The medieval definition makes no appeal to sense perception, defining a priori as a form of reasoning from cause to effect, such as from astronomical positions to eclipse, and a posteriori as reasoning from effect to cause, such as observing the sun hidden, and inferring there is an eclipse.

24. Or (to take a non-biblical example) we could introduce some person in a history of the US presidency as "a former governor of Nevada," and continue to identify him as "the former governor of Nevada," in a series of statements, which make it clear that the description is intended to co-refer with the proper name "Franklin Delano Roosevelt," which occurs in other US history books. But the other history books make it clear that FDR was never governor of Nevada. This is not a problem. Establishing co-reference between different texts involves techniques, which are different from the way we establish co-reference within the same text. See also chapter 9 on semantic relations between different historical texts. See also Soames, "Why Incomplete Definite Descriptions Do Not Defeat Russell's Theory of Descriptions," who points out that we don't want one explanation for the assertion of the contextually determined singular proposition when the incomplete description, *the F*, is a misdescription, but a different explanation for the case in which it is not. Why should a compositional semantic theory ignore the content clause of a description on one of its readings?

25. Strawson, *Individuals*, 18.

26. See 1 Kings 16:16–17. Mesha is the subject of 2 Kings 3.
27. Trans. King, *Moab's Patriarchal Stone*, ch. 3.
28. Perhaps by the same means that the rumrunners identified the two halves of the bills!
29. I shall discuss the so-called *Frege puzzle* of how identity statements can be meaningful in the next chapter.
30. See, for example, Cross, *Canaanite Myth and Hebrew Epic: Essays in the History of the Religion of Israel*, chapter 3 and *passim*, Dever, *Did God Have a Wife?*, 255ff.
31. Cleopas is not the Clopas of John 19:25, for "Cleopas" is a shortened form of the Greek name "Cleopatros," the masculine form of "Cleopatria," whereas "Clopas" is a Hebrew/Aramaic name. "Some have suggested that perhaps Cleopas was known to Luke's readers in the same way that Alexander and Rufus were known to Mark's (cf. Mark 15:21). This is purely speculation, and *even more speculative is discussion about who the other person was,*" Stein, "Luke":610, my emphasis.
32. Lemche, *Biblical Studies and the Failure of History*, 291ff.
33. As Whybray comments (*The Making of the Pentateuch*, 15) it would be a serious error to assume that the authors of the Pentateuch had the same notions of authorship, editorship, style, and other matters as ourselves. Rendtorff, *The Problem of the Process of Transmission in the Pentateuch*, 180, argues that there is no satisfactory way of dividing the whole text into individual sources. See also Wenham, "Pondering the Pentateuch: The search for a new paradigm."
34. *Ioannes Duns noster ex hac Dunsiorum propagine de Littledeno prodiisse videtur cum [pro] nepos ex fratre Eliae nominetur* (Brockie, *Monasticon Scoticanum*, 1298, cited in Docherty, "The Brockie Mss. and Duns Scotus," 354).
35. See e.g. Vos, *The Philosophy of John Duns Scotus*, 19, Hackett, *Dictionary of Literary Biography: Medieval Philosophers*, 441.
36. Kenny, *A New History of Western Philosophy*, 320, Little, "Chronological notes on the life of Duns Scotus," 569; Callebaut, "A propos du Bx. Jean Duns Scot de Littledean," 317.
37. Cited in Docherty, "The Brockie Mss. and Duns Scotus," 354.
38. *Archivum Franciscanum Historicum*, 22, 1929:588.
39. See "Documents I," Little, *Franciscan Papers, Lists, and Documents*, 235, starting with the tenth name: "Iohannem de Stapelton, Adam de Corf, Petrum de Todeswrth, Willelmum de Schirburn, Petrum de Baldeswell, Martinum de Alnewyk, Iohannem Douns, Fratrem Walterum Boseuille, Robertum de Couton, Rogerum de Alnewyk, Iohannem de Horley, Ricardum de Conigton, Thomam de Pontefracto." Cited in Vos, 19.
40. I have adapted this from Little (ibid.), who cautiously writes *Fr. Johannes Dons*, as it appears in the source.
41. Buckner, "On the authenticity of Scotus's logical works," 57.
42. Buckner and Zupko, *Duns Scotus On Time and Existence*, 55.
43. *Explicit lectura Doctoris Subtilis in Universitate Oxoniensi super primum librum Sentenciarum, sc.* Doctoris Johis. Duns *nati in quadam villicula parochiae de Emyldon vocata Dunstan, in Comitatu Northumbriae pertinente domui Scolarium*

de Merton halle in Oxonia, et quondam socii dicte domus. Script, per me Johannem Reynbold Almanicum de Monte Ornato Anno Dni. Millimo. ccccli . f 190v. "Johannes Reynbold" was from Zierenburg in Hesse, who copied a six-volume set (MS 59–64) of Scotus's *Sentences* and other works for Richard Scarborough at Merton College between 1451 and 1455. See Parkes, *Their Hands Before Our Eyes: A Closer Look at Scribes.*

44. Ridolfi, *Opera Quae Extant Omnia*, Sermo 1, p.5.

45. Ita accidit in mente oppressa, & procliva in terrenis desideriis: nam oportet sublevare mentem ab istis sensualibus ad insensualia, sicut accidit *Magistro subtili*, scilicet *Scoto*, qui ita fuit extractus de sensualibus ad insensualia, & ita fuit elevatus, quod fratres, qui *ignorabant hunc eius solitum morem*, credentes ipsum fore mortuum, subterraverunt eum vivum. Et postea venientes eius discipuli, scientes id sibi saepe accidere, quid foret de eius modo interrogantes, repererunt eum vivum subterratum fore, [id] est, suffocatum.

46. "Dum in gradibus mausolei devoratis manibus repertus est" Génébrard, *Chronographiæ libri quatuor*, 667.

47. Giovio, *Elogia virorum litteris illustrium*, cited in Wadding, *Opera omnia, quae hucusque reperiri potuerunt*, 14.

48. Quoted in Wiseman, *Essays on Various Subjects*, Vol. 3, 218.

49. Wadding, Ibid., 10, citing Pelbartus Temesvár, *Stellarium Coronae Mariae Virginis* lib 4 p.5 art. 4.

50. See e.g. Pitcher, *Writing Ancient History: An Introduction to Classical Historiography*, 72–78.

51. Ali, *The Lives of Muhammad*, 44.

52. See Little, *Franciscan Papers, Lists, and Documents*, 34. According to the Wellhausen-Horowitz scholarly tradition, al-Waqidi simply plagiarized Ishaq's work. A more recent tradition argues that the two authors drew upon a common fund of materials, consisting of traditions and popular stories that had already been formalized by the eighth century: see, for example, Jones, "Ibn Ishaq and al-Waqidi," 51.

53. For example, Guillaume, *The Life of Muhammad*, xiii.

Chapter 6

Reference and Identity

In the following two chapters, I shall explore consequences of the anaphoric thesis that conflict with fundamental principles of the classical semantic framework. The first consequence, which I shall explore in this chapter, is that proper name identity statements can be informative, in the sense that the names flanking them are not synonymous. The second consequence, which I shall explore in the next chapter, is that negative proper-name existential statements can be both true and informative.

It follows from the anaphoric co-reference thesis (and from standard semantics) that co-reference implies identity. If two terms "a" and "b" co-refer in the sense that I have defined, that is, anaphorically, and assuming that they have a referent at all,[1] the identity statement "a=b" is necessarily true. For example, "Herod is identical with himself." It is part of the meaning of the proper name-pronoun combination that if they have a referent, they have a common referent, so the identity statement, if true, is true in virtue of its meaning, and such a statement cannot come as news. On the other hand, I have argued that proper names in *independent* texts do not co-refer. Michael Jursa's discovery that that Jeremiah's Nebo-sarsekim was the same person as Nabu, the chief eunuch mentioned in the British Museum tablet, was an important archeological discovery,[2] and the names "Nabu" and "Nebo" are not synonymous. Co-reference implies identity, but identity does not imply co-reference.

This leads to the following puzzle. How can it come as news that Nebo is the same person as Nabu, although it is not news that Nebo is Nebo? If they are the same person, whatever is true of one statement, for example, newsworthiness, ought to be true of the other. If "Nebo" refers to Nebo, as we agree, and if Nebo is Nabu, why doesn't "Nebo" refer to Nabu? In this chapter, I shall defend my view of reference statements, namely that they have an illusory form, and shall explore its implications for two important contemporary views: the Russellian "direct reference" view of the proposition, and Kripke's thesis that identity statements involving proper names, if true, are necessarily true.

WHAT IS IDENTITY?

Beyond practical reasons, there is no need either for singular terms or for a relation of identity in a complete history of the world. Singular terms are a practical and important way of expanding a single indefinite proposition "some S was P" into two propositions: an indefinite proposition followed by a singular or definite one, "something is S and *it* is P," as in the move from (A) to (B).

(A) A eunuch called "Nebo" was an official called "Nabu."
(B) A eunuch was called "Nebo." Nebo was an official called "Nabu."
(C) A eunuch was called "Nebo." An official was called "Nabu." Nebo was Nabu.

(A) is a shorter way of representing (B); however, for a very long narrative, and particularly when we introduce new items such as "a king called 'Nebuchadnezzar,'" "a city called 'Babylon'" and so on, it would be inconvenient, and we would have to resort to a device something like the variables x, y, and so on, of predicate calculus. In fact (if I am right) proper names like "Nebo," "Babylon" and so on, are the equivalent of these variables, except each combination of function and variable expresses a complete proposition, unlike in predicate calculus. Identity statements such as (C) are a way of connecting different and independent indefinite descriptions into a more complex indefinite description. For example, Jeremiah gives us the indefinite description "a high ranking Babylonian official called 'Nebo' who witnessed the culmination of Nebuchadnezzar's second siege of Jerusalem in the summer of 587 BC," the Babylonian tablet gives us "a eunuch called 'Nabu' of Nebuchadnezzar who sent 0.75kg of gold to a temple in 595 BC." The proper name "Nebo" co-refers with the first description, "Nabu" with the second. Using the identity statement "Nebo was Nabu," we can combine these two descriptions into one, and we can eliminate one of the possible states of past reality consistent with the original sources. The original sources are consistent with there being two people, a eunuch and an official, the combined sources, if the identity statement is true, are consistent with there being only one such person.

Hence, we can interpret identity statements as a way of combining two less complex indefinite descriptions into a single more complex one. These give us important information about history, by reducing the number of possible items that *might* have existed, *for all the information available*. Think of them as a kind of statement about number. Instead of a man called "Fr. Johannes Dons" who was ordained priest on March 17, 1291, and a man called "Iohannes Douns" who was one of twenty-two Oxford Franciscans presented to Bishop Dalderby on July 26, 1300, we can eliminate the possibility that the man presented to Bishop Dalderby was another man, on the supposition that Fr. Johannes Dons was Iohannes Douns.

Identity statements can provide information about history, given the information we already have. They rule out the possibility that there were more people in history than there actually were. But this conflicts with two fundamental principles of the standard theory of reference. The first principle is that identity statements involving proper names are not informative. This conflicts with the fact that the discovery that Nebo was Nabu was historically important. It revealed a fact, namely that two descriptions ("high ranking Babylonian official"/"eunuch of Nebuchadnezzar") that *might* have been true of different people, were true only of one. The second principle is that identity is not contingent, hence necessary. Saul Kripke and others have persuasively argued that an identity statement a=b, if true, is necessarily true. For what objects a and b could be counterexamples? Not two distinct objects, for then the antecedent is false, nor an object and itself, for then the consequent is true.

INFORMATION VALUE

My claim that identity statements can be informative is in stark contrast to strong *Millianism* or "direct reference." This alludes to Mill's claim, "A proper name [is] a word which answers the purpose of showing what thing it is that we are talking about, but not of telling anything about it,"[3] although (as I discussed in chapter 2) the idea is older than Mill. The term "direct reference" was introduced by Kaplan in the mid-1970s in works on the semantics of demonstratives and indexicals,[4] and the theory was developed by a "new wave" of reference theorists such as Joseph Almog, Nathan Salmon, Scott Soames, and Howard Wettstein. It is sometimes called the "Fido"-Fido theory,[5] or "Millianism," but we should distinguish *weak* Millianism, namely Kripke's thesis that a proper name is not descriptive, from direct reference or *strong* Millianism. Millianism of both sorts is still central to contemporary philosophy of language. As Bianchi recently notes, "probably the majority of philosophers of language locate themselves in the camp generated by the work of Kripke and company in the late 1960s and early 1970s."[6]

My disagreement with Millianism turns on the view of the *proposition*, that is, that which is capable of truth and falsity. For Aristotle (and for traditional logic generally), a proposition (λόγος ἀποφαντικός, *oratio enuntiativa*) is a kind of sentence (λόγος, *oratio*), distinguished by its capability of being true or false. A prayer is not a proposition (nor is a question or a command). But as Kripke notes,[7] strong Millianism depends on the thesis that the proposition is not a linguistic item at all, but a *Russellian* proposition: an extralinguistic item that is expressed by an assertoric sentence.[8] On this view, the same proposition is expressed by "Herod feared John," "Herodes metuebat Iohannem," "Hérode craignait Jean," and so on. The proposition is supposed to have components that correspond to the *semantic values* of the components of the sentence. The semantic value of a proper name is the bearer itself, the semantic value of a predicate is a property, and the semantic value of a verb is a relation. The proposition expressed by "Peter preached in Galilee" is an extralinguistic item containing the relation expressed by "preached in," and Peter and Galilee themselves, *trapped* in the proposition.[9] If a singular term is directly referential, then its presence in an assertoric sentence contributes nothing to the meaning except the object that it refers to.[10]

On the strong Millian view of the proposition, no identity statement can be informative (at least, not for anyone who knows that every object is identical with itself). Defenders of the standard theory such as Nathan Salmon would argue that the information content of the sentence "Nebo was Nabu" is the Babylonian officer "taken twice" (i.e., on both sides of the identity sign) plus the relation of identity at the time 595 BC.[11] The proposition expressed by the sentence is an extralinguistic item, which consists of components that include Nebo himself. It follows that the information content of "Nebo is Nabu" is made of precisely the same components, in precisely the same way, and so the information content of any such identity statement is the trivial proposition about some object that it is identical with itself. It was trivial to discover that Nebo was Nabu, as Michael Jursa appears to have done.

Hence, if Salmon is right, many of our intuitions are mistaken. For example, Christopher Heard (theology professor at Pepperdine University) says:

> The tablet gives us a Chief Eunuch Nabu-sharrussu-ukin in 595 BCE; the biblical story gives us a Chief Eunuch Nebo-sarsekim in 587 BCE. Could these be the same person? Well, sure they could. My hunch is that it's more probable than not. However, *proof* for that hunch is lacking. (my emphasis)[12]

Salmon might say that Heard is mistaken.[13] We do *not* lack proof that Nebo is Nabu, for we have proof that Nebo is Nebo, in the form of the principle of identity, and "Nebo is Nebo" expresses exactly the same proposition as "Nebo is Nabu." Even Salmon concedes that "this seems to fly in the face of the fact that the two sentences differ dramatically in their informativeness," but he justifies it as follows.[14] Suppose a foreign-born person has not been taught that "ketchup" and "catsup" are synonyms,[15] but learns the words by reading the labels on the bottles, and accidentally forms the idea that "catsup" means a sauce eaten at breakfast, whereas "ketchup" means a sauce only consumed at lunch. Hence, for that person, the sentence "ketchup is ketchup" is uninformative, while the sentence "Catsup is ketchup" is as informative as "Nebo is Nabu." But that does not mean that the terms "catsup" and "ketchup" differ in information value. They are perfect synonyms, and so have the same information value, indeed it is possible they are merely two different spellings of the very same English word, like the American-English "color" and the British-English "colour." Thus, assuming that Nebo was in fact the same person as Nabu, "Nebo" and "Nabu" are perfect synonyms, and it would be no part of the semantic content of "Nebo is Nabu" to specify the way that a biblical archeologist takes the proposition.[16] When Heard claims, there is no proof that Nebo is Nabu, it is like the foreigner, ignorant of condiment labels, claiming there is no proof that catsup is ketchup.

But "Nebo" and "Nabu" are *not* synonymous. The information provided by the third sentence in the following passage adds to the information provided by the first two.

A man called "Nebo" was at Jerusalem. A man called "Nabu" was at Babylon.
Nebo was the same person as Nabu.

The first two sentences do not contain the information that Nebo was Nabu, for the subjects are indefinite noun phrases, which everyone agrees do not refer. What they convey is consistent with there being two people, or one. Only in the third sentence is the identity asserted. Since "Nebo" refers back to the indefinite noun phrase in the first sentence, likewise "Nabu" to the indefinite noun phrase in the second, they cannot be synonymous, for neither refers back to the other. So it is not like "catsup is ketchup," where the *transportable* meaning of the two terms is identical, and where the foreigner has not grasped the correct meaning. One can correctly grasp the meaning of the first two sentences given earlier, without also grasping that they are true of a single person. Furthermore, the first two sentences do not give the information that there is only one person rather than two: only the three sentences together do this. Therefore, the third sentence must be informative. Nor does any part of the meaning of "Nebo" constitute the man himself, an extralinguistic entity trapped in a proposition, likewise for "Nabu."

This does not mean that the information value of a proper name is something subjective, a conceptual representation, which can differ from person to person. As I argued earlier,[17] there must be some sort of rule or heuristic for determining reference, involving knowledge of the syntax and semantics of the language, literary genre, what the author knows about what we know, and so on. The purpose of language is to establish understanding.[18]

The three-sentence example given earlier is a simple one, but it is no different in principle from the longer and more complex example of the unknown traveler in Dumas' *The Vicomte de Bragellone*. The narrative begins "Cropole had, at the time, but *one single traveller* in his house. *This* was a man of scarcely thirty years of age." The indefinite antecedent "one single traveller" introduces a chain of anaphors, such as "this," "he," "this gentleman," and so on. The anaphors collect a whole set of predicates together into one subject, and so the anaphoric chain preceding chapter 9 is thus a long indefinite description: "a traveller, nearly years old, who arrived at Cropole's hotel in Blois in May 1660," and so on. It is no part of the *meaning* of the description to identify the Charles II of the history books, and so the identity statement reveals a significant piece of information: that in May 1660, Charles II had visited Blois, where he met D'Artagan, an officer of Louis XIV. The information is likely to be false, given there never was such a person as D'Artagan, and given that as far as we know (from other narratives) Charles stayed at Breda in the Netherlands in the first half of May 1660, and the Hague in the latter half from where he departed for England on June 2. Yet it is information for all that. In the gospel of Mark, by contrast, we never get this information. It is left open, that is, it is never *signified* whether the man mentioned in 14:51–52, the one who followed Jesus wrapped in a linen cloth, and who fled naked when the young men laid hold on him, is the same as or different from the man[19] mentioned in 16:5, the one whom the women saw sitting at the right side of the tomb, who told the women that Jesus should be sought in Galilee. "You cannot wring out of the Bible any more information than was already in there."

You will object that if a name has no descriptive content, then its meaning can be no other than its bearer. Devitt has called this the *Semantic Presupposition*: the meaning of a name is either descriptive or else it is the name's referent, and there are no other possible candidates for a name's meaning.[20] But it does not follow. It is essential to the theory I have defended above that there is no semantic difference between the following two narratives.

A man called "Peter" preached in Galilee.
There was a man called "Peter." Peter preached in Galilee.

The name "Peter" as used in the second sentence of the second narrative clearly has no descriptive content. It is merely a tag signifying that the predicate "preached in Galilee" is to be affirmed of the (indefinite) subject of the previous sentence. This does not require that the meaning of the proper name "Peter" is its referent.

Hence, identity statements can be of two kinds. Where the terms flanking the identity sign (anaphorically) co-refer, and if they have a referent, the statement will be necessarily true. Where they do not, the statement will semantically encode useful information, and will be contingently true only. What is it for an identity statement to be true? In what way must the world be different, if the statement is true, from the way it is if the statement is false? I have argued that an identity statement merges two distinct anaphoric chains, each of which involves many, perhaps *very* many separate sentences about each individual, expressing as a whole a large body of information about each. Thus, the general form of the merger is this.

There is some F called "M"
There is some G called "N"
M = N

The predicate F could represent all the information we have about Francis Bacon (was an English philosopher and statesman, served as Attorney General and as Lord Chancellor of England, etc.), the predicate G could represent all the information we have about William Shakespeare (was a playwright, an actor, England's national poet, author of *Hamlet*, etc.). Suppose we discover that Bacon and Shakespeare were one and the same person. Before the putative discovery these names are not synonyms: their signification lies solely in their anaphoric connection to the chain of propositions containing information about each man. Until the discovery, it is not part of the meaning of "Bacon" that it co-refers with the "Shakespeare" chain, nor part of the meaning of "Shakespeare" to co-refer with the "Bacon" chain.

So when it is discovered that Bacon was Shakespeare what fact is discovered? What fact is it that makes the identity statement true? Consider what is asserted by the first two statements mentioned earlier (i.e., that there is an F and there is a G) with what is asserted by those two statements plus the third. The first two statements are consistent with there being one or two things, that is, with there being one thing that is F, another thing that is G, or with there being just one thing that is both F and G. The world is such that there are one or two things that the statements are true of. But when we add the third statement, that is, the identity statement, the statements can be true of only one thing that is both F and G. In the case of the Bacon Shakespeare example, we have a set of statements that could be true of one person who was both a statesman and a playwright, or of two people, one of whom was a statesman, the other a playwright. The fact-that-makes-the-identity-statement-true is thus an important fact about the world, in that it reduces (as it were) the possible number of people who existed in the world by one.

Note that at the time of the discovery, "Bacon" and "Shakespeare" are not synonyms, but that does not rule out their becoming synonyms over time. We can imagine the Wikipedia entry for Francis Bacon opening "English philosopher and statesman, poet and playwright, also known as 'Shakespeare,'" with the two (current) articles merged into one, perhaps with a new section discussing the discovery of the identity. At some point in time, the names "Bacon" and "Shakespeare" would be synonymous, in just the way that "Hesperus" and "Venus" are now synonymous.

But now we must discuss Kripke's argument that identity statements involving proper names are not contingently true.

IDENTITY NOT NECESSARY

The question is whether true a posteriori identity statements are also *contingent*, that is, true but not necessarily true, or (which is the same thing) true but possibly false. The orthodox position is that if any individual a is *actually* identical to some individual b, a and b are *necessarily* identical. If a is identical with b, then necessarily a is identical with b, and by implication, if a and b are numerically different, then they are necessarily so. If the Nabusharrussu-ukin ("Nabu") mentioned by the Babylonian clay tablet was the same person as the Nebo-sarsekim ("Nebo") mentioned in Jeremiah 39:3, it is necessary that they were the same person. If they were different, then it is necessary that they were different. The principle seems to have been first stated by Ruth Barcan Marcus in 1947. Willard Van Orman Quine demonstrated it in 1953 by a shorter and more elegant argument,[21] and it became widely known and accepted after Saul Kripke's informal and entertaining *Naming and Necessity*, a work which established him as one of the foremost analytic philosophers of the twentieth century.

The principle seems to conflict with the idea that proper name identity statements convey information. Information is about how the world is, so if the information is correct, the world must be different from how it would be if the information were not correct. For example, if the identity statement "Nebo is Nabu" is true, there is one fewer person than if it were not. Moreover, the information *might* not be correct. It is possible that it is, but also possible that it is not. But if Kripke's thesis is right, both possibilities cannot stand together. It is possible that Nebo is Nebo, *or* it is possible that Nebo is not Nebo, but there is no *and*, which conflicts with our notion that both are possible. Indeed, Kripke concedes that both are possible, at least if "possible" means something like "possible *as far as we know*," but I shall discuss this idea shortly.[22]

I present his argument as follows.[23] Suppose that the person referred to or "designated"[24] by "Nebo" is identical with the person designated by "Nabu" in the actual world, and let's represent this as follows:

(1) des("Nebo,"@) = des("Nabu,"@)

where "@" represents the actual world, and "des" is the "designates"[25] relation. Kripke argues that proper names like "Nebo" are *rigid designators*. As he puts it, a proper name designates the same object in every possible world or possible situation, whereas a non-rigid or *accidental* designator does not.[26] For example, "Moses"[27] is a rigid designator because although Moses might not have been the man who led the Israelites out of Egypt, it could not have been the case that he was not Moses. By contrast "the man who led the Israelites out of Egypt" is an accidental designator, since the man who led the Israelites out of Egypt might have been other than Moses, for example, Aaron. The content of a proper name, as a proper name is typically used, cannot include any descriptive information that would be relevant to truth-evaluation in other possible worlds.

Thus, if "Nebo" is a rigid designator, it designates Nebo in any possible situation, say w, and likewise "Nabu" designates Nabu in that situation.

(2) des("Nebo,"w) = des("Nebo,"@)
(3) des("Nabu,"w) = des("Nabu,"@)

Then from the transitivity of identity (a=b and b=c implies a=c), it follows that the designation[28] of "Nebo" in w is identical with the designation of "Nabu."

(4) des("Nebo,"w) = des("Nabu,"w)

In other words, let a be the designation of "Nebo" in w, and b its designation in the actual world. Then by the rigidity hypothesis a=b. Assume that b=c, where c is the actual designation of "Nabu" in the actual world. So a=c. By rigidity, c=d, where d is the designation of "Nabu" in w. So a=d, and (4) is true. But w was any possible situation. It follows, purely from the assumption of rigid designation and transitivity, that if "Nebo" and "Nabu" *actually* designate the same person, then they *necessarily* designate the same person. This conflicts with the idea that the identity comes as news.

To resolve the problem, let's start by noting that in one sense of the word "designate," Kripke's master argument is entirely trivial. Suppose, for sake of argument, that the word "mutton" means or designates or signifies the same thing as what "lamb" signifies. Then obviously the statement "it is possible, as far as we know, that Dave is cooking mutton tonight" means, and therefore has the same truth value as when we replace the word "mutton" by the word "lamb." If the words mean the same, then it is necessary that lamb is mutton. Of course, it is not necessary that they do mean the same, given that words signify by convention, but as Kripke notes, the rigidity thesis does not depend on what the names mean in the *counterfactual* situation. We could all be speaking German in that counterfactual situation, or we could be speaking in a different way such that "Nebo" and "Nabu" meant something entirely different. Nonetheless, in describing that situation, Kripke says that we use English with its current meaning and the proper names *with their current designation.*[29]

But on this trivial reading of the argument, it doesn't work. If "Nebo" means the same as "Nabu" in the way that "mutton" means the same as "lamb," or "bachelor" means the same as "unmarried man," then the identity of Nebo and Nabu could not have been *discovered* by Jursa, any more than we could "discover" that Dave was cooking lamb from the knowledge that he was cooking mutton. We cannot read "designate" in this way, nor does Kripke mean to. He himself has not advocated a direct reference view of the proposition, distinguishing his doctrine of rigid designation from what he calls the "Millian," that is, *strong* Millian doctrine that only the referent of the name contributes to its meaning.[30] As Burgess has pointed out, if a=b is and if "a" and "b" are strongly Millian, then all three of the following propositions are true.

It is (metaphysically) necessary that a = b.
It is a priori that a = b.
It is analytic that a = b.[31]

But Kripke holds that only the first is true. The uncertainty expressed by the "may" of "Nebo may not be Nabu" is purely *epistemic*, and "merely expresses our present state of ignorance, or uncertainty." He distinguishes between this epistemic form of necessity and the "metaphysical" form.[32]

So if a proper name does not designate its bearer in the sense that "mutton" signifies lamb, or "bachelor" signifies being an unmarried man, what does Kripke mean? He suggests that "designate" is interchangeable with "refers to,"[33] but then we have the puzzle about what "refers" means, for his argument is only valid if the verb phrase "refers to" or "designates" expresses a genuine relation between a name and an object.

(5) There is a person called "Nebo."
(6) There is a person called "Nabu."
(7) It is possible that Nebo = Nabu.

(8) It is possible that Nebo <> Nabu.
(9) The tokens of "Nebo" in (7) and (8) designate *Nebo*.
(10) The tokens of "Nabu" in (7) and (8) designate *Nabu*.

Clearly it is possible that the indefinite propositions (5) and (6) are, or could be true of one person, or more than one, that is, it is possible that there is a single person with the names "Nebo" and "Nabu," or two people, one with each name, and it is these possibilities that sentences (7) and (8) express, by means of the co-reference mechanism: the tokens of "Nebo" are anaphors of the indefinite antecedent "a person called 'Nebo,'" and likewise the tokens of "Nabu" are anaphors of the indefinite antecedent "a person called 'Nabu.'"[34] But as I have argued (chapter 3 and *passim*, defending the reference thesis), the co-reference relation is purely intralinguistic. No bearer for the name "Nebo" has to exist in order for it to be an anaphor of "a person called 'Nebo,'" and likewise for "Nabu.'" Furthermore, the reference statements (9) and (10) express this co-reference but by using rather than mentioning the names. That is, the italicized "Nebo" in (9) continues the anaphoric chain "a person called 'Nebo,'" "Nebo" (7), and "Nebo" (8). The *reference thesis* is that a reference statement is true if *and only if* the token that is *used* co-refers with the one which is *mentioned*. For example, the reference statement

> In "Herod feared John$_1$, knowing that *he* was a just man," the term "he" refers to John$_2$.

is true because "John$_2$" co-refers with "he": the proper name in the reference statement itself has intralinguistic co-reference. The reference statement appears to express a relation between language and reality, even though what makes it true is a relation between linguistic items only. We can say that a pronoun *co-refers* with the name "John," expressing an intralinguistic relation, or we can say that it refers to *John*, apparently expressing an extralinguistic relation, but really stating the same fact in a different and perhaps illusory way.

But in no case does "Nebo" co-refer with "Nabu": their tokens form different anaphoric chains, and so we cannot establish (1) above, that is, that the actual designation of "Nebo" is the actual designation of "Nabu," nor are (2) and (3) true on the intralinguistic hypothesis.

It may be objected that this violates the principle of substitutivity, and indeed another argument for Kripke's conclusion goes as follows.[35]

1. If Nebo is Nabu, and F(Nebo) then F(Nabu)
2. It is necessary that Nebo is Nebo

3. If Nebo is Nabu, and it is necessary that Nebo is *Nebo*, then it is necessary that Nebo is *Nabu*
4. If Nebo is Nabu, is necessary that Nebo is Nabu

Step 1 is an instance of the principle of substitutivity. Whatever predicate we substitute for "F" expresses some attribute of an individual. It follows that he possesses this attribute regardless of how we designate him. If Nebo was a high-ranking official in Babylon, and if Nabu was him, then Nabu was a high-ranking official in Babylon too. (Indeed, forget the "too." There was just one of them, and so just one high-ranking official.) Step 2 expresses the trivial fact that Nebo is Nebo, or that Nebo is himself. Step 3 is simply step 1 with the function "it is necessary that Nebo is . . ." substituted for *F*. In this step, it is crucial that the reference of the names in "it is necessary that Nebo is Nabu" do not differ from their usual reference, otherwise the argument fails.

But this assumption is false. It does not follow, even if "a" designates (i.e., refers to) a and a is identical with b, that "a" designates b, or that "b" designates a. If the statement that the "Nebo" of Jeremiah 39 refers to *Nebo* is true because the italicized token of the name co-refers with the token in Jeremiah, then it cannot be true that "Nebo" of Jeremiah 39 refers to *Nabu*, for "Nabu" co-refers with the Babylonian tablet, not the Hebrew Bible. If we substitute the name in the reference statement, we change the truth value, even if Nebo and Nabu are the same man. "Nebo" does not refer back to the text in the Babylonian tablet, although "Nabu" does. In general, if "b" does not co-refer with "a," the reference statement "'b' refers to a" is false, *even if a is identical to b*. Being the reference of "b" is not a property of a—an extralinguistic item—at all. The term "the man in the linen cloth" does not *refer* to the man sitting in the tomb, even though it refers to a man who *may* have been the man sitting in the tomb. "Nabu" does not refer to the man mentioned by Jeremiah, even though Nabu may have been that man.[36]

This may seem absurd, and you may object, following David Wiggins[37] and others, that if a is the very same thing as b, then if something is true *of* the object a, it cannot fail to be true of the object b. After all, they are the same object! If it was true of Nebo that he was a high-ranking official in the court at Babylon, Nabu must have held the same rank, for they were the same person. If the man following Jesus was wearing a linen cloth, and if the man at the tomb was the same person as him, the man at the tomb would have been following Jesus in a linen cloth also. Of course, but does the reference statement that "Nebo" refers to Nebo express any genuine property of Nebo himself? If the cause of its truth, as I have suggested, lies not in reality but in some intralinguistic relation, then being the referent of a proper name is not a property of an individual at all. (Being *called* "Nebo" by one's contemporaries is a different matter, as I argued in the previous chapter.[38] That is like the Roman soldiers branded with the name or ensign of their general). Note that a reference statement can be true even if the name has no bearer at all. It is unlikely that there ever was such a being as Asmodeus, the demon in the book of Tobit. But, as I have argued, it is true that "Asmodeus" refers to *him*, because of the co-reference between the name mentioned (i.e., "Asmodeus" in the previous sentence) and the term used (i.e., the italicized "him" in this sentence). The terms co-refer whether or not there was such a person as Asmodeus, hence it is not a property *of* anyone that "Asmodeus" refers to him. Wiggins is correct that if something is true *of* the object a, it cannot fail to be true *of* the same object *b*. But is it true *of* Asmodeus that the name I use here designates *him*? In what sense is there any real connection between a name and a being who existed long ago, or who never existed at all? Was it true of anyone *then* that I am referring to him *now*? The only thing available at present is the semantic connection between the text I am writing here, and the texts that are available to you, the reader.

OBJECTIONS

Since the thesis of the necessity of proper name identity is one of the few philosophical claims that is almost universally accepted as incontrovertible, I shall consider other objections. Consider Kripke's claim that there can be *no question* about identity being necessary. No question about it! If "a" and "b" rigidly designate the same object x, then by definition in every possible world, they will designate x, so there is no possible situation where a is not identical with b, for "that would have to be a situation in which the object which we are also now calling 'x' would not have been identical with itself."[39] The argument is compelling, yet it involves a covert appeal to substitutivity. We agree that "Nebo" designates Nebo, and that "Nabu" designates Nabu, and suppose Nebo and Nabu are the same person. If the principle of substitution is invalid for reference (or 'designation') statements, as I claim, then it does not follow that "Nebo" designates Nabu. Nor does it follow that if X = Nebo=Nabu, that "Nebo" designates X. It may be true that "Nebo" rigidly designates Nebo. That is merely a consequence of how a name in a modal statement is available to co-refer with the same name outside a modal statement. For example, in "*Nebo* was an official, but it might not have been that *Nebo* (or 'he') was an official," the two tokens of the name co-refer (or the name and the pronoun). But, since it does not follow that "Nebo" designates Nabu or X, it does not follow that "Nebo" *rigidly* designates Nabu or X. We are *not* supposing a situation where Nebo is not identical with himself. "Nebo" always refers to Nebo, and "Nabu" always refers to Nabu. The rigidity thesis is impeccable. But it does not follow that the *identity* is rigid, for "Nebo" does not refer to

Nabu, as argued earlier. It follows on the assumption of substitutivity, but my central claim is that substitutivity is not valid.

Elsewhere, Kripke refers to Leibniz's law that identity is an "internal" relation: for all x, for all y, if x=y, necessarily x=y. For what pairs (x, y) *could* be counterexamples?

> Not pairs of distinct objects, for then the antecedent is false; nor any pair of an object and itself, for then the consequent is true. If "a" and "b" are rigid designators, it follows that "a = b," if true, is a necessary truth. If "a" and "b" are not rigid designators, no such conclusion follows about the statement "a = b" (though the objects designated by "a" and "b" will be necessarily identical.[40]

That is also compelling, but what does "x=y" mean? In the sense that Kripke requires, that x is self-identical, so the formula above says that if x is self-identical, then it is necessarily self-identical, which is certainly true. But I have argued that "x=y" is not asserting self-identity, but rather contains an important piece of information, and what information is that? Clearly about some fact in the world, which may or may not obtain, depending on whether the identity statement is true or false. But "may or may not obtain" means it is contingent, so the statement is not necessary after all.

Kripke's argument involves another covert appeal to substitution. He argues that if "x=y" is true of any pair of an object and itself, then the consequent, that is, nec(x=y) is true. But the real consequent is nec(x=x), the necessary identity of an object with *itself*: necessary because of the semantics of co-reference. Assuming that there is such a person as Nebo at all, "Nebo=Nebo" and "Nebo=himself" are necessarily true because the terms flanking the identity sign have guaranteed co-reference. Tokens of the same proper name in uninterrupted sequence co-refer, as do a pronoun and a name that immediately precedes it. But "Nebo" and "Nabu" do not co-refer in this way, for they co-refer with different anaphoric chains, and the substitution is not valid. While "Nebo is identical with himself" is necessarily true, it does not follow, unless we assume the universal validity of the principle of substitution, that "Nebo is identical with Nabu," even though Nebo *is* Nabu. Kripke's consequence is only valid for *self*-identity statements.

Marcus also makes the same covert appeal, saying that "if a=b is such a true identity, then a and b are the same thing. It doesn't say that a and b are two things which happen, through some accident, to be one."[41] But if I am right, the latter is exactly what "a=b" is saying. It does not say that a=a, that is, that *a* is identical with *itself*, which is necessarily true because of the guaranteed co-reference, but that a=b. The assumption that if a=b then "a=b" expresses the same thing as "a=itself" is founded once again on substitutivity. The same applies to her suggestion that proper names are a sort of tag that have no linguistic meaning.[42] In the same place, she claims that the kind of discovery that Nebo and Nabu are the same person, or (her example) Hesperus and Venus are the same planet, is the discovery that "a" and "b" tag a single object. Since it is not an "empirical fact" that Venus=Venus, it is not an empirical fact Venus=Hesperus. Again, this presumes the universal validity of substitution. For example, let F be "it is not an empirical fact that Venus=x," a Venus and b Hesperus. Then Fa is true, but Fb only follows assuming substitutivity of "b" for "a." Her claim also involves the presumption that there is some extralinguistic "tagging" relation between a name and an object, like a label on a suitcase. My core thesis is that there is no such relation.

SUMMARY

Co-reference implies identity, but identity does not imply co-reference. Hence, identity statements can come as news when the terms flanking the identity sign do not co-refer. This conflicts with two fundamental principles of the standard theory of reference: that identity statements using proper names are not informative, and that identity statements are not contingent.

I have replied as follows. First, it is easy to construct a simple example where the identity could be true, but the singular terms flanking the identity sign do not have the same meaning, such as when each term has a different indefinite antecedent. But everyone agrees that indefinite statements (e.g., "a planet appears in the morning and a planet appears in the evening") do not themselves tell us whether they are true of two planets, or just one. On the intralinguistic model of reference, the identity statement connects the two indefinite descriptions and provides that information. It follows that singular propositions are not *Russellian*, that is, they are not extralinguistic objects containing an object corresponding to the bearer of the proper name. The proposition "Nebo is Nabu" does not contain the Babylonian officer "taken twice," nor is it equivalent to the trivial "Nebo is Nebo." Nor, even if Nebo is the same person as Nabu, are their names synonymous as "catsup" and "ketchup" are synonymous. One name has the text of Jeremiah 39:3 as antecedent, the other a Babylonian clay tablet, and their meaning consists solely in their antecedent co-reference.

Second, this undermines the apparently compelling arguments of Kripke and others that true identity statements are necessary, not contingent. Clearly identity statements provide information about how the world *could* be. The Kripke objections covertly depend on the principle of substitution, but substitution is not valid for reference statements according to the reference thesis. Even if a=b, it does not follow that "a" refers to b, for a reference statement is true only if the mentioned and the used term co-refer, and it is not necessarily true that the used term "b" co-refers with "a." Identity is not an "internal" relation, so "a=b" does not mean that a is self-identical, assuming that "a" and "b" do not co-refer.

But this raises a further question. According to the reference thesis, "'Santa' refers to Santa" is true. But most think "'Santa' refers to Santa" entails "'Santa' refers to *something*," and many philosophers think this last claim is false, given that there is no such person as Santa. I shall address this question in the next chapter.

NOTES

1. For example, "a" refers to a, *and a exists*. I shall deal with the issue of existential statements in the next chapter.

2. The discovery in this case was getting hold of some important information, but the question of when we can be said to *have* the information that p is a difficult one that I shall set aside here. Jursa says, "Reading Babylonian tablets is often laborious, but also very satisfying: there is so much *new information* yet to be *discovered*" (British Museum press release, "Important breakthrough in Biblical archaeology," undated, probably July 2007, my emphasis), thus clearly identifying the discovery of the information with the translation of the cuneiform into English, although the British Museum acquired it in 1920, where it remained in storage. It was originally unearthed in the ancient city of Sippar near modern Baghdad in the 1870s, and before that had been in the ground for thousands of years. Did we have the information while it was in the ground? Part of the discovery of information consists in the understanding of the language. Cuneiform was deciphered through the Behistun (or *Bisitun*) inscriptions in Persia, carved in the reign of King Darius of Persia (522–486 BC), identical texts in the three official languages of the empire: Old Persian, Babylonian, and Elamite. The inscriptions were to cuneiform what the Rosetta Stone was to Egyptian hieroglyphs (see Adkins, *Empires of the Plain*, xxi). Having a *means* of decipherment, such as a trilingual inscription, is clearly a part of "having the information," but the question of exactly *when* we can be said to have it or have discovered it is complex and difficult.

3. Mill, *A System of Logic*, 1. ii. 5.

4. Devitt cites Kaplan, "Bob and Carol and Ted and Alice" among others.

5. I.e. the meaning of the name "Fido" is Fido himself. As far as I can tell this (intendedly pejorative) term was coined by Ryle, "The theory of meaning."

6. Bianchi, *On Reference*, 2.

7. Kripke, *Naming and Necessity*, 20.

8. See Burgess, "On a derivation of the necessity of identity," 22, and Kripke, *Naming and Necessity*, 20–21. "How this relates to the question what 'propositions' are expressed by these sentences, whether these 'propositions' are objects of knowledge and belief, and in general, how to treat names in epistemic contexts, are vexing questions. I have no 'official doctrine' concerning them, and in fact I am unsure that

the apparatus of 'propositions' does not break down in this area." Note that he calls *strong* Millianism "Millianism" only.

9. In Kaplan's picturesque phraseology ("Dthat," 13).

10. "The content of a directly referential expression, taken relative to a context, is that thing which the expression, taken relative to the context, has as a referent at any circumstance of evaluation" (Richard, "Direct reference and ascriptions of belief," 426); "a token of a singular term is directly referential provided its only contribution to the proposition expressed is its referent," Schiffer, "A problem for a direct-reference theory of belief reports," 361.

11. Salmon, "A Millian heir rejects the wages of *Sinn*," 5, see also 1986:117ff.

12. https://web.archive.org/web/20070927194301/http://www.heardworld.com/higgaion/?p=681.

13. Salmon might object that we should distinguish between information contained in propositions "semantically expressed," and other ways of conveying of information. For example, we sometimes use identity statements to convey the information that two names are synonymous. I discuss this case further down.

14. Salmon, "A Millian heir rejects the wages of *Sinn*," 7.

15. One theory is that ketchup is from the Cantonese dialect k'ē chap meaning "tomato juice." Another theory is that is derived from koe-chiap in the Amoy dialect, meaning the brine of pickled fish or shellfish. "Catsup" is an alternative transliteration.

16. Salmon, *Frege's Puzzle*, 117.

17. Chapter 2.

18. Ironically Salmon argues for the same view for pronouns ("A Millian heir rejects the wages of *Sinn*," 11). "A variable with an assigned value, or a pronoun with a particular referent, does not have in addition to its referent a Fregean sense—a conceptual representation that it contributes to semantic content." "Individual variables are singular terms that would be individual constants but for their promiscuity," whereas "individual constants are singular terms that would he variables but for their monogamy." "The proper names and demonstratives of ordinary language might be seen as nothing other than the hypothesized 'invariable variables.' Proper names and unrestricted variables are but the opposite limiting cases of a single phenomenon." This is similar to the view I have defended here, except that I do not substitute *objects* as the value of variables, given that propositions—being a kind of sentence—cannot contain objects. We do not "assign the planet Venus" to the variable "x," or to the pronoun "it." Rather, we assign a variable to an anaphoric chain or a subject *type*. The chain back-terminates in an indefinite term, not an object.

19. The other gospels refer to an angel rather than a man, and John and Luke say there were two of them. This is not necessarily inconsistent. Remember that "angel" means a messenger, which includes human messengers, and neither Mark nor Matthew say that there was only one man or messenger.

20. Devitt, "Against direct reference," 463, also holds that Semantic Presupposition is false, arguing that the meaning of a proper name is "a non-Fregean sense explained in terms of a causal network."

21. See Burgess, "On a derivation of the necessity of identity," for a history of the idea. An argument with the same conclusion but a more complex derivation is

in Marcus 1947. The simple derivation is due to Quine 1953 (who happened to be referee for Marcus's paper).

22. It may be objected that I am taking for granted that the information conveyed by an identity statement is the same thing as the proposition semantically expressed by the token of the identity statement. That is correct, but I don't see, apart from the special case mentioned by Salmon where we convey synonymity by an identity statement, that what is conveyed is any different from what is "semantically expressed." The Bacon-Shakespeare example makes this point clear.

23. Frustratingly, Kripke's actual argument is spread across his text and difficult to find. I have relied upon the reconstruction by Burgess, "On a derivation of the necessity of identity."

24. "Designate" is Kripke's term, which I shall assume here to be synonymous with "refer to."

25. Or "refers to."

26. Kripke, *Naming and Necessity*, 48. The definition is sometimes qualified as "the same object in all possible worlds *in which that object exists and never designates anything else*," but nothing of importance hangs upon this, as Bostock ("Kripke on identity and necessity," 314) rightly points out. The talk about "possible worlds" sounds like science fiction; I will talk about modal propositions or modal contexts. Kripke himself concedes (*Naming and Necessity*, 15) that the "worlds" terminology can often be replaced by modal talk such as "It is possible that . . ." According to the medieval logicians a modal proposition is one where we attach a *mode* such as "it is necessary that" or "it is possible that," or "it might be that" or "it cannot be that" and so on, to an assertoric proposition. According to Ockham (*Summa Logicae* II.1), "A modal proposition is that in which a modal term occurs. A assertoric proposition is one without a mode." Ockham includes "it is known that p" as a mode. He and other medieval writers distinguished between the *de dicto* meaning or "sense of composition" and the *de re* meaning, or "sense of division," but this does not matter much for my present purpose. Note that in medieval Latin, a *de contingenti* proposition is not one that is contingently true, but one in contingent mode, that is, prefixed by "it is not necessary that." A contingent proposition is one which is not necessary, or possibly not the case. It is customary to distinguish "counterfactual" modal statements from "epistemic" ones. See, for example, Ockham (1974 ed.) *Summa Logicae* II.1, II.9 and *passim*. Lewis (*A Survey of Symbolic Logic*, 5) claims that the history of symbolic logic and logistic properly begins with Leibniz, though in fact nearly all the terms of modern modal logic are etymologically and often semantically derived from the Latin terms used by the scholastics. For example, *possibile, necesse, contingenter*, and of course the term *modalis* itself, that is, "moodal" or "modal."

27. Kripke's example, for he was writing in the 1970s, is "Nixon."

28. For example, referent.

29. Kripke, *Naming and Necessity*, 77. "Designation" in this sense is clearly synonymous with "meaning."

30. Kripke, *Naming and Necessity*, 20.

31. Burgess, "On a derivation of the necessity of identity," proposition 40.

32. Kripke, *Naming and Necessity*, 103 and 49.

33. Kripke, *Naming and Necessity*, 139.

34. You may object that if (5) and (6) are false, then (7), (8), (9), and (10) are neither true nor false. You say "I saw a man. He smoked." You object that the utterance of "he smoked" is true only if you indeed saw a man who smoked. If you didn't see anyone, then "he smoked" is *neither* true nor false. In reply, I say that "He smoked" is false, not meaningless, but I address the question of anaphors with empty antecedents in the next chapter. Briefly "he smoked" asserts (i) that some man smoked, which could be true of anyone who smoked, and (ii) that that man was identical with the man *I said I saw*. A similar example is discussed by Geach at the end of chapter 16 of *Mental Acts*. I say "There's a man on the quarry-edge," then later say "Now he's gone—he must have fallen in!" If it turns out that I hallucinated the man, clearly "he" cannot be explained by bringing the man himself into the story, for there was no man. It means "the man I meant a little while ago. "What is required in my referring to him as 'he' is not a present *sense-perception* but a recent *thought*."

35. Kripke, "Identity and necessity," 136. I have replaced the variables x and y with the proper names "Nebo" and "Nabu."

36. Devitt, "Against direct reference," 468: "'a = a' and 'a = b' have differing cognitive values because they have different senses; for underlying 'a' and 'b' are different types of d-chain."

37. Wiggins, *Identity and Spatio-Temporal Continuity*, 5.

38. I.e. chapter 5.

39. Kripke, "Identity and necessity," 154.

40. Kripke, *Naming and Necessity*, 3, see also 1980:104.

41. Marcus, "Modalities and intensional languages," 308.

42. Marcus, "Modalities and intensional languages,"310: "This tag, a proper name, *has no meaning*. It simply tags." My emphasis.

Chapter 7

Existence

In this chapter, I want to address the question of how we can meaningfully use a name that may be empty, given that I want to answer the "Same God" question within a semantic framework that is acceptable to both atheists and fideists. We are asking whether Christians, Jews, and Muslims worship *God*, and we want the answer to be the same whether or not God exists. But there is an old and famously difficult problem about possibly-empty names such as "God."

The difficulty is that if the truth conditions or proposition expressed by a sentence, such as "The Greeks worshipped Zeus," are compositionally determined by the semantic values or referents of the terms in the sentence, then the proposition expressed must have the referent of "Zeus" as a constituent, which presupposes that Zeus exists. But what if "Zeus" does not have a referent, as most people now believe? Then no proposition is expressed, and the sentence has no content. It may have a meaning of some sort, but it cannot state anything, that is, it has no *semantic value*. How then can we meaningfully ask whether Christians, Jews, and Muslims worship *God*?

A similar difficulty attaches to the question of whether God actually exists. If atheists are right, there is no such being as God. *But what is the fact that they are right about*? For that fact would be compositionally determined by the semantic values or referents of the terms in the sentence "there is no such being as God," one of which would be the referent of the name "God." Yet there is no such referent, if there is such a fact, hence there can be no such fact. Mainstream semantics presupposes that every proper name has a referent.

The presupposition problem just described is specific to mainstream semantics, which requires that the referent of a name is a constituent of the proposition expressed. I argued in chapter 3 that we don't have to buy that requirement. But sentences with empty names present a general problem for *any* semantic framework. Consider the sentence "The Greeks worshipped Zeus." It is certainly true, but it seems to imply "The Greeks worshipped *something*," which, in turn, seems to imply "there is or was something such that the Greeks worshipped it," that is, it implies Zeus exists, or once existed. But it is doubtful that Zeus ever existed. If every proper name sentence implies a "something" sentence, and if every "something" sentence implies an existence sentence, it seems a lot of sentences we consider true, like "The Greeks worshipped Zeus," "some Greek myths were about Zeus," "Homer wrote that Zeus struck panic into the comrades"[1] and, of course, "Ζεὺς refers to Zeus" are false, if there was no such being as Zeus. For which reason, of course, even the sentence "there was no such being as Zeus" is false!

I shall defend a broadly Aristotelian view of the proposition against the standard or "Fregean" view of proper name sentences. First, I shall argue that the standard view is inconsistent with the anaphoric view of co-reference that I have defended throughout this book. Second, I shall show how the Aristotelian framework, which does not presuppose a referent for the proper name, can explain the puzzling sentences above.

ARISTOTLE VERSUS FREGE

In the first chapter, I contrasted the standard (essentially Fregean) account of a proper name proposition, whereby it is presupposed rather than asserted that the proper name has a referent, with the Aristotelian account, whereby the existence of a referent is asserted. I shall argue that the anaphoric account of co-reference is *wholly* inconsistent with the standard view of the proposition.

My starting point is the transportability argument of chapter 3. Consider

Some deity is called "Zeus."
Zeus is wise.
Therefore some deity called "Zeus" is wise.

The first premiss has the form "Ex Fx," where "F" is "is a deity called 'Zeus'," the second premiss has the form "Ga," where "a" is the proper name "Zeus," and "G" is "is wise." But the following argument is invalid:

Ex Fx
Ga
Ex (Fx & Gx)

It is clearly the anaphoric connection between the premisses that makes the argument valid, but no such connection exists in the formalized version of the argument. In predicate calculus, anaphor corresponds only to the relation between a bound variable and a quantifier, but the "Ex" of the first premiss is in a different sentence from the second premiss, so cannot bind the subject of the second. Moreover, "a" is not a bound variable, but a constant, and (as I argued in chapter 3) a constant must have a "transportable" meaning, independent of its position in the text. By contrast, the validity of the inference expressed by the corresponding ordinary language statement requires precisely that the sense of the name "Zeus" is *not* transportable: that it refers *back* to the indefinite term "some deity."

Note that it is not sufficient, in order to grasp the truth conditions of the second premiss, simply to suppose that "Zeus" has a referent. For then the syllogism would be

Some deity is called "Zeus."
Someone called "Zeus" is wise.
Therefore some deity called "Zeus" is wise. **

which is not valid, given that the first premiss could be satisfied by a different entity from the one satisfying the second. A proper name (or other appropriate singular term) is required in the second premiss in order to tell us *which* individual is said to satisfy "is wise," namely the individual who was the same as the individual asserted to exist by the first premiss, and it is the anaphoric connection which underpins the implication. But standard semantics has no role for such an connection. Standard semantic theory cannot explain how, given that the name "Zeus" lacks a referent, we can tell what the world would be like if a sentence containing an empty name were true. The second premiss lacks the sort of truth conditions required by the standard theory, that is, truth conditions that actually contain Zeus as a component.

Now it could be objected (i) that there is no such cross-sentential anaphoric relation, in which case, the entire premiss of this book is false, but that objection is totally implausible when it is precisely that relation, and only that relation, that underpins our ability to comprehend a narrative like the Hebrew Bible, with its 31,000 verses and 2,000 characters. As I argued in chapter 2, such a narrative (and many others like it) would make little sense if we were unable to tell whether the same character was the subject of any two of those verses, or not. In any case, it is wholly implausible that the syllogism above is not valid.

Or it could be objected (ii) that we cannot grasp the sentence "Zeus is wise" unless it "introduces" an object as argument to the function introduced by the concept-expression "ξ is wise"—"a function which maps all and only wise objects to the value True," in Evans' words.² But why should a proper name introduce such an object? To grasp a truth condition is to grasp what things would be like if the sentence were true, which is exactly what we can do in the case of the Zeus syllogism above. Although both premises are false—there was no deity called "Zeus," and so Zeus was not wise—we know the syllogism is valid because we can grasp how things would have to be if the premises were true. Namely, it would have to be true that there was some deity called "Zeus," and Zeus, that is, *that deity*, was (or is) wise. We can comprehend that the premises cannot be true with the conclusion false, which requires comprehending how things would be *if* the premises were true, so we can grasp the truth conditions of "Zeus is wise," even though the name "Zeus" is empty.³

Or (iii) you could object that the Fregean truth, function "ξ is wise" requires objects as arguments, in order that the function may map all and only wise objects to the value True. But why can't there be a function "ξ is the same person as Zeus" or just "ξ is Zeus," which maps all and only objects that are the same person as Zeus to the value True? If there is no such person as Zeus, the function will return the value False for every object in the domain. That fact would correspond to there being no object identical with Zeus, or that there is no *such* individual as Zeus. By the same reasoning, the anaphoric property, the proper name in the singular negative existential, "there is no such person as Zeus" tells us *which* person it is who there is no such person as. The anaphoric relation does not require the existence of a referent, only the existence of an antecedent. Thus, negative existentials, on the anaphoric thesis, do not deny what they presuppose. The only presupposition required is the anaphoric connection, which is needed in order for us to understand a proper name at all.

Nor do we need a function mapping objects to truth values in order to explain how proper name sentences can be true. The anaphoric conception of meaning explains how we can state what proposition is expressed by a sentence, thus state what makes the proposition true. Consider:

(1) One of the disciples is standing.
(2) The disciple is speaking.
(3) Proposition (2) says that *a* disciple is speaking.
(4) Proposition (2) says that *the* disciple is speaking.

Proposition (4) plainly requires a semantic connection between the definite "the disciple" and the indefinite "a disciple," as I have argued, but this connection does not have to be *extra*linguistic, but only *anaphoric*. If the proposition *says* that the disciple is speaking, it is true if and only if he is speaking. To say a proposition is true is to assert it, and to say it is false is to deny it, which is perfectly consistent with the classic definition of truth given by Aristotle.[4] To speak truly is to say of what is (τὸ ὄν), that it is (εἶναι), and of what is not (τὸ μὴ ὄν), that it is not (μὴ εἶναι). (It helps to read "is" as "is the case"). It is true to say of what is the case, such as snow being white, that it is the case, that is, that snow *is* white; and it is true to say of what is not the case, such as snow not being black, that it is not the case, that is, that snow is not black. Tarski[5] deferred to this classical conception in his well-known *semantic* formulation of truth: the sentence "snow is white" is true if and only if snow is white. The anaphoric proposal is entirely consistent with this conception of truth.[6] Hence, it is possible to state *what* a sentence states without invoking semantic dependence upon objects, or "introducing" a bearer for a name into a proposition or as argument to a propositional function.

It could be further objected (iv) that *if* the pronoun "he" in the truth condition "If the proposition says that *the disciple* is speaking, it is true if and only if *he* is speaking" co-refers intralinguistically with the description "the disciple," then a sentence expressing the truth condition is correct merely intralinguistically and hence necessarily correct. But if "the disciple" refers extralinguistically to an entity in the world, then the sentence "the disciple is speaking" is true if and only if *that entity* is speaking, where "that entity" refers extralinguistically to that entity, and if that extralinguistic relation is contingent, the truth condition is not necessarily correct.

In reply, I concede that there may be some extralinguistic relation between "the disciple" and some entity X in the world, and the same relation may hold between the pronoun "he" and X. But there is still an intralinguistic relation of co-reference between those terms, whether or not they are related externally to the entity in the world, indeed, whether or not there is any such entity. You say that the sentence "the disciple is speaking" is true "if and only if *that entity* is speaking," attempting to express some extralinguistic relation, yet you are compelled to use the expression "that entity," which is anaphorically dependent on your indefinite "a disciple." You want the expression to have a non-anaphoric sense that it cannot have. You want to signify something that you cannot signify, but you have no means of doing this.

It follows from all of this that, if the semantic value of a proper name consists solely in its anaphoric relation to its antecedent, then a sentence containing it can express a proposition capable of truth and falsity without the name having a referent, which is fully consistent with the Aristotelian view of the proposition. "Moses is a prophet" is true if there is such a person as Moses, and if he is a prophet. It is false if either (i) there is such a person as Moses, but he is not a prophet, or (ii) there is no such a person as Moses. Thus, the medieval scholastic philosophers thought that a negative proposition can have two causes of truth (*causae veritatis*), and that moving from the negative "it is not the case that Moses was a prophet" to the affirmative "Moses was a non-prophet" is the fallacy of affirming the consequent, "like moving from a disjunctive proposition to one of its parts."[7] The negation of a singular proposition has wide and narrow scope for the same reason. We must distinguish "Moses was not a prophet," which implies someone (Moses) was not a prophet, from "it was not the case that Moses was a prophet," understood in the sense "either there was a person such as Moses who was not a prophet, or there was no one such as Moses."

You may object (v) that if "there is a man called 'Moses' and he/Moses is a prophet" is equivalent to "there was a man called 'Moses', *who* was a prophet," then the joint content of the two sentences is no more than an general existential assertion: some x was an Israelite called "Moses," x was a prophet and so on. But as Geach has argued,[8] the negation of the general existential assertion is not equivalent to the negation of the two propositions. Suppose (his example) that (A) "Socrates owned a dog. It bit him" is really two separate propositions "p and q." But the negation ~A of "p and q" is equivalent to "not-p or (p and not-q)," that is, "Socrates did not own a dog; or Socrates owned a dog and it did not bite him." But a moment's reflection suggests that both A and ~A could be true (e.g., if Socrates owned two dogs, one of which bit him, the other of which did not).

Sommers has already pointed out the fallacy of this objection.[9] As Aristotle says,[10] two propositions form a contradiction so long as the subject in the affirmation means the same as the subject in the negation, and so long as the predicates also mean the same, and are not ambiguous or equivocal. Thus, if we are to represent the contradictory of A, we must ensure that the repetition of "it" in the negation has the same meaning as in the affirmation. That is, in the negation of "Socrates owned a dog_1. It_1 bit him," the pronoun "it" must have the same meaning, that is, the same *reference*. Representing co-reference by subscripts, the true negation ~A should be thus "Socrates did not own a dog, or Socrates owned a dog_2 and it_1 did not bite him," where "it_1" means the same dog introduced in the *affirmation* (A).

Sommers also points out that no separate sign for identity is needed if we drop the idea that there is some absolute category-difference between proper names and common names. If "Venus" and "the morning star" are proper names, then we have to render them as the lower-case letters "a" and "b" in logical notation, and then "a is b" is not well-formed, for "b" is not a predicate. So it is "obvious" that it must be rendered "F(a,b)" where "F" represents "is identical with." "It is only after one has adopted the syntax that prohibits the predication of proper names that one is forced to read 'a is b' dyadically and to see in it a sign of identity."[11]

Nor under the Aristotelian conception of the proposition is there any difficulty in explaining how atheists can express their view, using the proper name "God." The problem for classical semantics is that, the semantic value of "God" being God himself, the sentence "there is no such being as God," denies a referent, and hence a semantic value for the name "God," and so the sentence itself has no semantic value. But under the Aristotelian conception, the semantic value of "God" is *not* the referent of the name. Thus, Ockham says that "a chimera is a non-being" is literally false, because it can be analyzed into "a chimera is something" and "that thing is a non-entity," of which the first is false.[12] This means that both "the chimera is a man" and "the chimera is a non-man" are false, but as Ockham argues, this does not violate the principle of contradiction. Certainly *if* "the chimaera is something" were true, one or the other of "the chimaera is a man" or "the chimaera is a non-man" would be true. But the chimera isn't anything.[13]

In summary, the anaphoric account of co-reference is wholly inconsistent with the standard view of the proposition. On the standard view, the referent of a proper name is a constituent of the proposition expressed, so that the existence of a referent is presupposed rather than asserted. On the anaphoric view, the meaning of the name consists entirely in its semantic connection to its antecedent, for which a referent is unnecessary. Hence the existence of a referent is asserted rather than presupposed.

THE "SOMETHING" PROBLEM

This leaves us with the problem of what sentences containing "something" imply. Clearly "Moses is a prophet" implies "something is a prophet," and the latter seems to imply that some prophet exists. As Frege says:

> Once "Sachse is a man" expresses an actual judgment, the word "Sachse" must designate something, and in that case I do not need a further premise in order to infer "there are men" from it.[14]

But my *reference thesis* is that a reference statement "'a' refers to b" is true if and only if the term mentioned by "a" co-refers with "b." What if "b" is an empty name? Empty terms can co-refer if co-reference is an intralinguistic relation, so "'Asmodeus' refers to a demon" can be true. But how can it be true that "Asmodeus" refers to Asmodeus if there is no such thing as *him*? How is it that reference statements of the form "a refers to b" are consistent with statements of the form "there is no such thing as b"? The reference statement has the same grammatical form as "a touches b," but we cannot touch something that does not exist,[15] and so the proposition "a touches b" is not consistent with "there is no such thing as b." Why is reference not like touching?

One route out of this problem was famously taken by Alexius Meinong, who argued that there can be non-existing things. "Tom is thinking of a demon" implies that some demon is the object of Tom's thought, but demons don't exist, ergo some things, such as demons, do not exist. The adjective "existent" qualifies things that exist, the adjective "non-existent" qualifies all things (unicorns, round squares, golden mountains) that do not exist.

I reject such a route. The problem can be resolved by an account of the logic of verb phrases like "refers to," "is thinking of," "worships," and the like.[16] Reference (and worship, and thinking) is *not* like touching because the grammatical form of a reference statement differs from its logical form. The relation suggested by its grammatical structure, that is, between the name "Asmodeus" and some demon of that name, is not the relation that makes it true. Rather, some other relation, namely co-reference, makes it true, and the grammatical structure of the reference statement is misleading. I say that verb phrase R is *logically intransitive* if "a R b" is consistent with there being no such thing as b, otherwise it is *logically transitive*. A logically intransitive verb phrase R_i takes a grammatical accusative, but no logical accusative, that is, there doesn't have to be an object corresponding to the accusative. Thus, if R_i is logically intransitive and R_t is logically transitive, "a R_i b" does not imply "a R_t b," since the former is consistent with there being no such thing as b, whereas the latter is not, that is, the former can be true when the latter is not. For example, "Tobit refers to Asmodeus" does not imply "Tobit is related to Asmodeus," for the verb phrase "is related to" is logically transitive.

How can we tell the two forms apart, given their *grammatical* equivalence? This is not easy, and it is doubtful whether there is a single rule for this. For example, the verb phrase "is missing" in "this chair is missing a leg" is logically intransitive. The statement is consistent with nothing whatsoever being a chair leg. Likewise "Tobit needs a wife," which is true precisely because there is no wife to be needed. But it is difficult to see any common explanation of why this is so, or why it would apply to "Tobit is referring to a demon." It is not my intention to supply any general theory here, so I shall restrict myself to some brief remarks. Starting with the verb "is," it is plain that there must be *some* sense of this verb which is logically transitive, otherwise logic would collapse. There must be a sense of "some A is a B," which is *in*consistent with "nothing is a B." Aristotle's whole theory of contraries in *Perihermenias* chapter 7 is based on this, and in modern formal logic, this is the sense of the so-called existential quantifier. "∃x (Ax & Bx)" is *always* inconsistent with "~∃x Bx." This should not be confused with Quine's thesis that the existential quantifier really expresses existence, which is about the meaning of the verb "exists," that is, that "some demons are red" means exactly the same as "red demons exist."[17] The inconsistency between "∃x (Ax and Bx)" and "~∃x Bx" remains even if the quantifier is supposed to range over non-existent things. However, not all senses if "is" are transitive. "Tobit is referring to Asmodeus" is not logically transitive. Yet the active "is referring to" can easily be turned into the passive "is referred to by," giving the sentence "Asmodeus (or: some demon) *is* referred to by Tobit," and on the assumption that the passive has the same meaning as the active, which is surely a matter of convention, it follows that the "is" of the passive form is logically *in*transitive. This is probably why English has the unambiguous form "is *such that it is*." Tobit is referring to something, so in some sense something is referred to by Tobit, but it does not follow that something is *such that it is* referred to by Tobit.

What I say is true so long as "is referred to by" is read as the passive form of a logically intransitive verb phrase. Clearly "something is touched by Tobit" implies that "something is such that it is touched by Tobit," because "is touched by" is the passive form of a logically *transitive* verb phrase. In the passive form of a logically intransitive verb phrase, the word "is" is not being used as a copula, that is, it does not express a relation between subject and predicate, but is merely a means of reversing the order of grammatical subject and object. In Latin, the present passive does not use the word "is" (*est*) at all. *Cogitatur res cum vox eam significans cogitatur*—"A thing *is* thought when the word signifying it *is* thought."[18] The passive form "cogitatur" is the equivalent of the English "is thought." When we say "some A is such that it is B," it is just a convention for unambiguously communicating "some A is B" *in the sense contrary to "nothing is B."* I could say that this is the "existential" sense of the verb "is," but, once again, I am *not* proposing a theory about the meaning of the English verb "exists." My point is that there must be two senses of the verb "is," one of which is unambiguously expressed by "is such that it is," the other of which (in English at least)[19] is auxiliary to the passive form of a logically intransitive verb.

This account does not require two domains of quantification. Philosophers and logicians talk about the domain of quantification, or about the range of a quantifier, or the "set of values" that a variable can take, and they say, for example, or that the domain *includes* some object *a*, or *contains* it. Clearly passive verb phrases like "includes" and "contains" are logically transitive by definition, for they are informal expressions capturing formal concepts. If *a* is in the domain, then for some x, x = *a*, which is by definition inconsistent with "for all x, ~x = *a*." This is another reason why the accusatives of a logically intransitive verb phrase do not correspond to objects in some wider domain. For in order to *say* that the objects are in the domain, that is, that they *are included in* the domain, we have to use the passive forms of logically transitive verb phrases, such as "are included in" or "are contained in." But that would be false, as well as an unwarranted inference from the statements containing the accusatives. "Tom is thinking of a demon" does not imply "some demon is in the domain."

For this reason, we cannot represent logically intransitive statements in formal logic. The standard sense of the verb phrase "is related to" is logically transitive, as is its corresponding schematic R in formal logic. The English statement "a is related to b" conventionally implies that *something* is (identical with) b, or, strictly speaking, that something is *such that* it is b, just as "aRb" always implies "for some x, aRx." But if we represent "Tobit is talking about Asmodeus" as "For some x, x = Asmodeus & Tobit is talking about x," then we have automatically but incorrectly represented it as contrary to "Not for some x, x = Asmodeus."

Hence the truth of reference statements such as "'Asmodeus' refers to Asmodeus" is consistent with the name being empty, and does not commit us to non-existent or "intentional" entities or anything of that sort. Reference is not a relation, although the grammatical form of sentences like "'Asmodeus' refers to Asmodeus" can mislead us into supposing that verb phrases, such as "refers to" express relations like the verbs "touch" and "hear." This avoids any commitment to Meinongian non-existent things, intentional entities, and other strange beings conjured up by the fertile imagination of some philosophers. When I say that "Asmodeus" refers to Asmodeus, I do *not* mean that some non-existent individual is the referent of the name. Not at all: there isn't and wasn't such an individual, in the widest possible sense of *isn't*.[20]

SUMMARY

The anaphoric account of co-reference is inconsistent with the classical view of proper name subject-predicate sentences, for it requires that the semantic value of the name (the value by which the name shows us *which* individual satisfies the predicate of the sentence) is not a referent, but rather the name's anaphoric connection to some antecedent. If we buy the anaphoric connection, we have to take a broadly Aristotelian view of the proposition, which has two conditions of truth. The sentence "God is good" is true if and only if there is such a being as God, and that being is good. This account is radically different from classical semantics, but there is no compelling reason to accept classical semantics. I have defended the anti-Meinongian view that "something (is such that it) is P" is logically equivalent to "some P exists," but sentences taking "something" as grammatical object to some verb phrase do not imply the corresponding existential statement if the verb phrase is what I call "logically intransitive."

This chapter and the previous one highlight the inconsistencies between the anaphoric theory and classical semantics, and argue in defense of the anaphoric theory. In the next chapter, I return to the question of how we are to interpret the term "God." Is it a definite description or a proper name?

NOTES

1. *Odyssey*, 14.268, ἐν δὲ Ζεὺς τερπικέραυνος φύζαν ἐμοῖς ἑτάροισι κακὴν βάλεν.
2. Quoted in chapter 1.
3. Empty names troubled Sommers (*The Logic of Natural Language*, 333), who saw them as a challenge to his thesis that proper names are special duty pronouns replacing common pronouns like "it" or "he" in pronominal sentences. He was worried that if we introduce Homer (his example) by the general existential statement "a blind poet called 'Homer' wrote the *Odyssey*," and the statement is false, "Homer" could not be a proper name. His worry is groundless. The statement claims that *someone* who was a blind and a poet (and called "Homer"), wrote the *Odyssey*. One could clearly go on to deny that *that person* was blind, or a poet, or the author of the *Odyssey*. One could utter, for example, "no, he wasn't blind" or "he wasn't really the author of the *Odyssey*" and so on. This is not the same as denying there was *such* a person, as I have argued earlier. The antecedent for "he" in "he wasn't a poet" is not some blind poet, but rather someone who has, in the corrector's view, wrongly been *claimed* to be a blind poet.
4. *Metaphysics*, 1011 b25.
5. "We should like our definition to do justice to the intuitions which adhere to the classical *Aristotelian* conception of truth—intuitions which find their expression in the well-known words of Aristotle's Metaphysics: To say of what is that it is not, or of what is not that it is, is false, while to say of what is that it is, or of what is not that it is not, is true. If we wished to adapt ourselves to modern philosophical terminology, we could perhaps express this conception by means of the familiar formula: The truth of a sentence consists in its agreement with (or correspondence to) reality" (Tarski, "The semantic conception of truth and the foundations of semantics," 53fn, my emphasis).
6. Cumming ("The dilemma of indefinites," Bianchi, ed., 335–49) imagines that an indefinite statement of the form "An F is G" has an *object-containing* semantic content, that is, it contains the F, but not an *object-dependent* truth condition (p. 337). He imagines this because "A woman called 'Julia Gallard' is Prime Minister of Australia" *seems* to communicate the very same information as "Julia Gallard is Prime Minister of Australia," and so appears to transmit a singular proposition about Julia Gallard (ibid., 339). He calls this *epistemic specificity* (ibid., 342). But this semantic content is not sufficient to determine truth-value, therefore the semantic content must be different from the truth condition. I have already discussed this confusion in chapter 3 (on "indefinite reference"). The confusion results from the illusion that the anaphor sentence refers, that is, its sense depends or contains some extra-linguistic object, even though the antecedent clearly does not. But this is only a puzzle on the assumption that a reference statement expresses an external "reference relation" between language and reality. We can state the truth condition of "Julia Gallard is Prime Minister of Australia," by using a token of the proper name whose meaning depends on back-reference with the appropriate "Julia Gallard" anaphoric chain. This does not require any external reference relation, although it does require

that the mentioned sentence also has such a back-reference. But that truth condition is not the same as for "A woman called 'Julia Gallard' is Prime Minister of Australia," which does not have such a back-reference, and so is true for *any* such woman so-called.

7. For example, incorrectly moving from the disjunction "Moses was a non-prophet or Moses did not exist" to "Moses was a non-prophet." The question is discussed extensively in Buckner and Zupko, *Duns Scotus On Time and Existence*, 335–43. Scotus was not the first to address it, and it dates back at least to John le Page and Nicholas of Paris, both of whom flourished at the University of Paris in the second quarter of the thirteenth century. See, for example, Peter of Auvergne, *Questiones super librum Peryermenias*, 42: "Utrum ad negativam de praedicato finito sequatur affirmativa de praedicato infinito" (ms. Madrid, Biblioteca Nacional 1565, f.10ra–va; quoted in Tabarroni, "Tenth thesis in logic," 354): "certain persons have said that the affirmation of the indefinite predicate does not follow from the negation of the finite predicate. Certain persons have said that the negation of the finite predicate has two causes of truth, because the negation precedes the verb 'is' and the finite predicate. And so they proposed a sense of being, and a sense of not being. For example, 'a man is not just' can have two senses, either because the man does not exist, and so is not just, and this is the 'sense of not being,' or because the man exists, but is not just, and this is the 'sense of being.' They have said also that the affirmative of the indefinite predicate only has the 'sense of being,' for they have said that the indefinite term posits some being of itself. And furthermore, they have said that the verb 'is' posits a sort of being, if not preceded by negation. And therefore they have proposed that the affirmation of the indefinite predicate does not follow from the negation of the finite predicate, because [otherwise] there would be a passage from two causes of truth to one, and thus there would be the 'figure of speech' fallacy." Translated in Buckner and Zupko, *Duns Scotus on Time and Existence*, 341.

8. Geach, "Logical procedures and the identity of expressions," 118 ff.
9. Sommers, *The Logic of Natural Language*, 77 ff.
10. Aristotle, *On Interpretation*, 17a35, see also Chapter 1.
11. Sommers, *The Logic of Natural Language*, 121ff.
12. *Summa Logicae*, II.14.
13. *Summa Logicae*, II.12.
14. Frege, *Posthumous Writings*, 60.
15. "And if someone touches something, he touches some one thing, and a thing which *is*?" Plato, *Theaetetus*, 189 a6, trans. McDowell, 73, my emphasis.
16. Sainsbury (*Thinking about Things*, chapter 2) argues for a solution also based on evaluating the logic of "thinking" and "referring" sentences, but he focuses on the logic of the word "something" itself, which he claims does not function in the way that the existential quantifier "∃" does. For example, "something" can bind "a wide variety of positions, including adjective position, as in 'You are something I am not—kind.'" The inference from "she is thinking about unicorns" to "there is something she is thinking about" is clearly valid, but the consequent is *not* equivalent to "$\exists x$, she is thinking about x" (ibid., 29).

17. See, for example, Quine, *Word and Object*, 242, also cited in Van Inwagen "Existence, ontological commitment, and fictional entities."

18. Anselm, *Proslogion* (Schmitt, 1946), 103.

19. Geach, ("A medieval discussion of intentionality," in *Logic Matters*, 131, also "The perils of Pauline," 1972, 159) mentions a distinction in medieval Latin between putting an object term before and after the verb, citing Buridan. He may have had sophism 15, chapter 4 of Buridan's *Sophismata* in mind. Buridan writes: "It should be added that it makes a great difference whether we place 'horse' before or after [the verb], for the aforementioned verbs, because of the appellation of the concept, somehow confuse the [supposition of the] terms that follow them, so that it is not possible to descend to the singulars by means of a disjunctive proposition. For example, this is not valid: 'I owe you a horse; therefore, I owe you Tawny, or I owe you Blackie,' and so forth; for each [member of this disjunction] is false. But before [the verb] the term is not thus confused; therefore, it is possible to descend by means of a disjunctive [proposition]. Therefore, if 'horse is owed by me to you' is true, then it follows that either Tawny is owed by me to you or Blackie is owed by me to you, and so forth." (*Summulae de Dialectica*, "Sophismata," chapter 4, trans. Klima, *John Buridan: "Summulae de Dialectica,"* 909).

20. On this view, identity statements involving empty terms are *false*. "Moses is Moses" is false if "Moses" is an empty name. This may seem paradoxical. How can nothing be identical with x if there is at least one thing, namely x, which is identical with x? But there are no non-self-identical objects, for we cannot infer from "nothing is identical with x" that something is not identical with x. "Nothing is identical with x" means the same as "there is no such thing as x," and "there is no such thing as" is a verb phrase which has a grammatical accusative ("x") but no logical accusative. A proposition of the form "a = a" is true only if there is such a thing as a, otherwise it is false. On the opposite side, Duns Scotus argues in an early work that "a chimera is a chimera" can be true even though there are no chimeras, given that "composition in the understanding" (*compositio apud intellectum*) of subject and predicate may be sufficient. It is not clear why composition in the understanding would make it true. See Buckner and Zupko, *Duns Scotus On Time and Existence*, 16.

Chapter 8

The God of the Philosophers

I have argued that proper names for *non*-divine individuals, names such as "Noah," "Abraham," and "Moses," have the same reference, that is, *co-reference*, in the Christian Bible and in the Quran. We must treat the three scriptures as though they were a single book with a single editor, and apply the rules for co-reference accordingly. Just as we do not question that all tokens of the name "Moses" in the Hebrew Bible co-refer, so we should not question the co-reference of all the tokens in all the three scriptures. It is as though they were written by a single author.

The same reasoning applies to the other 2,000 non-divine persons mentioned in the Hebrew Bible. What about names for *God*? God occupies a prominent place in the biblical narrative, as well as in the New Testament and (arguably) the Quran. If the semantics of God's name are identical to those of names for non-divine persons, it follows that "God" and "Allah" co-refer, by the same logic that "Noah" in English translations of the Hebrew Bible and "Nūḥ" in the Quran have the same reference. The difference is merely the effect of translation from one language to another. If these terms for God are really proper names, that is, if they are words for a *person*, a being capable of knowledge, intentional action, and interpersonal relationships, then they have the same reference, that is, they co-refer. If this is so, the logic that demonstrates that "Moses" has the same reference in the Hebrew Bible, the New Testament and the Quran, shows that "God," "Allah," and "Yhwh" co-refer.

This depends upon a particular assumption about the meaning of proper names and definite descriptions. What if the name "God" has some descriptive sense and does not refer back to the scriptures in the way that I have argued? Perhaps God is *not* a person in the sense of something with a material body, or even something that is necessarily located at some particular place at some particular time, *whatever* its shape or substance. Perhaps God is a divine reality who is not corporeal. Why should the semantic rules that apply to personal reference also apply to the divine reality? I turn to the long-standing philosophical debate about the proper analysis of definite descriptions, and the parallel theological debate about the distinction between the personal or anthropomorphic conception of God, and the classical theistic conception.

CORPOREALISM

There is a tradition in both Judaism and Christianity (but not in Islam)[1] that the *anthropomorphic* descriptions of God that we find, mostly in the Hebrew Bible, should be taken at face value. "Anthropomorphic" is from the Greek ἀνθρωπόμορφος, having the form or shape of a human, sometimes used in a wider sense as having human characteristics, or behavior. "Anthropopathic" is a related term meaning an attribution of human emotions to a nonhuman being. For example, in Genesis 2.7, God blows the breath of life into the first human, suggesting that God has a mouth or some organ with which to breathe out of. In Genesis 3.8, Adam and Eve hear the *sound* of the Lord God as he was *walking* in the garden in the cool of the day, suggesting that God can make a sound, and that he can walk on two legs. In Genesis 11:5, God *comes down* to *see* the city and the tower the people were building, implying that God could have a spatial position, also that he had eyes, and that his vision was limited enough that it was necessary to "come down" in order to see what was going on at Babel. Genesis 18 says that God *appeared* in human form to Abraham near the great trees of Mamre while he was sitting at the entrance to his tent in the heat of the day (see 18:13, possibly 18:3). As Sommer comments:

> The divine body portrayed in these texts was located at a particular place at a particular time. It was possible to say that God's body was here (near Abraham's tent, for example) and not there (inside the tent itself), even if God's knowledge and influence went far beyond that particular place.[2]

Exodus 25–40 describes in detail the building of a home where God can *reside* on earth. In Exodus 33, we are told how Moses would pitch a "tent of meeting" outside the camp, and whenever Moses went into the tent, people saw a pillar of cloud come down to the entrance, while God spoke to Moses inside, *face to face, as one speaks to a friend*. Shortly after, Moses asks God if he can see his "glory." God tells him (33.20) that no one can see him and live, but allows him to stand in a split in a rock, where he will cover him with his (very large?) hand, while his glory passes by. "Then I will remove my hand and you will see my *back*; but my *face* must not be seen."

There are many other passages that suggest that God has a form similar to that of a human, that he wears clothes (Isaiah 6.1), that he stands (Amos 9:1), that he has a figure "like that of a man" (Ezekiel 1:26). Ezekiel 1:28 explains that God's glory (*kabod*) appears like a radiant rainbow, or as brilliant light. It is well known that the light can be fatal. See Genesis 32:30, Exodus 33:20, Isa 6:5, Judges 13:22. All of this, not forgetting the well-known passage in Gen 1:26 saying that humans were created in the image (*bə·ṣal·mê·nū*) and in the likeness (*kiḏ·mū·ṯê·nū*) of God, suggests that when God comes down from the heights and appears to humans, he has a human form, emits a brilliant light, and speaks in a language understood by the people he is addressing.

Some early Christians believed in a corporeal God. The Audians were fourth-century Syrian Christians named after their founder, Audius, who took Genesis 1:27 literally, although Jerome called it a "rustic" view, and "a most foolish heresy."[3] Cyril of Alexandria (376–444) mentions anthropomorphites among the Egyptian monks, and published a refutation of their error.[4] Supposedly Melito (bishop of Sardis, died c. 180) had believed in the corporeality of God.[5] According to Paulsen, for at least the first three centuries, ordinary Christians believed God to be corporeal.[6] "The belief was abandoned (and then only gradually) as Neoplatonism became more and more entrenched as the dominant world view of Christian thinkers." Writing in the seventeenth century, Spinoza contended that scriptural anthropomorphisms were originally meant to be taken literally. Today, Mormons believe in the corporeality of God,[7] and Sommer has argued that a proper understanding of the Hebrew Bible requires not only that God has a body, but that God has *many* bodies "located in sundry places in the world that God created." As he says,[8] if the authors of the Hebrew Bible had intended their anthropomorphic language to be understood figuratively, why did they not say so? The Bible contains a wide variety of texts in different genres, but there is no hint of this, the closest hint being the statement of Deuteronomy 4:15 that the people did not see any form when the Ten Commandments were revealed at Sinai. Eichrodt says that the Old Testament emphasizes God's personal side while *leaving veiled* the fact that he was also spiritual, but the claim that his spiritual nature is left veiled is, as Sommer says, "but a clever way of importing into the Hebrew scriptures a notion they lack."[9] Hopkins argues that we would expect God to be honest in his dealings with humans. "If He appeared to Men in human form, but was not Himself human, one would expect that, at some point, He would reveal that fact. Yet there is no indication in scripture that God is something other than what He has appeared to be during His many visits to Men."[10] It has been objected that some passages say that God has wings (e.g. Ps. 17:8 "hide me in the shadow of your wings"), and since this is obviously figurative, references to God's physical body must be also. Hopkins objects that this has no hermeneutic validity. The passages about wings are in the Book of Psalms, which is a book of Hebrew poetry, and "poetic language is normally interpreted more figuratively than the language of eyewitness accounts."[11]

INCORPOREALISM

Opposed to this is the tradition that the anthropomorphic descriptions of God in the Hebrew Bible should be understood figuratively. It is not clear precisely how or when this tradition developed, given that allegorical exegesis has always been considered as dangerous to religion, given the tendency for the whole biblical and interpretative tradition to evaporate into allegory, but it is implicit[12] in the *Targum Onkelos* of c. 110 BC, a translation of the Hebrew Bible into Aramaic by Onkelos the proselyte, a Roman convert to Judaism. Onkelos strictly avoided anthropomorphic modes of expression, so that God does not "hear" in Genesis 2:24 or "see" in 2:25. "Mountain of God" in 3:1 is rendered as "mountain upon which the glory of the Lord was revealed,"[13] "the Lord will come down" (Exod. 19:11), as "The Lord will manifest Himself," and so on.

Following Onkelos,[14] the Jewish philosopher and commentator Moses Maimonides devoted the first seventy chapters of his monumental twelfth-century *Guide of the Perplexed* to demonstrating how a proper understanding of the Hebrew Bible excludes corporeality. For example (chapter 26), expressions like "to descend," "to ascend," "to walk," "to place," "to stand," "to surround," "to sit," "to dwell," "to depart," "to enter," "to pass," and others imply corporeality, but Maimonides says that God is not corporeal, so none of these terms apply strictly to him. He explains that God's existence is shown to ordinary men by means of similes taken from physical bodies, and that we ascribe such actions to God only figuratively. Again (chapter 46), since we can perform these actions only by means of bodily organs, such as feet, hands, and fingers palm, we figuratively ascribe such things to God, "to express that he performs certain acts."

The Christian tradition was influenced by the Hellenistic Jewish philosopher Philo of Alexandria (25 BC–c. 50 AD), who also dismissed the anthropomorphic conception.

> For to think that the divinity can go towards, or go from, or go down, or go to meet, or, in short, that it has the same positions and motions as particular animals, and that it is susceptible of real motion at all, is, to use a common proverb, an impiety deserving of being banished beyond the sea and beyond the world.[15]

Philo explains the miraculous events described in the Bible as having natural causes. The miracle at the Red Sea was a "prodigy of nature,"[16] the plague of darkness was a total eclipse,[17] although his view was actually not naturalistic in the modern sense, but more in the Stoic sense, whereby miracles are predetermined in nature by divine power.

Both Maimonides and Philo were influenced by Greek philosophy. Maimonides by Aristotle, whom he frequently cites, writing in a period (the twelfth century) when the works of Greek science and philosophy were being translated from the original Greek into modern languages such as the Arabic that Maimonides spoke. For example, in Guide II.30, in his "Philosophical Interpretation" of the creation story in Genesis, Maimonides must reconcile the biblical account with scientific views such as found in Aristotle's *Meteorology*. Although the view he cites is not actually found in Aristotle,[18] it is evidence of the need to reconcile the biblical view of the universe with the twelfth-century understanding of Greek science. By contrast, Philo was influenced by Plato, whom he called "the sweetest of writers,"[19] impressed by the Platonic view of the material world and the human body as locked into a spatio-temporal prison, in contrast with God who is unlimited, eternal, and perfect. He speaks in Platonic spirit of the "unspeakable contemplation of all the things on the earth"[20] and of the body as an evil, dead and injurious thing, which is connected to, and which has no other purpose than to harm, his living soul. It may have been Philo[21] who introduced the Greek concept of the *logos* to Christian theology. Logos strictly means word or language, but has a much wider connotation, embracing thought or reasoning, and was used in Greek philosophy to signify a rational, life-giving principle of the universe. Philo posits two supreme and principal powers in God, namely benevolence and authority, but *logos* is a third between these two which brings them together, "for it was owing to reason that God was both a ruler and good."[22] He explains that in Genesis 18:2, where the three men meet Abraham by the tent, God appeared together with his "two powers," benevolence and authority, appearing as three to the human mind.[23] And when the passage says that Moses "lifted up his eyes," this does not mean the eyes of the body, for it is not possible to perceive God with the senses, but with the eyes of the soul.[24] The apparently strong similarities between Philo's conception of *logos* and the Gospel of John (as well as the Book of Hebrews) has suggested to some that this was a direct influence on the Gospel itself, but as Nash points out,[25] Philo's Platonism, and particularly his view of the body as a dead encumbrance upon the soul, rules out God becoming man, and participating in all that is human, including even the temptation to sin (Hebrews 4:15).

Philo influenced later Christian writers, such as Clement of Alexandria (150–c. 215), who is the first to mention Philo by name. In the *Stromateis*, or Patchworks, Clement cites him four times,[26] and he adopts his ideas extensively.[27] Later Origen (c.185–c.254), who probably succeeded Clement as head of the catechetical school in Alexandria, argued forcefully against literal interpretations of scripture that make God a corporeal being. Referring to the passage in Genesis (3:8) where God is heard "walking in the garden in the cool of the day," he asks if we are to imagine that God, who fills all of heaven and earth, is contained by a tiny garden that is not filled by him, but rather greatly exceeds him in magnitude? "Absurder still on this interpretation is the hiding of Adam and Eve, in fear of God by reason of their transgression, from before God amid the wood of the Garden."[28] He says that the cause of false opinions and impious statements about God is the failure to read scripture not according to its spiritual meaning, but understanding "to the mere letter,"[29] citing anthropathic passages like Deut. 5:9 ("I am a jealous God, visiting the iniquities of the fathers *upon the children unto the third and fourth generation*," Deut 32:22 ("A fire has been kindled in Mine anger"), and many others, which if understood literally "would not be believed of the most savage and unjust man."[30]

The incorporealist conception underpins the theological tradition of the later Middle Ages. Thomas Aquinas (1225–1274) says that God is a spirit, quoting the proof text John 4:24.[31] Concerning Exodus 33:11 where God "spoke to Moses face to face, as a man is wont to speak to his friend," he objects that the scripture speaks "according to the opinion of the people," who thought that Moses was speaking with God "mouth to mouth" (*ore ad os*), whereas Moses was actually speaking through an subordinate being, such as an angel. Or perhaps, he adds, "face to face" means an apprehension of God that was inferior to the vision of the divine essence. He contrasts this form of indirect reception of the law via the ministers of God, the angels, with the direct reception from the incarnate God (*per ipsum Deum hominem factum*), that is, Christ.[32] On the idea that man is "the image and likeness of God," he claims that this refers to a likeness of man's intellectual nature. Man "is most perfectly like God according to that in which he can best imitate God in his intellectual nature."[33]

CLASSICAL THEISM

These essentially philosophical ideas about the nature of God became a collection of doctrines now known as *classical theism*, closely associated with medieval figures like Anselm, Aquinas, Maimonides, and Avicenna, and which remain central to the thinking of many modern theologians.[34] The foundational assumption of classical theism is that God is the most perfect possible being, leading to its core tenets that God is omnipotent or all-powerful, omniscient or all-knowing, and omnibenevolent or completely good. Other attributes include uniqueness, simplicity, impassability, and immutability (all of which follow from being omnipotent), being everywhere or omnipresent (which follows both from omnipotence and omniscience), and so on. There are philosophical difficulties with the doctrine of classical theism, which I shall outline further (a full treatment would be a work of many volumes). Then I shall present the difficulties that my theory of reference presents for classical theism.

The problem of supposing that God is omnipotent is to explain how he can intervene in the universe. It is difficult for him to do so because, as McCabe puts it, "not because he has not the power but because, so to speak, he has too much," that is, we cannot *intervene* in what we are already doing ourselves.[35] On this supposition, it also seems difficult to explain how we can pray to God to intercede. If human affairs are not governed by God, or if everything happens by necessity, then prayer can have no efficacy. Yet if it is possible to change God's mind (as it were) that implies God is changeable, or lacked foresight, or the power to anticipate the need for prayers. Pope Gregory (540–604) resolved this by saying that a prayer brings about what was from all eternity predestined to be obtained by it, thus meriting us to receive what God had already determined to give us.[36] Aquinas followed him,[37] saying that prayer does not change the divine disposition, but rather allows us "to fulfil certain effects according to the order of the Divine disposition," so that we do not change what God has (already) settled, but rather accomplish what God has settled to be fulfilled by our prayers. The Quran rejects intercession in some cases (2:47–48, 2:122–123, 2:254), although appears to allow it in others (2:255, 3:159, 47:19, 40:7-9). There is a similar problem with supposing that God is immutable ("I the Lord do not change"[38]), which suggests that God is somehow indifferent to the world. Yet in the Hebrew Bible, God commands, forgives, controls history, predicts the future, occasionally appears in humanoid form, enters contracts with human beings, and sends prophets, whom he occasionally allows to argue with him.[39]

The problem of supposing that God is omniscient seems inconsistent with God needing to intercede, suggesting imperfect knowledge of what will happen. As everyone knows, it seems to conflict with the possibility of human freedom. If God knows that things will happen in that way, then isn't it *necessary* that they happen that way? And if it is necessary for them to happen that way, how can we be free to do otherwise? For to be free is to have the ability to do otherwise, that is, for it to be possible for us to do otherwise, which is inconsistent with the apparent necessity of our not doing otherwise. Too much ink has been spilled on this question for me to say anything useful here.

The doctrine of divine *simplicity* is also central to classical theism. "Simple" here means not having parts, either in the material sense, or in the metaphysical sense, as when Philo asserts that in God there is no distinction of genus and species. "For God is not only devoid of peculiar qualities, but he is likewise not of the form of man."[40] This idea is developed systematically by the neo-Platonist Plotinus (204/5–270 AD), who developed a spiritual cosmology based on The One, a being that is absolutely simple yet also the cause of everything:

> self-gathered not inter-blended with the forms that rise from it, and yet able in some mode of its own to be present to those others ... authentically a unity, not merely something elaborated into unity and so in reality no more than unity's counterfeit; it will debar all telling and knowing except that it may be described as transcending Being- for if there were nothing outside all alliance and compromise, nothing authentically one, there would be no Source. Untouched by multiplicity, it will be wholly self-sufficing, an absolute First, whereas any not-first demands its earlier, and any non-simplex needs the simplicities within itself as the very foundations of its composite existence.[41]

As he suggests, this absolutely simple being debars all telling and knowing. This is puzzling. If we are to pass over The One in silence, how can we conceive of it at all? Plotinus answers that while we do not grasp it by knowledge, we are not utterly devoid of it. "We hold it not so as to state it, but so as to be able to speak about it. And we can and do state what it is not, while we are silent as to what it is: we are, in fact, speaking of it in the light of its sequels; unable to state it, we may still possess it."[42] This consequence is known as negative or apophatic theology, and it has a long tradition in the theology of all three religions. Gregory of Nyssa (c. 335–c. 395) may have read Plotinus, and there is a similarity of topic in both writers. "By what name can I describe the incomprehensible? By what speech can I declare the unspeakable?"[43] Later on, Maimonides and the Islamic philosophers were influenced by a work titled *Theology of Aristotle*, actually an edited summary of parts of books four to six of Plotinus' *Enneads*. Maimonides argues that negative theology follows directly from the doctrine of simplicity, for God's existence is not merely an accident added onto his essence, as for things whose existence is due to some external cause. God has no cause, and so his existence is absolute, and identical with his essence. Consequently, he exists without possessing the attribute of existence, "lives without possessing the attribute of life; knows, without possessing the attribute of knowledge; is omnipotent without possessing the attribute of omnipotence; is wise, without possessing the attribute of wisdom: all this reduces itself to one and the same entity." Furthermore, his unity or oneness is not an element added. God is One without possessing the attribute of unity. He has no accidental attributes and no constituent elements, which would detract from this absolutely unity. "Hence it is clear that He has no positive attribute whatever."[44] As far as we have any knowledge of God, it is only through negations, which do not convey a true idea of the being to which they refer. Thus, God cannot be the object of human comprehension. No one but God truly comprehends what he is and our knowledge consists in knowing that we are unable truly to comprehend him.

> All philosophers say, "He has overpowered us by His grace, and is invisible to us through the intensity of His light," like the sun which cannot be perceived by eyes which are too weak to bear its rays. Much more has been said on this topic, but it is useless to repeat it here. The idea is best expressed in the book of Psalms, "Silence is praise to Thee."[45]

The simplicity of God is the *de fide* teaching of the Catholic Church, affirmed at the fourth Lateran council of 1213,[46] and the first Vatican council of 1869–1870, the denial of which amounts to heresy. There are also statements of the doctrine in Augustine (354–430, *City of God* XI.10), Anselm (1033–1109, *Proslogion* 18), and Aquinas (1225–1274, *Summa* I Q3). Aquinas says that God is *ipsum esse subsistens*, subsistent existence itself (*Summa* I q. 11 a. 4). Its negative consequences have been questioned by many philosophers and theologians, including Aquinas himself.[47] Duns Scotus (c.1265–1308) argued that there is no point distinguishing between positive and negative knowledge, for negation is only comprehended through affirmation, therefore we only know negations about God through affirmations, in order to remove inconsistencies from those affirmations. Moreover, "negations are not the object of our greatest love."[48] And how is the view of divine simplicity, and consequent unintelligibility, consistent with the view of God as a person? A person has a mind whose thoughts and feelings are distinct and successive. As Hume (1711–1776) argued, a being who is simple has "no thought, no reason, no will, no sentiment, no love, no hatred; or in a word, is no mind at all."[49] Yet God is obviously a person, according to Plantinga and others.[50] Then he is obviously not simple.[51]

SEMANTIC DEPENDENCE

The contrast between the anthropomorphic and the theistic conception of God belongs to theology, but corresponding to this, as I have pointed out, there is a philosophical distinction between the *co-referential* and the *descriptive* interpretation of the term "God." On the co-referential interpretation, "God" is a proper name that has no descriptive content. It tells us which individual is the subject of predication by telling us, as it were, which individual it is the same as. Thus, Genesis 2:8 says "God planted a garden in Eden," 1 Kings

4:29 says, "God gave Solomon unusual wisdom and insight," telling us that the individual who gave Solomon wisdom and insight around the tenth century BC was *one and the same individual* who planted a garden in Eden at the beginning of the universe. In the terminology I have adopted here, the two tokens of "God" *co-refer*, and the second token (which occurs later in the text) is *semantically dependent* on the series of earlier tokens. On the descriptive interpretation, by contrast, "God" means something like "an omnipotent, omniscient, omnibenevolent being," which is not semantically dependent on any text except the English dictionary.

Neither interpretation requires that "God exists" is necessary. First, we can understand the *descriptive* interpretation even if nothing satisfies it. As Anselm observed, even a foolish atheist understands the proposition that God exists, "and what he understands is in his understanding; even if he does not understand it to exist. For, it is one thing for a thing to be in the understanding, *but another* to understand that the thing exists."[52] The fool can understand the proposition "God exists" because he understands the proposition that there is or there exists a being than which nothing greater can be conceived, but he does not have to believe it, nor does God have to exist for the proposition to make sense.

Second, we can understand the co-referential interpretation even when the subject of predication is empty.

(A) A being called "God" created the sky, and created the land.
(B) A being called "God" created the sky, and *God* (or *he*) created the land.

As I have argued, (A) and (B) express the same thing in a different grammatical form. Given that (A) can be empty, it follows that (B) can be empty also. Yet the proper name is meaningful, for it signifies that the predicate "created the land" attaches to the subject of the antecedent proposition. Thus, the semantics of the proper name do not involve any connection with reality, and God's existence does not follow from the co-referential use of "God." Semantic dependence is not *object* dependence, that is, dependence upon an object in extralinguistic reality.

Thus, neither God nor Moses have to exist in order for us to understand "God" or "Moses" in the co-referential sense, *pace* strong Millians. But do the *scriptures* have to exist? Could we refer to, and think about the scriptural God if, by some accident, the scriptures had never come down to us? As I argued (chapter 5), the meaning of the second token of the name "Omri" in the Mesha stele is dependent on the different fragments being cemented together. Some of the meaning was lost when the stone was broken, namely the co-reference of the second token of the name. When separated, one fragment would inform us someone called "Omri" was king of Israel, the other that someone called "Omri" took the land of Madeba. No identity would be signified. But once the fragments were cemented together, the co-reference was signified just as it was when the stele was first inscribed. The co-reference or *semantic* dependence depended on the tablet being in one piece and understood as a single text. Even identification by *definite* description (as opposed to by *in*definite description, such as "an officer called *Nabu-sharrussu-ukin*") involves identifying some textual antecedent that it co-refers with. But if we lost the scriptures, and all memory of them had perished, could we still construct a noun phrase from the words of our ordinary language that would have the same sense as the co-referring term?

My arguments in chapter 3 show that we cannot construct such a noun phrase. A co-referring singular term does not have a *transportable* sense, that is, a sense that can belong to any token, regardless of context or order, and by the same reasoning, a general or indefinite term is indifferent to what came before. "A young man" means any young man, not necessarily a specific man already mentioned, "an omniscient being" means any such being, not necessarily already mentioned. Now if the central claim of the Hebrew Bible is that there is *a* being that is all-powerful, omniscient or all-knowing, and omnibenevolent, we have the problem that this being is referred to as "God" or "Yhwh," but the antecedent description "a being that is all-powerful, omniscient or all-knowing, and omnibenevolent" and so on is general and indefinite so, while it necessarily refers *forward* to subsequent occurrences of "Yhwh," it cannot refer *back*, for the reasons I have given. It is indifferent to any singular term that comes before. If there were a term that had the same meaning as "Yhwh," but which had a sense that was independent of the Bible, we could coherently deny the identity.

You will object that the uniqueness of the description guarantees co-reference. But this is not the case. Consider

A: There is a girl called "Sally." Sally is the tallest girl in the class.
B: Sally is not the tallest girl in the class. Jane is.

It is not part of the meaning of the name "Sally" that she is the tallest in the class, so it is not self-contradictory to say that she is not. What if we let the name "Sally" denote *whoever* is the tallest in the class, even though she may not be so-called in real life? Clearly someone must be the tallest. Let the name "Sally" refer to her, you object. In reply, (1) the Hebrew Bible does not specify the name "Yhwh" as arbitrarily referring to *whoever* is the most powerful, most high, all-knowing, and so on. Rather, tells the story of a being who created the heavens and earth, saying that the being's name is "Yhwh" in Gen 2:4. Somewhat later we learn of the attributes such as all-powerful (Job 37:23), all-knowing (Isaiah 40:13). Thus, it is clearly not a contradiction to claim that, for example, Vishnu is not the same being as Yhwh, that Vishnu is the supremely powerful being and that Yhwh is not, which it would be if the *meaning* of "Yhwh" as it occurs in the Bible was "the most powerful being" or something like that. And (2) even if we allow "Sally" to denote the tallest girl in the class, I doubt it is *contradictory* to claim subsequently that she isn't. We are *letting* "Sally" denote someone, then we are *claiming* that she is tallest in the class. So it is clearly contradictory to say that Sally is not Sally, for "letting" the name have that meaning is not a claim. But it is not contradictory to deny the claim that she is tallest in the class, for any claim may be legitimately be denied.

Hence, no descriptive interpretation of "God" (*a* first mover, *a* first efficient cause, *some entity* by whom all natural things are directed to their end, etc.) can *refer* to the God of the scriptures. Such a description requires no engagement with the scriptures, and is independent of any revelation, for it is semantically independent. It is what Strawson calls a "pure individuating description," that is, one which is free of a proper name of a person, or of a place, or a date, or any kind of demonstrative indicator. Strawson gives the examples "first dog born at sea" and "only dog to be born at sea which subsequently saved a monarch's life,"[53] but "being than which nothing greater can be conceived" (*aliquid quo nihil maius cogitari possit*) will do equally well. To grasp the meaning of a pure individuating description, it is enough to have a good grasp of one's own language, whatever the language, so long as it has appropriate terms like "dog" or "monarch." Thus, the description "omnipotent being" identifies in some sense a single being, on the assumption that only one being can be all-powerful, and it is purely individuating or semantically independent in that one needs merely to understand the dictionary term "powerful," and to grasp the grammatical comparative, that is, *most* powerful. We understand the description "being than which nothing greater can be conceived" as long we understand the meanings of standard English words, that is, the meanings of "being," "than," "which," and so on. The descriptive conception is equally accessible to one and all, which is probably the reason for Kant's claim that no doctrine that comes from revelation alone should be taken as essential to our religious calling, being a violation of "ought implies can."[54] *But this would not be a conception of the scriptural God.* (You may object that some person in Africa was never saved by missionaries and never encountered the scriptures, but God appeared before this person. Couldn't this person have a conception of the God of the Scriptures? I shall address this objection in the next chapter).

This brings us to identity. I argued in the previous chapter that a true identity statement is necessarily true when the terms flanking the identity sign anaphorically co-refer, but contingently true otherwise. Thus, the proposition "God is identical with *Dieu*" is necessarily true if "God" refers back to the

Christian or Hebrew Bible in English translation, and "Dieu" refers back to a French translation of the same scripture. One name has simply been translated for another. Likewise, on the assumption that some proper names in the Quran co-refer with names in the Hebrew Bible, and that "Allah" and "Yhwh" co-refer, "God is identical with Allah," if true, is necessarily true. But, as I argued earlier, the description of God embedded in classical theism cannot capture the content of any name that is semantically dependent on the scriptures.[55] Such a description does not require any engagement with the scriptures, and is independent of any revelation, for it is semantically independent of scripture or revelation, and so the two names, that is, "God" of the scriptures and the "God" of the philosophers, do not co-refer. It is not a semantic property of "God of the philosophers" that it co-refers with "God of the Bible." If Maimonides and Aquinas and the others are right, they *descriptively* identify the same being. But the identity is not necessary. As Aquinas points out in a different context,[56] a proposition can be self-evident in two ways: in itself, although not to us, or in itself and to us as well. It is self-evident when the essence of the predicate is included in (or is the same as) the essence of the subject, and so if predicate and subject are signified for what they are ("are known to all"), then the truth of the proposition will be evident. But if not, the proposition will be self-evident in itself, although not to those "who have no knowledge of (*qui ignorant*) the predicate and subject of the proposition."[57] It follows that the identity of the God of the philosophers with the God of the scriptures, if it exists, is contingent, that is, not necessary. It does not follow, even if the God of the scriptures is identical with the God of the philosophers, that they are *necessarily* identical. Likewise "God is Vishnu," even if true, is not necessarily true, since the two tokens do not co-refer, one being from the Christian Bible, the other being from the Vedas. It is the same as the example of the Nebo-sarsekim mentioned by Jeremiah, and the Nabu-sharrussu-ukin mentioned in the Babylonian clay tablet. They are probably the same person, but that is a contingent and a posteriori truth only.[58] Some other being than the greatest possible being might have been the greatest possible being, although *no being other than God might have been God.*

SUMMARY

The philosophical and scriptural conceptions of God correspond to a logical distinction between description and reference. The philosophical conception of God is available to anyone who understands the meaning of "omnipotent," "omniscient," and of other common dictionary terms. The scriptural or coreferential conception is available only to those who have read the appropriate scripture. All definite reference to the scriptures, or to any other narrative, whether it involves definite descriptions, proper names and pronouns and indeed any other singular term, has the same underlying explanation, namely co-reference or semantic dependence. This explains how propositions can be definite without being *object dependent*. An object dependent proposition is one that is in some sense *about* a particular individual, and which could not express what it is intended to express if that individual failed to exist.[59] The semantics depends on the existence of an external object, and should not be confused with the semantic dependence of co-referring terms.

I have also argued that a semantically independent conception of God, that is, which is available to anyone who understands the meaning of "omnipotent," "omniscient," and so on, is essentially an indefinite description, but no indefinite description on its own, not even a unique description, can capture the content of a *definite* description. Russell's theory of descriptions, which analyzes a definite proposition as an indefinite one, is inadequate to capture the sense of "sameness" that is asserted or implied to hold between the subjects of different propositions. Just as we cannot understand the proper name "Frodo Baggins" unless we have read *The Lord of the Rings*,[60] so we cannot understand the term "God" unless we have read the Bible, or some text that is dependent on it. If Moses had not been handed the Torah, and the Hebrew Bible had never been written, we would not be able to understand the name "God" in its co-referential sense, although perhaps some descriptive but indefinite sense would still be available. Nor is the God of the Hebrew Bible *necessarily* identical with the God of the philosophers. The identity is contingent, and a posteriori, although if it is a truth, it is not a truth we could ever discover in this life. The question is which conception of "God" is the *standard* one, which I shall discuss next.

NOTES

1. There are a few verses in the Quran suggesting this, for example, 6:52 "And do not send away those who call upon their Lord morning and afternoon, seeking His *countenance*," or 2:255 "His Kursi [throne] extends over the heavens and the earth, and their preservation tires Him not. And He is the Most High, the Most Great"; 5:64 "both His hands are extended; He spends however He wills." However these all seem to be figurative. See Peters 1993:259 for a summary of early debates on the subject.

2. Sommer, *The Bodies of God and the World of Ancient Israel*, 2, passim. According to Sommer, Babylonians, Assyrians, Canaanites, Arameans, and Egyptians thought that a single deity could exist simultaneously in several bodies. "Avatars usually are understood to be only partial manifestations of the deity who assumes them" (ibid., 15).

3. "You spoke, forsooth, with indignant rage against the Anthropomorphites, who, with rustic simplicity, think that God has actually the members of which we

read in Scripture; and showed by your eyes, hands, and every gesture that you had the old man in view, and wished him to be suspected of that most foolish heresy." "To Pammachius against John of Jerusalem" Gregory of Nyssa, *Against Eunomius*, trans. H.A. Wilson, 430.

4. Cyril of Alexandria, *Against the Anthropomorphites*. Cyril says their argument is that since sacred scripture says that man is made in the image of God, then God must be of human species or human form. But this is altogether absurd, and extremely impious, for the similitude of man to God is not corporeal (p.1067). But see Patterson (*Visions of Christ: The Anthropomorphite Controversy of 399 CE*, 90) who argues that the anthromorphites, while seeking a vision of Christ in prayer, were not merely seeking Christ *incarnate*, but rather a vision of the eternal, divine body of the Word.

5. Origen, *Selecta in Genesim*, I.26, Migne, *Patrologia Graeca*, 12.94 "*Faciamus hominem ad imaginem nostram et similitudinem*" *[Gen. I.26]. Prius discutiendum est ubi consistat illud, ad imaginem, in corpore, an in anima. Et in primis videamus, quibis utantur qui prius asserunt; e quorum numero est Melito, qui scripta reliquit, quibus asserit Deum corporeum esse. Membra enim Dei appellata cum reperiunt, oculos Dei respicientes terram [Ps. 101:6], et aures eius intentas esse ad preces iustorum [Ps. 34:15] et: Olfecit Dominus odorem suavitatis [Gen. 8:21] et : Os Domini locutum est ista [Isa 1:20], et brachium Dei, et manus, et pedes, et digitos; statim inferunt haec nihil aliud docere quam formam Dei.* "'Let us make mankind in our image and in [our] likeness.' First we must discuss where that 'in [our] likeness' may be situated, in the body or in the soul? And in the first place we must see which [passages] are used by those who assert the former, among whom is Melito, who left writings where he asserts that God is corporeal. For when they discover the body parts named—the *eyes* of God looking at the earth, and his ears attending to the prayers of the righteous, and 'the Lord smelled the scent of pleasantness' and 'the mouth of the Lord has spoken,' and 'the arm of God,' and the feet, and the fingers—they immediately conclude that these things tell us [about] nothing other than the form of God." My translation of Migne's Latin.

6. Paulsen, "Early Christian belief in a corporeal deity," 105–116.

7. See, for example, Beckwith, "Philosophical problems with the Mormon concept of God," chapter 2 for a summary of Mormon "finistic theism," and chapter 3 for some of the philosophical problems with this view. According to Beckwith, Mormon belief is that God is (1) a contingent being, who was at one time not God; (2) finite in knowledge (not truly omniscient), power (not omnipotent), and being (not omnipresent or immutable); (3) one of many gods; (4) a corporeal (bodily) being, who physically dwells at a particular spatio-temporal location and is therefore not omnipresent like the classical God, and (5) a being who is subject to the laws and principles of a beginningless universe with an infinite number of entities in it. "Mormon and classical theism stand in starkest contradiction" (40).

8. Sommer, *The Bodies of God and the World of Ancient Israel*, 9.

9. Ibid., 6.

10. Hopkins, *How Greek Philosophy Corrupted the Christian Concept of God*, 253.

11. Swinburne considers a similar view, toward the end of *The Christian God*, 238.

12. "The primary preoccupation of his translation of the Torah into Aramaic was precisely to dispose of the corporealistic suggestions of the original. Maimonides . . . does *explicitly* what Onkelos did *implicitly*" (*Leo Strauss on Maimonides*, 505).

13. Drazin, *Onkelos on the Torah*, xxiv.

14. Whose influence Maimonides acknowledges at the beginning of chapter xxvii of the *Guide*.

15. *A Treatise on the Confusion of Languages* XXVII (134), Yonge (trans.) 1993, 246.

16. *A Treatise on the Life of Moses*, I.165; Yonge, *Works of Philo Judaeus* trans., 474.

17. Ibid., 1.123; Yonge, 470.

18. Davidson, *Moses Maimonides*, 100.

19. *A Treatise to Prove that Every Man Who Is Virtuous Is Also Free*, I.13; Yonge, 1993, 683.

20. *A Treatise on Those Special Laws*, III.I.2; Yonge, 1993, 594.

21. I say "may." Despite the longstanding view that the fourth Gospel was influenced by Philo's use of *logos*, the recent drift of scholarship has been away from Philo as a source for the *logos* doctrine. See Nash 1993.

22. Philo, *De Cherubim*, 1.27–28.

23. *Quaestiones et Solutiones in Genesim*, IV.2.

24. *Quaestiones et Solutiones in Genesim*, I.39.

25. Nash, "Was the New Testament influenced by Pagan philosophy?" 16–19, 35–38, see also Nash, *The Gospel and the Greeks, Did the New Testament Borrow from Pagan Thought?*, passim.

26. Runia, *Philo and the Church Fathers: A Collection of Papers*, 54, Casey, "Clement of Alexandria and the beginnings of Christian Platonism," 39–45, 73–101.

27. "Some 300 times, as has been ably demonstrated and analysed by Annewies van den Hoek," referring to Hoek "How Alexandrian was Clement of Alexandria?"

28. *Libellus de oratione* (On Prayer) Migne *Patrologia Graeca* XI.490, see also *De principiis* IV (*Patrologia Graeca* XI, 378).

29. *De Principiis* IV, *Patrologia Graeca* XI 359 "secundum sonum litterae."

30. *Patrologia Graeca* XI, 360.

31. *Summa* I Q3.

32. *Summa* I^a–IIae q. 98 a. 3 arg. 2.

33. *Summa* Q 93.1.

34. As is evident from introductory books such as Inbody (*The Faith of the Christian Church*, 95). "Central to the theistic idea is the assumption that anything less than perfection is inappropriate to the concept of God. *Who would disagree?*" (my emphasis), although he adds (Ibid., 96), "Classical theism *does not adequately represent* the complex and subtle thought of most theologians, and few of the great theologians have restricted their thinking about God to only this concept" (my emphasis). See also Beckwith, "Philosophical problems with the Mormon concept of God," chapter 1.

35. McCabe "Creation" in Davies, ed., 199.

36. *Dialogues* I.8 (Warner, *The Dialogues of St Gregory*, 30) As Gregory points out, Isaac prayed for his wife to have children, and she conceived (Gen. 25:21), yet God had already told Abraham he had appointed him to be the father of many nations (Genesis 17:5).
37. *Summa* IIb Q83.
38. Malachi 3:6.
39. I owe this formulation to Dale Tuggy.
40. *Legum Allegoriarum* 1.36.
41. Ennead V.4.1 (MacKenna, *The Enneads* (trans.), 400).
42. Ennead V.3.14 (MacKenna, *The Enneads* (trans.), 396).
43. *Against Eunomius* III. 5. The context is John 4:22 "You worship what you do not know; we worship what we know."
44. *The Guide for the Perplexed*, I.57.
45. *The Guide for the Perplexed*, I.59.
46. Saying that God is a *substantia seu natura simplex omnino* (a substance or nature that is entirely simple).
47. *Summa Theologiae* Part I Q13 a2 co.
48. Ord. I, d. 3, qq. 1–2, n. 10, Vat. III:5.
49. Hume, *Dialogues Concerning Natural Religion*, Popkin, ed., 1980, part 4.
50. See e.g. Plantinga, *Does God Have a Nature?*; Stump, *The God of the Bible and the God of the Philosophers*.
51. Although Stump, *The God of the Bible and the God of the Philosophers*, 104, argues cogently for the consistency of a simple God, in the classical sense, who is also personal.
52. *Quod intelligit in intellectu eius est, etiam si non intelligat illud esse. Aliud enim est rem esse in intellectu, aliud intelligere rem esse* (Schmitt, *S. Anselmi Cantuariensis Archepiscopi opera omnia*, 101).
53. Strawson, *Individuals*, 26. I have removed the definite article from Strawson's examples for reasons which should be obvious.
54. *Religion within the Boundaries of Mere Reason and Other Writings* 6:103, 154–55.
55. It also tells against the idea of *reference-fixing* descriptions, that is, using a definite description like "all-powerful being," or "all-knowing being" to pick out some being, or to single him out for thought, and that we can give a proper name to the being thus singled out. For example, we can use the term "God" as his name.
56. *Summa Theologica* I Question 2 a1. The context is the proposition "God exists."
57. Bauder, "The difficulties surrounded the relationship between knowledge and language. If humans cannot know God's essence, how can they give Him any name that is not equivocal?" Aquinas addresses this issue in *Summa Theologica* I, q. 13, especially articles 1–2, 5, and 10. For comparison with other authors, see Ashworth 1980.
58. Kripke also mentions the contingent *a priori*, which I shall not discuss here. See Donnellan, "The contingent a priori and rigid designators"; Hughes, *Kripke: Names, Necessity, and Identity*, 84–107; Plantinga, *The Nature of Necessity*, 8–9n.;

Salmon, "How to measure the standard metre"; cf. Oppy, "Salmon on the contingent a priori and the necessary a posteriori."

59. Neale, *Descriptions*, 19, but note that his formulation is slightly different because of his use of the term "proposition" for a mental or Platonic entity that is expressed by a *sentence*. As explained in the first chapter, I use "proposition" for a type of sentence that expresses a truth, or a falsehood.

60. Or some work or commentary which is referentially dependent on that work.

Chapter 9

Identification in the Present

I have contrasted the descriptive use of the name "God," corresponding to the philosophical conception of God as omniscient, omnipotent, omnibenevolent, and so on, with the referential use, corresponding to the conception of the being who is central to the Hebrew, Christian, and Muslim scriptures. But Aquinas says, "it is necessary to posit a first efficient cause, to which *everyone* gives the name of God," referring to everyone who uses the name "God," not just the prophets (the authors of the scriptures) and the generations of philosopher-theologians who wrote the monumental works that defined the high middle ages. What is the common or *everyday* use of the name? When the Reverend Dr. Magdy Gendy said "I worship the triune God," in what sense did *he* understand the proper name "God," and how did he intend *us* to understand it? When a person feels that God is speaking to her, and she says "God is speaking to me," how are we to understand her? When a Muslim asserts "God is not a trinity" and a Christian says "God *is* a trinity" are they using the name in the same sense, so that they contradict one another? Or are they simply asserting contradictory predicates of different things?

THE PADEREWSKI PROBLEM

The purpose of language is to establish understanding, that is, mutual understanding. As Locke says, "When a man speaks to another, it is that he may be understood: and the end of speech is, that those sounds, as marks, may make known his ideas to the hearer."[1] This can only be achieved when different people understand the same words, in the same context, in the *same* way. We achieve this by imposition, a convention whereby we attach (as it were) a particular or *standard* meaning to a particular expression. So what is the standard sense of the name "God"? Do we use it to signify the God of the scriptures, or the God of the philosophers? Generally, what counts as the standard meaning of a proper name, and how is it imposed?

As soon as we approach the question of standard or ordinary meaning, we come up against what I call the *Paderewski problem*, made famous by Kripke.[2] The problem is to justify the move from a quotation context, where we specify what someone uttered ("God is speaking to me"), to a *dis*quotation context, where we use the speaker's words instead of quoting them ("Sarah says *that* God is speaking to her"). The audience must understand the way we standardly use the words, and the meaning it attaches to them must be the meaning Sarah attaches to them. When Sarah says "*God* is speaking to me," what she means by "God" must be the same as what we mean by it when I say "Sarah believes that God is speaking to her," otherwise we are not correctly reporting what she means to say. What if Sarah worships Baal (whom she calls "God") instead of God? How then do we justify the move from quotation to disquotation? How do we justify the assumption that everyone will understand the disquoted name in the way we intend and that the person we are quoting meant it that way?

Kripke asks us to consider a man called "Peter" who first learns the name "Paderewski" under the description "famous pianist." Later, Peter learns of someone called "Paderewski" who was a Polish nationalist leader and prime minister. Believing that politicians have no musical ability, he concludes that there are two different people both named "Paderewski." So Peter assents to both "Paderewski is musical" and "Paderewski is not musical." On the principle (which Kripke calls the *disquotational principle*) that assenting to "p" entails believing that p, it follows that Peter believes that Paderewski is musical and that Paderewski is *not* musical. Peter, a rational being, believes two contradictory statements. How can he believe opposite things of one and the same person? How can he believe that Paderewski has musical talent, and also believe that *the very same person* has no musical talent? Of course, Peter believes that there are two people called "Peter," one of whom is a pianist, the other of whom is a politician, but nonetheless he would *assent* to statements "Paderewski has musical talent" and "it is not the case that Paderewski has musical talent," and if we accept the disquotational principle, for which Kripke provides compelling evidence, it logically follows that Peter has contradictory beliefs. Kripke made no attempt at resolving the paradox. "My main thesis is a simple one: that the puzzle is a puzzle," he said, noting, "As any theory of truth must deal with the Liar Paradox, so any theory of belief and names must deal with this puzzle." The puzzle quickly became famous, and has intrigued a generation of philosophers.

I shall begin by setting out the puzzle as a set of five mutually inconsistent assumptions, all of which have strong but competing claims to plausibility.[3]

(1) *Assent*: Peter assents[4] to the statements "Paderewski is musical" and "Paderewski is not musical," at the same time. *Supple* "at the same time": clearly we are not supposing that he assents to the first statement at one time, then later changes his mind to assent to the second. Indeed, Kripke remarks that Peter is "set in his ways," and refuses to give up his previous belief.[5]
(2) *Understanding*: Peter understands each occurrence of the proper name under its standard or normal meaning. Kripke says, "The speaker should satisfy *normal* criteria for using 'London' as a name of London." He says, in formulating the "disquotational principle" (see further), that the speaker must use words in the *standard* way, that is, use them to mean what a *normal* speaker should mean by them.[6]
(3) *Disquotation*: If a normal English speaker S sincerely and reflectively assents to "p," then S believes that p, where "p" is to be replaced, inside and outside quotation marks, by a standard English sentence whose words are used in the *standard* way as given earlier.
(4) *Contradiction*. First definition: contradictory statements are where the same predicate is simultaneously affirmed and denied of co-referring terms. Second definition: contradictory statements are statements that cannot have the same truth value. I shall consider the first definition only. Clearly anything falling under the first also falls under the second.
(5) *Rationality*: No one rationally believes contradictory statements. Kripke imagines (p. 257) that Peter is actually a logician, and would never let a contradiction pass. So clearly Peter would not assent to the statement "some musical person is not musical."

At least one of these assumptions has to be false. If the first and second are true, Peter simultaneously assents to, and correctly understands, the two statements. Adding the third (disquotation), it follows that, at the same time, he believes that Paderewski *is* musical and that Paderewski is *not* musical. Adding the fourth implies that he simultaneously believes contradictory statements. But this conflicts with the fifth assumption, that no rational person—including Peter—simultaneously believes contradictory statements.

We can engage with the puzzle using the notion of *co-reference*. It should be clear from the definition of co-reference I gave in chapter 2 that we cannot understand two co-referring propositions without also understanding that the predicates are signified to be affirmed (or denied) of a single individual. In the conjunction "Peter preached at Jerusalem and Peter preached in Galilee," it is signified, that is, it is part of the meaning, that the predicates "preached at Jerusalem" and "preached in Galilee" are true of the same person. Thus, in the conjunction "Paderewski is musical and Paderewski is not musical," it is signified that the predicate "is musical" is both asserted and denied of co-referring terms, and so to understand what is signified is to understand that a contradiction is signified. It is no different from "Paderewski is musical and *he* is not musical." Thus, Kripke's puzzle cannot arise when two terms co-refer, as I have defined co-reference, that is, as *anaphoric* co-reference. We cannot understand the terms without understanding that their predicates are signified to be true of a single thing.

You may object that we could understand the terms without understanding that they co-refer. What if they co-refer, but Peter does not know it? I reply that my definition of co-reference precludes such a thing. Clearly we cannot understand pronoun use—short-range anaphora—without understanding that a pronoun co-refers with its antecedent. But I have argued also (see chapter 2 and *passim*) that there are rules for long-range anaphoric co-reference, which are clearly understood by both authors and readers. For example, the convention in all three scriptures is that "Moses" is an unambiguous name, that is, that all occurrences of "Moses" co-refer. Someone might not realize this convention and might suppose, in the manner of Peter and "Paderewski," that the name "Moses" as it appears in the Pentateuch does not co-refer with the same name as it appears in Malachi ("Remember the law of my servant Moses").[7] But that would be a result of misunderstanding the convention, which would be a form of misunderstanding. If there are commonly understood rules for determining co-reference, then either the author has failed to apply the rules correctly, in which case they are not making sense, or they have been applied correctly by the author, but the interpreter has not applied them, meaning that the interpreter has misunderstood. It is impossible, as I have defined co-reference, to understand two co-referring terms, hence understanding and applying the rules of co-reference, but not to understand what the terms mean. The meaning of a singular term *is* its co-reference.

For the same reason, the puzzle cannot arise with a narrative constructed to avoid confusion about naming by using the informal rule system discussed in chapter 2. If there are two or more people called "Mary," the name should be appropriately qualified, so it is clear their reference is different. Mary Magdalene is qualified as *Magdalene*, as is Mary *the mother of James and Joseph*, who is also called the *other* Mary (Matthew 27:61, 28:1).[8] If there is no such qualification, the default is that the reference is the same, although the author may also qualify this. Thus, John 11:2 states, "This Mary, whose brother Lazarus now lay sick, *was the same one who poured perfume on the Lord and wiped his feet with her hair*," in case we think she is a different Mary, although Luke does not say whether they are the same or different. Likewise, Acts 13:14 tells us that the Apostles came to Antioch *in Pisidia*, to distinguish it from the Antioch in *Syria*. Or the ambiguity can be resolved by the passage of time. There are two people called "Herod" in the gospels. The first, the infant boy slayer of Matthew 2, was Herod the Great (74 BC–4

BC), whereas the person to whom Jesus was sent before his crucifixion (and the one who had John the Baptist murdered) was Herod the Great's son Herod Antipas (Matthew 14:1; Luke 3:1). There is no overt disambiguation in Luke. Luke 1:5 says "In the time of Herod king of Judea," and Luke 3:1 "In the fifteenth year of the reign of Tiberius Caesar—when Pontius Pilate was governor of Judea, Herod tetrarch of Galilee." However, the infant killing episode took place at Jesus' birth, whereas Luke 3 explicitly states that Jesus was about thirty.

The same techniques can be used when the author of one part of a text is different from the author of an earlier part. As mentioned in chapter 2, the author of Psalm 106 who says that Phinehas "stayed the plague," is almost certainly different from the author of Numbers 25:7, who says that Phinehas, "son of Eleazar," kills an Israelite man and a Midianite woman, but the author (or editor) of the Psalm is presumably aware of other characters called by the same name, and so is able to disambiguate their names. There is no reason why multiple authors cannot achieve the same as a single one, just like the different people who write the different episodes of a television soap series, and so there is no essential difference between the multiply authored books of the Bible and the multiply authored propositions of everyday speech and journalism, given that both have an *expected* order of reading, that is, an ordering which may be explicit or implicit, and such that both authors and readers are conscious of what the texts are and the order in which they should be read, and whose semantics are broadly as if they had been physically bound in that order. The ordering is merely understood or presumed, or signified in some way other than a physical order such as a binding. I call such a collection a *virtual narrative*. Printed news is a virtual narrative. There are many hundreds or thousands of people who write it or produce it. They are conscious of what was in the news the day, the week, the year, even the decade before, and even longer before that. They are conscious of what is available to their audience, and the order in which they are likely to have received it. The readers are also conscious of this. We cannot read tomorrow's copy of the paper today, and even if we deliberately read the news in the wrong order, for example, by reading last week's news immediately after today's, this is not the order it is *meant* to be read, and we must interpret the texts in the intended or expected order of reading, rather than actual. Just as the author of Deuteronomy knows the order in which the previous books of the *Torah* are presented, and just as the reader knows that he knows, and just as the meaning depends on that expected order, so it is with journalism.

A virtual narrative allows a writer to use names unambiguously, which would otherwise be ambiguous outside it. Consider news that was written a long time ago. I own copies of *The Illustrated London News* from the 1870s.

They are bound together in date order, so they have become an actual rather than a virtual narrative, but they were originally separate, and if they are read through in the appropriate order it is evident how the semantics of proper names is dependent on this ordering. For example:

> *Earl Russell* asked the government to make a statement in reference to the Franco-Prussian war.
> *Earl Russell* introduced a bill for the reorganization of the militia.[9]

As I read the copies reproduced in *this* text (i.e., my own, the one you are reading now), they signify co-reference, because of the physical ordering in my text. They also signified the same thing in the *original* texts, because the ordering was expected or understood: both the writers and the readers in the 1870s were aware of the texts and the order in which they should be read. Thus, they were presumed to have the same reference as would have applied to an actual text. This partly depends on collective memory, which is why the following text, published in 1961, is not virtually a part of those 1870s texts:

> London police today prevented *Earl Russell* from addressing a mass meeting at Hyde Park organized as a sequel to this morning's Whitehall demonstration in observation of Hiroshima Day.[10]

This was written much later, in 1961, and so the writer was almost certainly not aware of the existence of the 1870 texts, he would not assume the readers were aware of them, and likewise the readers would not be aware. The name "Earl Russell" therefore is not presumed to signify the same person in the 1961 text as in the 1870 texts. Hence, the three texts, at least in their original form, do not together imply that a single person asked the government to make a statement about the Franco-Prussian war of 1870, *and* addressed a crowd on Hiroshima Day in 1961. The reference rule for a single text is that the same proper name always refers in the same way unless indicated otherwise, and so it is part of the *meaning* of the 1870s texts given earlier, taken together, that a single person, whoever he was, asked the government to make a statement in reference to the Franco-Prussian war, introduced a bill for the reorganization of the militia, and moved the second reading of the same bill. The virtual binding, that is, the expected order of reading, ensured that a potentially ambiguous name like "Earl Russell" was not ambiguous in that context, for exactly the same reason that "Edward" is not ambiguous in a single text about Edward I or Edward II.

Other forms of disambiguation include titles and dates or both. "The first Earl Russell" is a unique description for John Russell (1792–1878), "the third Earl Russell" for Bertrand Russell (1872–1970), and so on. Knowing the dates of death, we can often eliminate the numbering. Thus, someone who sincerely assents to "Earl Russell addressed a meeting of the Campaign for Nuclear Disarmament in 1961" clearly does not have to believe that the *first* Earl Russell, who died in 1878, addressed a meeting in 1961, nor does assenting to "London police [in 1961] prevented Earl Russell from addressing a mass meeting at Hyde Park," require believing that Earl Russell, that is, the present Earl Russell,[11] addressed a meeting ten years before he was born. Surnames are another common device, and in the Hebrew Bible, disambiguation is achieved by a form of family tree, for example, 1 Samuel 9:1, referring to Saul, son of "Kish, son of Abiel, the son of Zeror, the son of Bekorath, the son of Aphiah of Benjamin."

The examples here are taken from written language, but the same applies to spoken language. A friend of mine (a philosopher) has a cat called "Max Black," punning upon the name of a well-known Anglo-American philosopher (1909–1988) and a cat who happens to be black. If he uses the name at a conference of philosophers, it will be understood as co-referring with tokens occurring in philosophical texts like this one by Baldwin:

> In the first paper of the symposium, *Black* was mainly concerned to differentiate "logical" analysis from "philosophical" analysis.[12]

The virtual narrative incorporates a set of philosophical texts where the name "Black" or "Max Black" is unique. In the domestic environment, by contrast, the narrative incorporates all spoken (possibly written) utterances of a domestic nature, in which the name "Max" or "Max Black" is also unique. The main difference between spoken and written narrative is that the former only lasts as long as the people who remember it, whereas written language persists as long as the medium in which it is written.[13]

Likewise, as Jeffery notes, the author of the Quran seems to have used proper names that were familiar to his audience.[14] It was the first book written in Arabic, and the Arabia of Muhammad was not isolated from the rest of the world. As a consequence, many of the words, including proper names, were borrowed from other languages of the region. There is surprisingly little reference to the religious and cultural terms of Arabian paganism, apart from the names of a few ancient deities.[15] Most of the proper names are the then familiar place names ("Babil" [Babylon], "Rum" [Rome], "Madyan" [Midian], "Firdaus" [Paradise], "Janannam" [Hell]), names borrowed from Hebrew, probably via Syriac ("Ibrahim," "Musa," "Dawud," "Sulaiman," "Nuh," "Isa," etc.). Jeffrey concludes that "not only the greater part of the religious vocabulary, but also most of the cultural vocabulary of the Quran is of non-Arabic origin." Now these Arabic-Syriac names would have been familiar to the original readers of the Quran because of texts that were available then, now lost. We have few of the Syriac texts, but most of the names in the Quran have counterparts in Greek or Hebrew, and we understand the names in *English* translations of the Quran by reference to *English* translations of the Old or New Testament. Thus, we understand "*Noah* and *Abraham* and *Moses* and *Jesus* son of *Mary*" because the very same names appear in the other scriptures. But that, as discussed earlier, is simply because the translators have imposed their own interpretation of the meaning of the names. Where they are less certain, they provide a transliteration of the Arabic. Thus, Dawood does not translate "Idris" as "Enoch," although he says in a footnote that Idris is Enoch.

Hence, the main assumption that generates Kripke's puzzle is faulty. He assumes throughout the text he wrote in 1979 that there is such a thing as the standard meaning of a proper name, as though we could look a name up in a dictionary.[16] In discussing the "London" puzzle, he asks "Does Pierre, or does he not, believe that London (not the city satisfying such-and-such description, but *London*) is pretty?" The italics betray his assumption that *his* readers understand the name "London," an assumption which is valid in a journal with an international readership, but not valid if made in, say, a newspaper published in London Ontario. He claims that when we infer "Peter believes that Paderewski had musical talent," we are using the name 'Paderewski', as we *usually* do.[17] He says, setting Peter's past history aside, we would judge him to be using "Paderewski" in a *normal way*, with the normal *reference*. He talks about the *conventional, community-wide* connotation of the names "Holland" and "the Netherlands" (which he regards as synonymous). He uses these names as though his readers will understand them, just as he assumes they understand other English dictionary words such as "believe," "musical," and "talent." Yet all such names ("London," "Holland")[18] are essentially ambiguous. Kripke's assumption is justified only because his readers understand the background narrative, and so understand that when he says "London," the narrative includes texts such as the international section of newspapers, rather than the "local" section of *The London Free Press*, Ontario, or the kinds of books and information that he would expect his readers to be familiar with, such as basic information about other authors of other philosophical papers. This means he can use the short form of the name "Russell," knowing that his readers will know that the unqualified "Russell" in *any* philosophical paper has the same reference in *all* philosophical books and papers, and should not be confused with the first or second Earl Russell. This is in contrast to the readers of *The Illustrated London News*, who would have expected it to refer to the ex-prime minister of that name. This is not to deny that Kripke's assumption about the *context* of his own utterance of "London" is valid, but the point is that the meaning of *any* proper name is determined by context, and that there is no such thing as a "conventional, community-wide" meaning that is independent of context.

What about the name "Paderewski"? Would Peter understand it as I use it *here*, for example when I ask whether Peter believes that *Paderewski* is musical? Suppose Peter is reading this text. He would have to understand that it is about the philosophy of language, and so part of a wider virtual narrative using the same rules that would apply were the texts bound together in the right way. Any unqualified name must have the same reference in any part of a virtual narrative, namely other philosophy papers, books, and articles of general intellectual interest. Thus, he might come across Kripke's original paper about him, reading with interest the story of his own apparent confusion. He might refer to any of the hundreds of papers written since then. He might look up the name in Wikipedia article, which redirects to the unambiguous name [[Ignacy Jan Paderewski]], with the comment that

> Wikipedia has only one biographical article of a person by this surname, or because one individual is *ubiquitously*[19] known by this surname (other persons sharing this name might be listed at a primary topic disambiguation page).

That is, the name "Paderewski," in its *everyday* use (and not in its use by Paderewski's family and friends, or by other Polish families of the same name), refers to the same individual, namely *Paderewski*, the person you understand me to be "talking about"[20] right now. It follows that if Peter did not originally understand the co-reference, he did not understand the name. Likewise, if Peter fails to understand that there is a certain place whose name is used everywhere in the international sections of newspapers to apply to a single world city, that is, that everywhere the name "London" occurs in such a section (not necessarily in a local section, or in a newspaper published in London Ontario) it refers to the same city, he fails to understand the name in its conventional journalistic sense, and so has no beliefs about *London* (I use the name "London" in its conventional journalistic sense). He recognizes now that his earlier beliefs were not really *about* anything, because he did not understand the name at that time. Thus, the notion of a "normal" or "standard" meaning of a proper name only makes sense in the context of some assumed background or "virtual" narrative. These remarks apply to proper names like "Shakespeare," "Paderewski," "Holland," "London," and so on, which are in *common use*, that is, which are not ambiguous in the background text, although potentially ambiguous anywhere else. This is not to say that a proper name does not have a meaning outside any context. For example, while the conditional "If a man owns a donkey, he beats Socrates" is puzzling, we would typically read the proper name as referring to the Greek philosopher, given no other obvious meaning. But as soon as a context is given, that is, "If a man owns a donkey *called* Socrates, he beats Socrates," we read the name as referring back to whatever donkey the man owns.

You might object that Peter could have a belief about London even if he fails to understand the name in its conventional journalistic sense. Is that really so? Could it be that a person who lives in London and uses the name in the ordinary way, but doesn't know enough about newspapers, has no beliefs about London? That is hard to believe. In reply, it is perhaps possible, though unlikely, that someone could live in London without having any knowledge of newspapers or mainstream media. But there are other parts or passages of the virtual narrative that he will have encountered, such as postal addresses, directions, station names, and maps. How will he negotiate the *London* underground, or catch a *London* bus? Perhaps you object that Peter has been kidnapped, blindfolded, and deposited in a windowless basement. He looks at the wall. Doesn't he have a belief about a *London* wall? I shall address the question of perceptual information in the next chapter, where I shall argue that perceptual information is essentially of an *indefinite* nature, because there is nothing in the information *itself* that identifies it as belonging to an object that is numerically the same as some object it previously belonged to.

Thus, assumption (ii) of Kripke's puzzle—that Peter understands each occurrence of the proper name *under its standard or normal meaning*—is false. There is no "standard" meaning of a proper name outside a specific context (journalism, philosophical papers, scriptures, etc.), and to understand the name in context requires that the appropriate parts of the narrative, or the virtual narrative, are available. We can move from "S assents to *p*" to "S believes that p" so long as the name that is mentioned in the proposition assented to co-refers with the name that is used in the "that" clause, where the test for co-reference involves the rules of disambiguation common to all narratives.

REFERENCE-PRESERVING LINKS

I have argued that we can explain the reference-preserving use of names in ordinary speech exactly as we would explain it in the case of multiple authorship of a canonical text. Multiple authorship means that a new author must "receive" the names in the earlier books or chapter, and must use it with the same reference as the previous author. Let's suppose the Bible has been written as far as Deuteronomy (book five), and that Moses was the author of all five books. We now have a new author who is taking over to write the Book of Joshua, who is traditionally regarded as Joshua himself. The book begins "After the death of *Moses*." How can he use the name "Moses" with the same reference as the man (Moses) from whom he heard it? Well, he needs to use the word "Moses" so as to continue the anaphoric chain that runs through the first five books, so all he has to do is to use the anaphoric rules that I discussed in chapter 2 and *passim*. His intentions are irrelevant, except as he realizes his intention by using the name in the correct way. Using the name with the same reference is simply using the rules for co-reference to extend the "Moses" anaphoric chain.

Thus, my theory of reference transmission is purely semantic. Kripke, by contrast, is associated with a so-called *causal* theory of names.[21] According to the theory, the use of the name is connected to an external object, the referent, by a "causal" *chain* or *passage* of communication.[22] The chain is anchored or tethered to the referent by means of an initial baptism or description,[23] the chain is constructed as the name is spread from person to person across a community "from link to link as if by a chain."[24] Thus, a person at one end of the chain can refer to the individual anchoring it at the other end.

> A speaker who is on the far end of this chain, who has heard about, say Richard Feynman, in the market place or elsewhere, may be referring to Richard Feynman even though he can't remember from whom he first heard of Feynman or from whom he ever heard of Feynman. He knows that Feynman is a famous physicist. A certain passage of communication reaching ultimately to the man himself does reach the speaker. He then is referring to Feynman even though he can't identify him uniquely.[25]

So the name "N" refers to some x if there is a chain of *reference-preserving links* originating in the baptism or dubbing, which fixes x to the name "N." But the model as described by Kripke bears no resemblance to the multiple-authorship model I described earlier. In the case of the author taking over from Moses, he needs to use the word "Moses" so as to continue the anaphoric chain that runs through the first five books, which requires some knowledge of that actual chain of tokens, the rules of use for that text, conventions of that genre, and so on. He is not taking over, as in the case of Kripke's Feynmann example, with some vague knowledge of the name "Moses" mentioned to him when he took over as the new author. It would be the same for a writer taking over authorship of a serial drama. For example, "Jac is characterised as a highly ambitious, forthright surgeon who is career-oriented. Her backstory states that her mother placed her in foster care aged twelve. Jac struggles to form relationships, but establishes rivalries and uses sexual manipulation to her benefit, engaging in romances with multiple colleagues." The author must come to the serial drama with a precise knowledge of everything the audience knows (or would be expected to know) about the specific character. Journalists follow similar rules, namely using those that would apply were the appropriate texts bound together in an appropriate order of reading.

By contrast, on Kripke's account the answer to the question about the reference of "God" and "Allah" would depend on which supernatural being the respective chains of reference are attached to (assuming there is any such being). Niketas of Byzantium argued that the revelations of Muhammad were really from some kind of demon, so that the chain of communication extending from the Prophet to the Quran, and then to millions of believers, originated in that demon. Thus, when the Quran uses the indexical "we," it is the demon who is speaking, and so "we" refers to him, not to the Christian or Hebrew God. More recently, Lydia McGrew of the Gospel Coalition has defended a similar idea.

> Suppose I invent a religion according to which I, Lydia McGrew, am identical to the One who made special revelations to Abraham as told in the biblical stories. My sincere followers sincerely think they are worshiping the God of Abraham when they worship me. Does that mean Lydians, Christians, and Jews all worship the same God?[26]

McGrew would argue that it does not follow that we have the same object of worship, since there is no single being that is causally responsible for the beliefs of the Lydians and the Christians, or the beliefs of the Lydians and Jews. One is McGrew herself, the other is God himself. Lydians and Christians worship different beings (even if they don't realize this) because the cause of their beliefs would be different.

The causal theory is attended by a number of problems. The most well known is finding a criterion for the *right* kind of causal chain. As Kripke himself notes, "not every sort of causal chain reaching from me to a certain man will do for me to make a reference."[27] For example, there is a causal chain from our use of the proper name "Santa Claus" to a certain historical character, but Kripke thinks it unlikely that the name refers to *him*. Even if a name does refer, the causal link must be of the right kind. If I hear the name "Napoleon" and decide it would be a nice name for my pet aardvark, my new imposition does not refer to the French emperor of that name. Kripke suggests, "The receiver of the name must, I think, *intend* when he learns it to use it *with the same reference* as the man from whom he heard it."[28] But to use it with the same *reference*, the name must have the same *referent*, yet Kripke has claimed that someone can refer to, for example, Feynman, even though he can't *identify him uniquely*. How can we intend to refer to someone who we can't identify, given we agree on the pre-theoretical notion of reference as telling the hearer *which* person we are talking about?

Bianchi and others have suggested that reference is somehow *borrowed*, and that this is achieved by *repetition* of the singular term introduced by some fixing process.[29] However, as I have argued, mere repetition is not enough where there are potentially ambiguous names, which is why Mary Magdalene is qualified as *Magdalene*, similarly Mary *the mother of James and Joseph*. Nor is reference borrowed in any sense, for reference is under the continued ownership and possession of the text: it is the *pen* which is borrowed. Think of the different authors of the books of the Hebrew Bible using the name "Moses," or the different writers of a serial who want to write (as it were) *about* the same fictional character. It is enough, when they take up the pen, that they have acquired a knowledge of the twists and turns of the plot and of the different characters in the plot, real or imaginary, the conventions of the genre, and so on, and they must have a strong sense of which names or descriptions the readers might find ambiguous. If they are able to do so, the text alone determines the reference, that is, the *co*-reference of the names.

As I have argued earlier, we can apply the same rule to virtual texts, both written and spoken. Suppose a reporter moves to some region of a distant English-speaking country to work in the local media. He comes across the name "John Smith" that recurs in recent reports. He knows immediately that if he uses that name without qualification, the readers will take it as co-referential with the previous recurring tokens, otherwise he would have qualified it accordingly. If he receives a story containing that name, he will (if he is a good journalist) check that it does co-refer. So he has borrowed the pen, or shared it with other reporters of the same set of stories. But the reference itself belongs to the tokens of the words in their specific context, and is not "borrowed." Hence repetition by itself is not sufficient for the reference of a proper name, but rather its context within a text or virtual text determines its reference.

For the same reason, I can talk about *Goliath*, that is, the Philistine who was said to have been killed by David in 1 Samuel 17. If I use the name, as I do now, indicating its origin in that passage, my use of the name co-refers with the name in the passage. Its use outside that context is irrelevant, contrary to what Evans has concluded from the fact that, according to modern biblical scholarship, the man that the *Philistines* knew as "Goliath" was killed by Elhanan of Bethlehem, as stated in 2 Samuel 21:19,[30] and that David actually killed another Philistine, the man referred to mostly as "the Philistine" in 1 Samuel 17.[31] This leads Evans to use the name to refer to the Philistine that Elhanan killed, saying "David is thought [i.e., by scholars] to have killed a Philistine but not *Goliath*."[32] This is wrong. 1 Samuel 17:4 says that there was *a* champion from the camp of the Philistines, whom the *text* calls "Goliath." The indefinite description "a champion" introduces a term to which terms like "the champion," "the Philistine," and "Goliath" can refer back. Verse 23 says that *Goliath* spoke to David, from which point on he is referred to as "this Philistine" or "the Philistine."[33] For example, verse 49 says that David killed *the* Philistine, that is, the very same Philistine referred to earlier as "Goliath."

So it *was* Goliath that David killed, for the name "Goliath" as I use it here, co-refers with verse 23. When I use the proper name "Goliath" here, I am continuing the chain of co-reference originating in 1 Samuel 17. It may also be true, if the scholars are right, that Goliath was not called "Goliath" back in the day, and that someone else was so-called, but that is irrelevant to the meaning of the name as *we* use it. The original context of its use is no longer available. David may not have killed a Philistine so-called by his contemporaries, but he was said to have killed a man so-called by *us*. For the name "Goliath" to refer to Goliath, my use of the name in this text must co-refer with the name as it is used in 1 Samuel 17.

Likewise, the *intended* reference is irrelevant. Evans clearly intends "Goliath," as *he* uses it, to refer to a different Philistine from the one that David is supposed to have killed. As I argued before (chapter 2), there is nearly always a natural interpretation of the reference of any part of a text, suggesting that co-reference is a real and objective property of a text, rather than the author's *unmediated* intention, which is necessarily unknown unless we are telepathic. If Evans indicates he is referring to a biblical text (as he does), then any name he uses from that text must have the same reference as it would have *in that text*. Thus, when he uses the name "Goliath," the natural reference is to the Philistine that David is said to have killed, in 1 Samuel 17.[34]

Nor can the causal thesis easily explain the supposed "reference shift" of a proper name. In the thirteenth century, "Madagascar" was a local name for part of mainland Africa (modern day Mogadishu). Marco Polo, mistakenly thinking that he was following local usage, applied the name to the island 1,500 miles to the South. So the name has shifted from meaning "a part of mainland Africa," to "the island now so-called."[35]

Note that reference shift makes sense only if we conceive of reference as a relation between names and things. There can be no *co*-reference shift. The name "Moses" as it occurs at the end of the Hebrew Bible cannot shift its reference from when it occurs at the beginning. Either we understand that it co-refers, or not, and if not, we have not understood the name at all. For precisely the same reason, pronouns cannot "shift their reference."

That is true for an *actual* text, but as I have argued, it is true for a virtual text, such as the utterances and writings of the local community of users in thirteenth-century Mogadishu. The locals would have used the name "Madagascar" on the understanding that it co-referred with the other tokens of that name as used in that community. If no co-reference was possible, then there was nothing to understand. Note once again that the author's intentions or mental states or acquaintance with any individual are irrelevant. For example, Burgess suggests that when a reference is passed on from X to Y, Y needs to be "sufficiently acquainted" with the object referred to.[36] But this type of acquaintance is irrelevant. Marco Polo's acquaintance with a geographical location in Africa was a psychological state he could not share with his Western European readers, who were not part of the African community of name users. The only relevant acquaintance was the scholarly community in Western Europe, outside the African tradition. Hence, for Marco's Western readers, the African sense of "Madagascar" was unavailable, although they would have understood names like "Rome," "London," and "Paris,"[37] just as a modern audience would understand them, although with that audience being international, they would now understand "Mogadishu" and "Madagascar." But no one in Western Europe had come across that name until Marco (or rather his co-writer Rustichello da Pisa) effectively introduced a new chain of co-reference: "Madagascar . . . it . . . this island . . . the island. . . ." Since he was *introducing* a name to his readers, there was no "reference shift" because there was no reference to begin with, and so the name had a different sense from the one understood in the African community of reference.

Another problem for the causal theory is explaining how the chain becomes anchored to the referent, particularly in cases where the name is introduced in circumstances where we are unable to identify the referent. Mark indicates that he knows who the young fugitive is, but he declines to tell us. The purpose of the indefinite noun phrase "a certain man" is precisely to avoid telling us *who* the man is. We can form a referential chain of co-referring terms starting with the indefinite introduction, but the chain is not *tethered* to any fixed point. There is the illusion of such a fixed point, in that we can form a reference statement, which mentions some token in the chain, then uses a token that co-refers with the chain, thus "the term 'he' refers to *the young man*." But as explained in chapter 3, this is an illusion, just like the illusion that the earth is a fixed point in absolute space.

As for Niketas' argument that the revelations of Muhammad were really received from some kind of devil or demon, suppose I hack into Donald Trump's Twitter account and write "I have just converted to Marxism, and I support the historically determined rights of the oppressed proletariat to overthrow capitalism and take control of the means of production," or some other statement expressing views hitherto not associated with Trump. I am not the same person as Trump, and if my post causes people to believe that Trump has converted to Marxism, my action has been the direct cause of this false belief. Hence, according to the causal theory, they have a belief about *me*. But the term "I" appearing in a post or article accredited to "Donald Trump," is equivalent to the "I" in "'I am a Marxist' *said* Donald Trump," so that the indexical "I" refers to Trump, and is understood as such, and so people believe that *Trump* has converted to Marxism, and not that I have.[38] Of course, they believe that the author of the post is a Marxist, and I am the author of the post. But they also believe that the author of the post is Trump.

The reference of the pronoun, in that context, is to him and not to me. Niketas argues that there is a kind of fraud involved in cases like this, which is true, but it can only be fraud if people have a false belief because of it, and, of course, the false belief is precisely that *God*, that is, the Christian God, has no partners, that is, is not triune: it would not be a deception if they thought that it was the *demon* who has no partners. And the demon is silent about his real name precisely to avoid Muslims thinking that the demon is responsible for all this. It is only by successful reference to the true God that the deceiver convinces Muslims to have false thoughts *about* him. Thus, the causal connection between author of the utterance and the utterance is irrelevant. It is how the authorship is signified that matters, and that is all.

In summary, "chains of communication" certainly exist, but the paradigm is the chain of reference that connects the multiple tokens of "Moses" in the multiple-authored texts of the Hebrew, Christian, and Islamic scriptures. The identity of the author is almost immaterial. We don't know for certain who wrote "*Moses* was tending the flock of Jethro" (Ex. 3:1), "the law was given through *Moses*" (John 1:17) or "Allah spoke to Moses with [direct] speech." (Quran 4:164), but the meaning of the names is given through the meaning of the three texts as a whole. The reference is not borrowed, for it belongs to the texts, nor does the chain of communication need to be anchored to reality via some extralinguistic relation. The causal theory, by contrast, is hardly a theory, as Kripke seems to acknowledge:

> I may not have presented a theory, but I do think that I have presented a *better picture* than that given by description theorists.[39]

But hardly a *good* picture, for the reasons noted. Thus, Bianchi, writing more than forty years after Kripke's seminal work, complains that we still do not possess a fully blown theory built on the sketch provided by Kripke.[40]

THE NAME "GOD"

With the above in mind, I turn to the central question of whether the *everyday* use of the name "God" is referential or descriptive. As I argued earlier (chapter 5), a scriptural commentary has to use the name in the referential sense. When Spinoza writes "God [Deus] was angry with him [Balak],"[41] he is referring back to Exodus 4:24–26.[42] Scripture and commentary together form a virtual narrative, where every token of the name "God" co-refers. The same applies to any form of prayer that is explicitly connected to the scriptures. For example, "God loved the world so much that he gave his one and only Son," which is from John 3:16, but also part of the Anglican

Common Prayer. There are also formulas whose connection is implicit only, such as Nicene Creed, based on Paul's letter to the Colossians ("For in him all things were created").[43] The Magnificat, which has many settings from composers as Palestrina, Bach and Mozart, and which is a standard part of the Anglican liturgy, is taken directly from Luke 1:46–55, which, in turn, seems to be modeled on Hannah's song in 1 Samuel 2:1–10. Any usage with such a location in the scriptures, or in dogma, doctrine, liturgy, and so on, has to be referential rather than descriptive. To understand the reference, *qua* reference, that is, in order to know which being is being referred to when we hear, for example, "My soul glorifies *the Lord*, and my spirit rejoices in *God my Saviour*," it is both sufficient to understand the text on which it is based, and we do not have to have any particular conception of God to do so. When the Archbishop of Canterbury says "God has no ambitions and seeks no final goal beyond restored relationship," we understand the allusion to Romans 5:10. Indeed, even if we *don't* grasp the allusion, it is sufficient that a senior Anglican churchman, and not the Dalai Lama, has uttered it (although the Dalai Lama would be more likely to say something like "God exists or God does not exist").

To be sure, the meaning of a popular or everyday name may change over time. The name "Allah" may have had a different meaning before Islam. The name itself probably predates Islam, as attested by the Quran itself. "If you asked them, 'Who created the heavens and earth and subjected the sun and the moon?' they would surely say, 'Allah.' . . . And if you asked them, 'Who sends down rain from the sky and gives life thereby to the earth after its lifelessness?' they would surely say 'Allah.'"[44] But we have little idea what the name meant before Islam, and in any case it is *the Quran itself* that establishes its meaning now. It abjures believers not to bow down "before Sun and Moon" (Quran 41:37), meaning that Allah cannot be identified with gods of Sun or Moon. It is possible that Allah was worshipped as one of many gods, explaining the injunction not to associate partners with Allah. For this reason, Christian apologists sometimes argue that "Allah" cannot refer to God, but this does not follow. Muslims in the Islamic period only had the Quranic text as a starting point. If they believed that the Quran was referring to the God of Abraham, that is, if that is how they understood the reference of "Allah," then that was how it referred, and that is how it refers now, as I have argued, because we still have access to the text of the Quran.

Once again, this does not mean that personal conceptions are relevant to understanding the name "God." According to Michael Sudduth, if Jake thinks of God as a being with properties A, B, C, and D, and Mark thinks of him as possessing properties B, C, D, and E, then these descriptive conceptions are broadly aligned (so long as A and E are not inconsistent, such as being triune and not triune respectively), and so these conceptions are as it were *of* or *about* the same God, whereas if Mary thinks of God as a being possessing properties E, F, G, and H, then there is less reason to believe that she is thinking of the same God.⁴⁵ But this would not explain how we understand surveys, such as those conducted by the Pew Research Center, such as the one in 2009, which stated that "more than eight in ten Americans (83%) say they believe in *God* and 12% believe in *a universal spirit or higher power.*"⁴⁶ Although "a universal spirit or higher power" is clearly a form of description, "God" must refer to the God of the Christian scriptures, given that the survey was of Americans. Note the disquotational move from assent to a proposition containing the name "God" (in the replies to the survey) to a report about the belief, which *uses* the name. The report assumes the reader will understand the virtual narrative that is its context, and their personal conceptions of God are irrelevant. Someone who thinks of God as a kindly man can understand the reference equally well as one who thinks of him as an avatar emitting a brilliant radiance that is fatal to humans. Even an atheist can understand the proposition that eight in ten Americans say they believe in *God*.

What about the philosopher-theologians who have used the term "God" through the centuries? Their use of the name is semantically dependent on the scriptures also. When Aquinas says "It is said in the person of *God*: 'I am Who I am'" (*Summa* I q. 2 a. 3, quoting Exodus 3:14), he clearly does not mean the existence of some abstract being, but rather of the being who is quoted in Exodus as uttering the words "I am Who am."⁴⁷ This assumption extended to the translations from Arabic of the works of Islamic philosophers into Latin. The Arabic term "Allah" was always translated "deus," while the epithets of Allah were rendered in Latin as "altissimus" (the most high) and "gloriosissimus" (the most glorious), and the "basmalla" ("bismi al-lāhi al-rraḥmāni al-rraḥīmi"—in the name of Allah, the Beneficent, the Merciful), with which every Islamic author's work began, was regularly translated as "In nomine Dei pii et misericordis."⁴⁸

Of course, Aquinas assigns a set of divine attributes to God, such as a first mover, first efficient cause, cause of the being of all beings, their goodness, and so on. But this does not mean that these attributes figure in the *meaning* of the name "God." In question 6 of Part I of his *Summa Theologiae*, he asks whether God is good. But if "good" were part of the meaning of "God," why would he be asking that? And why does he adduce a biblical quotation in support of God being good (Lamentations 3:25: "The Lord is good to those whose hope is in him")? It would be like asking if any bachelor was unmarried, then quoting the dictionary. In question 7, he asks whether God is infinite, in question 9 whether he is immutable, and so on. In each case he quotes the Bible, or some biblical authority in support of his claim. Of course, God is good, but we can always wonder whether he might not have been good, or ponder the counterfactual situation in which he was not. As I argued in the chapter on identity, even if the God of the scriptures is identical with the God of the philosophers, it does not follow that they are *necessarily* identical. Not only is the everyday use of the name "God" co-referential, rather than descriptive, so also is the name as used by the philosopher-theologians themselves.

SUMMARY

Aquinas claims that *everyone* calls the first cause "God." But this is an unjustified assumption about the everyday use of the name "God." I have argued that there is no "standard" use of a proper name outside of a specific context (journalism, philosophical papers, scriptures, works of theology), and to understand the name in context requires the availability of an appropriate narrative, or *virtual* narrative. Such a narrative is available in the scriptures, which even Aquinas and the classical theists depend on to determine a reference for "God," using the sorts of rule for co-reference that I discussed earlier, and earlier. Aquinas does not mean what 12 percent of Americans mean by "a universal spirit or higher power" (which could be any universal spirit such as the "Great Mystery" of the American Sioux, or Vishnu, or Zeus or Mazda), but rather the being that 83 percent of Americans refer to as "God," the God of the Christian scriptures and liturgy. The classical conception involves identifying God by some set of attributes that uniquely characterize *some* being, that is, in the Russellian way where every term can be understood by someone who understands standard English, independent of any semantic connection with the scriptures. But such a description does not tell us which being this is, and is thus not equivalent to an ordinary language description, such as "the God of Abraham" and "the Lord of hosts." The everyday use of the name "God" is referential, therefore *co*-referential.

This suggests a further problem. If all definite referential identification is relative to a text, and if the text as a whole amounts to a huge indefinite description, how can we refer to the world itself? How can we refer to *God* himself? Next, I shall consider whether some *demonstrative* or indexical conception of reality is available to us.

NOTES

1. Locke, *An Essay Concerning Human Understanding*, III.ii.2.
2. Kripke, "A puzzle about belief."
3. Kripke gives two formulations of the puzzle, the first concerning the name "London" (Ibid., 119), which has an extra layer of mostly irrelevant complexity, and

the second about "Paderewski" (Ibid., 130). The assumptions that follow are common to both.

4. Kripke stipulates "sincere and reflective" assent. Since I feel these qualifications are built into the meaning of "assent" (which is more than just saying "yes"), I omit the stipulation. Readers who feel that they are necessary can mentally supply them.

5. Kripke, "A puzzle about belief," 256. This is in the context of Peter's beliefs about London, rather than Paderewski, but the same point applies.

6. Kripke, "A puzzle about belief," 249.

7. Malachi 4:4.

8. Other than Mary Magdalene, of course, since there were only two Marys at the tomb. Mary, mother of Jesus, was not present at that point, although confusingly she also had sons called James and Joseph, common names in first-century Galilee.

9. (i) Parliamentary report for Monday July 18, 1870, Saturday July 23, 1870 edition, (ii) Parliamentary report for Monday August 1, 1870, Saturday August 6, 1870 edition.

10. *Mainichi Daily News*, August 8, 1961, quoted in *Bertrand Russell's America*, 135. Lightly edited. The occasion was the sixteenth anniversary of the dropping atomic bomb on Hiroshima. There is a recording in the McMaster archives, http://pw20c.mcmaster.ca/case-study/fused-fizzing-and-ready-go-bertrand-russell-takes-streets.

11. John Francis Russell, 7th Earl Russell, born 1971, succeeded to the title in 2014. Devitt, "Against direct reference," 488 makes a similar point about Russell the *logician* and Russell the *peace marcher*.

12. Baldwin, "G.E. Moore and the Cambridge School of Analysis," 446.

13. Perhaps a very long time, given that the very oldest writing dates back to the seventh millennium BC.

14. For example, of the name Gabriel (Jibril) "Muhammad seems to have been able to assume in his Madinan audience *some familiarity with the name*, and the probabilities are that it came to him in its Syriac form" (Jeffery, *The Foreign Vocabulary of the Qur'ān*, 101).

15. Jeffery, *The Foreign Vocabulary of the Qur'ān*, 1.

16. A similar assumption is made by Marcus ("Discussion on the paper of Ruth B. Marcus," 142): a genuine proper name is really a tag, and even if its bearer had more than one such tag, "there would be a way of finding out such as having recourse to a dictionary or some analogous inquiry, which would resolve the question as to whether the two tags denote the same thing."

17. Kripke, "A puzzle about belief," 265.

18. For example, London Ontario, Holland Manitoba.

19. My emphasis. Similarly, "Kylie" redirects to Kylie Minogue, Einstein to Albert Einstein.

20. I put scare quotes around "talking about" given that, in the view presented here, there is no word-world relation corresponding to "about." See chapter 10 on intentionality.

21. Outlined in Kripke, *Naming and Necessity*, 95 and *passim*.

22. Kripke, *Naming and Necessity*, 95. According to Wettstein ("On referents and reference fixing," 117n), Kripke has denied in conversation that he meant to emphasize "causal."

23. Kripke, *Naming and Necessity*, 96.

24. Ibid., 91.

25. Ibid.

26. "The 'Same God' debate is too important to leave to philosophers," Lydia Mcgrew, 2016, https://www.thegospelcoalition.org/article/the-same-god-debate-is-too-important-to-leave-to-philosophers.

27. Kripke, *Naming and Necessity*, 93.

28. Ibid., 96.

29. "What makes it the case that the sound with which my earlier utterance of the sentence 'Giulia is not in the room' began referring to Giulia? Well, precisely the fact that that sound was a repetition of a linguistic particular that had been introduced, more than twenty-four years ago, for Giulia" (Bianchi, *On Reference*, 103).

30. Evans, "The causal theory of names," 12. In fact, there is no scholarly consensus, and the reading depends on which of 2 Samuel 21:19 and 1 Chronicles 20:5 is corrupt. The theory mentioned by Evans, citing Robinson *A History of Israel*, is that 1 Chronicles, which says that Elhanan killed Lahmi, the *brother* of Goliath, is corrupt. However Provan (*A Biblical History of Israel*, 224–5) suggests that 2 Samuel is equally likely to be a scribal error, resulting from a confusion between eṭ-laḥmî (Lahmi) and bêṯhallaḥmî (Bethlehem).

31. For example, 1 Samuel 17:50 "David prevailed over *the Philistine* with a sling and with a stone, and smote *the Philistine*, and slew *him*." "The Philistine" is only referred to as Goliath in verses 4 and 23, and once again in 1 Sam 21:9. Another theory is that David was the same person as Elhanan. See Ps Jerome in his questions on Samuel, and the medieval Jewish authors of the Targum Jonathan.

32. Evans, "The causal theory of names," 11.

33. In the translation, of course.

34. Of course, some scholars may themselves use the name "Goliath" in a different way, to refer to the other Philistine mentioned in 2 Samuel 21, and so long as they restrict their use to scholarly discourse, the reference will be unambiguous. Perhaps Professor Robinson utters "David did not kill Goliath." Then, so long as this is part of scholarly discourse, his intended referent (the Philistine of 2 Samuel 21) will be the natural referent. But if, outside this context, we apply disquotation "Robinson thinks *that* David did not kill Goliath," then the natural reference is to 1 Samuel 17. This is why Evans' remark that "David is *thought* [by scholars] to have killed a Philistine but not Goliath" is confusing and wrong. These scholars *do* think that David killed Goliath, but (like the Philistines) they don't call him by that name, and when they utter "David did not kill Goliath," they are not referring to Goliath.

35. Evans, "The causal theory of names," 195. As Burgess ("Madagascar revisited") has pointed out, and as Marco Polo's *Travels* makes clear, Evans does not correctly describe the situation. Marco *was* talking about the place now known as Mogadishu. He says it is a thousand miles of the island of Soccotera (Socotra), and

what he says about it agrees with what we know of fourteenth-century Mogadishu. However, he wrongly believed it was an island, rather than part of mainland Africa. Later cartographers, for example, Ortelius, not finding an island in the horn of Africa, transferred the name to the island we now know as Madagascar.

36. Burgess, "Madagascar revisited," 198.

37. Ockham writes "Pepper is sold here and at *Rome*" (*Summa Logicae* I.66) and "Socrates is in *London*" (*Summa Logicae* III.3.45), confident that his readers understand those names. Not necessarily because they are physically acquainted with either place, but because they understand the co-reference.

38. Likewise, the book *David Copperfield* begins "I am born," yet I don't believe that David Copperfield actually wrote that, nor do I think that "I" refers to Charles Dickens.

39. Kripke, *Naming and Necessity*, 97, my emphasis.

40. *On Reference*, 2015, 94.

41. *Theological-Political Treatise* ch. 3 (2007 ed., 51).

42. Spinoza also mentions a figurative use of the name, such as "a wind was sent by God," meaning a powerful wind occurred. "Spirit of God" can mean a dry or violent wind (see Isa. 40:7, or Gen. 1:2) where "spirit of God" means a dry, violent, and fatal wind, "a wind of God," or it can mean a great heart (Ex. 31.3), or the mental depression of Saul is called "an evil spirit from God" (1 Samuel 16:14). But "the patience of Job," while used figuratively, nonetheless refers to Job.

43. Colossians 1:16.

44. Quran 29:61, 63.

45. Sudduth, *The Reformed Objection to Natural Theology*, 196.

46. David Masci, "Religion and Science in the United States," Pew Research Centre, 2009.

47. Sudduth, *The Reformed Objection to Natural Theology*, 197: "In natural theology . . . God is described in a way that at least overlaps with *the biblical description of God*, for traditionally natural theology describes God as an immaterial person with unlimited power, knowledge, and goodness, and who is the independent, eternal, and unchanging creator of the universe." See also Stump, *The God of the Bible and the God of the Philosophers*, who notes (37) how the great medieval thinkers also wrote biblical commentaries "without giving any indication of unease at the combination of biblical stories and classical theism. And there are really are not two Aquinas's, one who wrote the questions of the divine attributes in the Prima Pars of the Summa, and one who wrote biblical commentaries" (Ibid., 55).

48. Thanks to Charles Burnett and Olga Lizzini for their help with this question.

Chapter 10

Revelation

Years ago a picture was sent to a London auction house for valuation. The expert who examined it failed to recognize the subject and sent it to auction entitled "Three Figures in a Landscape." There is a sort of irony here, since the subject of the picture was a story about people who, like the expert, were unable to recognize an individual whose identity they already knew. The story (Luke 24) tells how two disciples were returning from Jerusalem to a village called Emmaus, when a man came and walked beside them, "but they were kept from recognising him." They told the man about a prophet who was sentenced and crucified three days ago, and how their companions went to the tomb but did not see him. They ate with the stranger, who took bread, gave thanks, broke it, and began to give it to them. Then they recognized him.

There are many stories about those who have initially failed to identify God or his avatars, but later come to recognize him, often through a sudden realization or revelation. Genesis 32 tells how Jacob, waiting in the darkness at the ford of the Jabbok River, was set upon by a stranger who wrestled with him until dawn. Jacob overcame him, though not without injuring his hip. "Please tell me your name," asked Jacob, upon which the man revealed his identity. Samuel heard a voice calling, and ran to Eli. "Here I am; *you* called me."[1] Eli had not called him, and told him to go back and lie down. Samuel heard the voice again, and again ran to Eli, who again had not called. The third time it was Eli who realized who was calling, and who set Samuel straight. While Gideon was under the oak in Ophrah threshing wheat in a winepress (Judges 6), he heard God commanding him to save Israel. Yet he oddly asked for a sign "that it is really *you* talking to me."[2] The Jews gathered around Jesus (John 10) and asked him to tell who he was. Jesus said he had already told them, but they did not believe. "My sheep listen to my voice; I know them, and they follow me."[3] As Mary Magdalene was weeping by the tomb (John 20), she turned round to see a man who she at first took to be the gardener. "Woman, why are you weeping? Whom are you seeking?" After he uttered her name, she recognized him. Muhammad had doubts whether it was really the angel Gabriel who was revealed the Quran to him. "So *if you are in doubt*, [O Muhammad], about that which We [God] have revealed to you, then ask those who have been reading the Scripture before you. The truth has *certainly* come to you from your Lord, so never be among the *doubters*."[4]

The forms of reference and identification I have discussed so far involve an *intra*linguistic semantic connection between propositions that allows us to identify a character within the framework of a narrative by grasping, which individual a character is the *same* as. There is a straightforward understanding of reference statements under which reference statements using proper names, pronouns, or definite descriptions are themselves true only for intralinguistic reasons. The fact that "Moses" refers to the prophet of the Torah is not true because of any relation between language and reality. But there are ways of identifying a person which require an individual to be revealed to us through some form of extralinguistic perception (perhaps extra-sensory or supernatural perception) that would be impossible through solely linguistic means. Anglican bishop Mouneer Hanna Anis of Egypt said "For us as Christians, and only by his grace, God has *revealed* himself in the person of his son Jesus Christ, whom Muslims do not *know* in this way." If God is revealed to us in this way, perhaps we can say (pointing to God) that "God" refers to *this being*. If the world is available to us through direct perception, perhaps God is available to us through divine revelation. It is time to discuss demonstrative identification.

DEMONSTRATIVE IDENTIFICATION

If all reference is intralinguistic, and thus in a sense *relative* to a text, how can identification be extralinguistic? The question prompted Strawson to seek "a requirement stringent enough to eliminate relative identification."[5] He sought to ground identification in terms of *demonstrative* identification, arguing that even if an individual cannot itself be demonstratively identified, "it may be identified by a description which relates it uniquely to another particular which can be demonstratively identified."[6] Many other philosophers of language have respected demonstrative identification as the archetype of genuine reference. It requires, as Castañeda says,[7] items that are "present in experience," and it is supposedly "our most basic means of identifying the objects and events we experience and think about." It attains an almost mystical prominence in the work of Gareth Evans, who claims that a genuinely singular proposition expresses a *Russellian* thought: one that simply cannot exist in the absence of the object thought about:

> [Philosophers] recognise the possibility, perhaps as a limiting case, of thinking of an object by description: as one may think of a man, some African warrior perhaps,[8] when one thinks that the tallest man in the world is thus and so. But, again ... they cherish the idea of a more "intimate," more "direct" relation in which a subject may stand to an object (a situation in which the subject would be "en rapport with" with the object), and the idea that when a subject and his audience are both situated vis-a-vis an object in this way, there exists the possibility of using singular terms to refer to, and to talk about, that object in quite a different way—expressing thoughts *which would not have been available to be thought and expressed if the object had not existed.*[9]

If this is correct, demonstrative thought is semantically dependent not on other linguistic items, but on reality itself. I shall argue that it is not thus dependent.

I shall discuss mostly visual information, which requires *images*, that is, structured light sources of any kind. Images can be natural, such as the light-reflecting surfaces of material objects, the reflections from the silvered surface of a mirror, or they can be artificial. Before the nineteenth century, artificial images included colored pigment on parchment, and oil on canvas, painted murals. After the development of photography and other technology, images include photographic film, the phosphor used in cathode ray tubes, and liquid crystal, currently the source for all the images projected by the internet, and the words on the screen that I am typing now.

Images in this sense should *not* be confused with philosophical "sense data," supposedly mental representations of external objects, having only an internal or psychical mode of existence, private to the one perceiving. The eighteenth-century philosopher David Hume (1711–1766) called these representations "impressions"—entities that cease to exist when we shut our eyes, and begin to exist again when we open them, which (according to Hume) we mistakenly identify with the visible surfaces of material objects. These are *not* what I have in mind. The images I have in mind have an objective, verifiable and public existence. They include the virtual images lurking behind mirrors, or beneath the surface of the water, for other people can see such images, they can be photographed, and their location measured. We can *see* images, whereas we cannot "see" sense data, but supposedly stand in a different relation to them, such as sensing or intuiting. *Pace* Hume, the image of the bowl on this table does not cease to exist when I shut my eyes, assuming there is still a light source, but maintains its being until the room is in complete darkness. Furthermore, it constitutes the *whole* surface of an object, whereas a sense datum, as early twentieth-century philosophers understood it, is defined by the observer's point of view. When I look at the front of the bowl, the sense datum corresponds to the front surface "as I sense it." I can go round to the back, and thus have a sense datum corresponding to the back surface of the bowl. But I cannot have both; such a thing would be impossible to imagine. Yet, so long as light is striking the bowl, its image belongs to its entire surface.

Images, as I define them, do not persist in time, since the light emitted or reflected from the surface of the object is different at any point in time. But unless the surface of the object changes significantly, the images belonging to it will be qualitatively (although not numerically) identical. I shall speak of qualitative identity in two senses. Two images have strict qualitative identity when every point in one image has the same tone and hue as the corresponding point in the other, as with a digital copy of an image, or two photographs made from the same negative. They are loosely identical or similar when people would be likely to identify them as belonging to the same object, even when under different lighting conditions, or their surfaces are similar but undetectably different. Think of different images of identical twins.

SAMENESS OF CHARACTER

An image can be *of* an object in two senses. It can *belong* to an object, by being the light-emitting surface of it. The pigments of a painting of the Last Supper *belong* to the canvas. But it can also *represent* a scene such as the Last Supper. Likewise, a picture of the prime minister on television represents her, but it *belongs* to the phosphor screen, or the light-emitting liquid crystals that project the image. The façade of a film set may represent a city street, but it belongs to the various bits of scaffolding and the carpentry behind the paint and so forth. All pictorial representation involves a sort of illusion, namely that the image we see belongs to a different object than the one in fact it belongs to: that it is not the light reflected from painted canvas, or emitted from a liquid crystal screen, but rather from the skin of a person's face. It represents a state of affairs—possibly a non-existing state of affairs—that there is a person somewhere of such-and-such an appearance, that this person is speaking, or acting, in a certain way.

Hence, the verb "belongs to" is *logically transitive* in the sense I introduced earlier.[10] The light-emitting surface *of* a picture is "of" or belongs to the picture in the sense that it is a part of it, and so belongs to it, and so the picture (the canvas, the gilt frame, the nails which attach them, and so on) must exist. If some image belongs to an F, there must be such a thing as an F. Verbs of representation by contrast are "logically intransitive." The "of" in the verb phrase "is a picture of" does not signify belonging in this sense, and the phrase is logically intransitive. The statement "this is a picture *of* a centaur" can be true even though there is no such a thing as a centaur.

Contrary to the standard theory espoused by Evans and others, it is not necessary that an object exist for us to demonstratively express a thought that can be understood by others. I point to the image of Mitchell Lewis, the actor playing Herod in the 1923 silent film *Salomé*,[11] uttering "*that* is Herod." So long as you can see his image on the screen, you understand me. Yet Herod does not exist any longer. I can also say "that is Mitchell Lewis," meaning the actor who is (or rather *was*) playing Herod. Lewis no longer exists either, having died in 1956. We can look to a Poussin and think "*that* is Venus" or "*that* is a faun," but as far as we know there was never any person such as Venus, nor any such things as fauns. Of course, there is a sense in which the identification is more intimate in virtue of the characters being portrayed vividly in a work of art, but we can have no intimate relation with Venus and the fauns, given that they do not exist.

Nor is it necessary, *pace* Castañeda, for an object to be before us in order to make a demonstrative reference. "If *you* (pointing to the actor playing Pilate) let *this man* (pointing to the actor playing Jesus) go, you are no friend of Caesar." The demonstrative terms "you" and "this man" clearly do not refer to the actors playing Pilate and Jesus, respectively, who the audience perceive, but to Pilate and Jesus, who they do not perceive, at least not in any standard sense of the verb "perceive." We use names as symbols for objects when it is not possible to have the objects before us, but demonstrative terms are no different. Even when the objects are "before" us, they are always hidden by their images. We point to "the" moon, but the moon is forever hidden by its surface. We say "*this* is France" as we approach the shore at Calais, even though most of France is hidden by the curvature of the earth.

Hence, we can tell stories with pictures just we can as with words. With such pictorial stories, there is an analog to co-reference, which I shall call "sameness of character." A *character* is an individual portrayed or depicted to exist in some image. The character will typically be different from the person to whom the image belongs. When we cannot specify the characters depicted by two different images without using a singular term, then I shall say that the images depict the *same* character. For example:

> On the last word of the rhyme, *he* swings the axe towards the door, splitting the top door panel. The camera then turns to the other side of the door though which we see *him* fit *his* head in the gap, saying "here's Johnny."

We cannot specify what is depicted in the sequence of different images without saying that a single individual swings the axe, splits the panel, and fits his head through the gap. The sequence depicts the same character.

Usually, the same actor plays the same character, but not always. A double is an actor who plays the same character as the main actor, typically in scenes which are too dangerous for the main actor, or require specific skills, or where the main actor, usually an actress, is portrayed in a situation, which she (rather than the character) would find embarrassing.[12] In Cameron's 1991 film, *Terminator 2: Judgment Day*, the T-1000 Terminator can shift his shape into any form he wants. He initially appears as a policeman, a form to which he continually returns throughout the plot, presumably to convey a continued identity to the audience. In one scene, he usurps the appearance of the prison guard Lewis, in another, the appearance of the Sarah Connor character. This was achieved in both cases by identical twin *actors*. Don Stanton plays the prison guard Lewis, his twin Dan Stanton plays the T-1000 taking on the appearance of Lewis. More confusingly, Linda Hamilton plays both Sarah Connor and the T-1000, while her twin Leslie plays Connor in the scene where Linda plays the T-1000.

The actors do not even have to resemble one another in order to portray the same character. In the film *That Obscure Object of Desire* (Luis Bunuel, 1977), the two main characters are Mathieu, a middle-aged wealthy Frenchman, and Conchita, a beautiful Spanish dancer who ensnares Mathieu. Remarkably, the character of Conchita is played by two actresses, Carole Bouquet and Angela Molina, who switch roles in alternate scenes and sometimes even in the middle of a scene. For example, Molina walks behind a curtain and Bouquet emerges from the other. Mathieu shows Bouquet through the door, cut to interior of house, where he accompanies Molina into the living room. The identity is expressed by the context. We see a woman walk through a door in the exterior, the scene cuts to a woman walking through a door into the interior, so we assume it is the same door, and the same woman. This is similar to Linda and Leslie Hamilton both playing Sarah Connor, except Bouquet and Molina don't even look remotely alike. It is all fiction— there is no woman, but the film is portraying that there *is* a woman, and that it is the *same* woman. Though the actresses do not even look similar, the context (the dress, the action and the logic of the scene) signifies the identity so convincingly that many people have seen the entire film without realizing there were different actresses (I plead guilty). Even those who realized that different actresses were playing the same character understood the *meaning* perfectly well.

Exactly how we understand when the same character is depicted is a complex question, but it is a question for semantics, not the theory of knowledge. The valuer who failed to realize that the three figures in the landscape were Christ and the two disciples simply failed to understand the picture. It was presumably in the genre of Emmaus paintings: small figures dwarfed by a landscape rendered in whatever style was fashionable in the period, such as tall trees, the remains of ancient buildings, tombs with classical inscriptions, and so on, Christ portrayed in the manner of patient teacher, perhaps dressed in white, the two disciples listening in puzzlement. These are all signs that should be understood by those taught to read classical paintings. Which is not to say that someone may fail to understand the references in a work of art. Many people do, like the valuer, but the concept of *understanding* is relevant here, not knowledge.

SAMENESS OF OBJECT

Sameness of character is when different images *represent* the same individual. Sameness of object, by contrast, is when different images *belong* to the same individual. There is a table lamp next to me while I am writing, which has been emitting a series of qualitatively identical images for the past half hour. I assume that these all belong to the same object, the lamp, and indeed I assume the same object has been emitting similar images ever since I put it there. We readily suppose, as Hume awkwardly suggests,[13] that an object may "continue individually the same, though several times absent from and present to the senses," although it is perfectly possible that someone changed the original lamp to another that exactly resembles it. What justifies this assumption? Hume argues, correctly I think, that we reason from cause and effect. We note the strong resemblance between the images, and we consider whether such a resemblance is common or not, perhaps with regard to the locality of the images. In the case of the lamp, it is highly unusual, so I assume that any image resembling it must belong to it. By contrast, the type of 60 W lightbulb that powers it is common, and while I suspect the bulb has not been changed recently, as it is mostly I who use the room, I have no strong reason to suppose that the image from it that I see now belongs to the same object as the image I saw yesterday, or a month ago.

But this sameness of object is not *signified*, as it is in art. Resemblance in art always has a reason. Similar images typically represent the same character, just as tokens of the same proper name have the same reference. Virginia Maksymowicz's *Stations of the Cross* shows the different stages of the crucifixion without any identifiable image of Jesus at all. Station I (Jesus condemned to death) shows a pair of hands, tied together, II (Jesus carries his cross) shows a single hand holding a plank of wood, III (Jesus falls the first time) shows a hand and a knee together on the ground. There is no "uncommon resemblance" in Hume's sense, but rather a series of images of body parts, which perfectly resemble any such part. But this is narrative art, in a familiar genre, and in that sense, the resemblance is uncommon. We know, or rather we *understand*, that the different images, while they could easily belong to different people, represent a single character. It is pointless to ask whether identical-looking characters in a play are identical twins, if the play never mentions the existence of such twins. Even if the same character is played by twin *actors*, it is pointless to speculate whether the *characters* are twins, unless it is the subject of the play, such as *Twelfth Night*. If the twins appear in different scenes, they might even be played by the same actor. Coincidences are rare in art, and even when they happen, it is by design. Where two images represent the same character, this is signified by a relation between the images. If the image representing a woman entering a door is followed immediately by a qualitatively similar image representing a woman coming out of the door, the same woman is signified. The director would not have placed the images in that sequence if he or she intended something else.

By contrast, where there is no art or direction, there is no signification: we simply assume that similar images belong to the same object. The armor-bearer sees a man alive at midday, and the image he sees is qualitatively identical to that of Saul, although, unbeknownst to him, it belongs to Saul's identical twin. He sees another man dead at midday, who he takes—correctly this time—to be Saul, so he infers that a man who was alive this morning is now dead. But suppose Saul was killed yesterday, and no one was killed this morning, so it is false that there was someone alive this morning who is now dead. While the image he saw in the morning was qualitatively identical to that of Saul, his inference is not valid. The images were in some sense veridical—one represented a man who was alive, the other a man who is now dead. But the second image cannot represent *the same man* as dead, for the two identical twins are not the same person.

The contrast I have drawn between sameness of character and sameness of object corresponds to my earlier contrast between referential and descriptive identity. The existence of a document describing a man called "Ioannes Duns" who was born in Maxton near Roxburgh, and of another document about a man called "Iohannes Douns" who was licensed to hear confession in 1300, makes it probable that a person born in Maxton was licensed to hear confession in 1300. Likewise, the uncommon resemblance between the woman who is passing my window now, and the woman who lives next door, suggests that she is the same person, and not some identical twin, up from the country. But these are assumptions. By contrast, if I say that Scotus was born in Maxton and *he* was licensed to hear confession in 1300, the pronoun signifies identity. Similarly if a documentary of life in our street showed first the neighbor in her house, then a person with the exactly same appearance passing our house, the identity would be signified.

It follows that the information presented by images about the objects they belong to (as opposed to the characters they represent) is of a purely indefinite character. You see a man on the road who you think you recognize. The informational content of the image is "a man who looks so-and-so."[14] You might go on to think "he is John" but, as I have argued, the identity with John is something you assume or infer, and is not any part of the informational content of the visual image.[15] You could say that perceptual information has no *thisness*. It is not a feature of perceptual content that it unambiguously identifies *this* image as belonging to *this* object.

This is not to deny the unique relationship between a definite term and its antecedent, whether the antecedent is linguistic, or an extralinguistic image. Clearly there must be such a relationship or anaphor could not exist, and a proper antecedent for a subsequent anaphoric pronoun must involve some connotation of uniqueness. But such a connotation does not have to depend on properties of *objects*. Consider story that begins "there were two identical twins," and that continues "the first (or the former) was blond, as was the second (or the latter)." Definite terms like "the former" or "the first" identify the antecedent, but without using any property that would apply in reality. It is not a property of the first twin that he is the former, nor of the second that he is the latter. Such terms identify intralinguistically. Likewise, the images that we identify by pointing, or by location are an adjunct to the language we use, and are in some sense a part of our language, and must be uniquely identified in some way.

DEMONSTRATIVE REFERENCE

We can point to the image of Christ in the Emmaus painting and say "*this* is Christ," using the demonstrative "this," but we are not referring to the *image*, which is all we perceive, but rather to Christ. (Of course, we can say "This is a *picture* of Christ," but then the demonstrative refers to the picture to which the image *belongs*.)[16] Now I have just said that *the demonstrative refers to Christ*, so aren't I making a reference statement? What makes the statement true? I have established truth conditions for *non*-demonstrative reference statements, where the statement is true if and only if the mentioned term co-refers with the used term. How do demonstrative terms co-refer?

According to the standard theory, any two terms, including demonstratives, co-refer if and only if they both pick out some object in reality by means of an extralinguistic reference relation. I have questioned the existence of such a relation where ordinary singular terms (proper names, pronouns, etc.) are involved. Such a relation may seem more plausible for demonstratives, where we seem to be in a more "intimate," more "direct" relation with the object, making it possible to express thoughts, which would not have been available to be thought and expressed if the object had not existed. But as I shall argue, even demonstrative co-reference can be explained without invoking object dependence. Consider:

This is a man (pointing to picture of Paul)
This is not a man (pointing to picture of Priscilla)

I am a man (in man's voice)
I am not a man (in woman's voice)

In each case, there is no contradiction, even though the statements have the *linguistic* form of a contradiction. "A is F" and "A is not F" cannot both be true (or both false), if both tokens of "A" have the same meaning. But clearly they don't. We cannot explain this by object dependence, for the object does not enter into the proposition. In the first case, the picture could be of a man long dead, or of a fictional character, in the second case, we could be listening to a radio program with a male and a female actor playing the different parts. It could even be the same actor uttering the female part in falsetto. It cannot be the object that explains the co-reference. Clearly the image, or the sound of the voice, is acting as a kind of supplementary sign. The demonstrative "this" is like a pronoun in that its (co)reference is constantly changing and is entirely dependent on context, but is different in that the context for a pronoun is purely linguistic, whereas the context for "this" and other indexicals is purely perceptual. It is not as though the pointing finger hits an object in reality, indicating which object satisfies a predicate, such as "being a man," or "not being a man." Rather, the sense data are a kind of addition to spoken language, where the pointing figure indicates a part of the image, and thus identifies the right *sign*, rather than the right *object*. We are not in any intimate relation with a man long dead when we point to a picture of Moses saying "this is Moses," nor does Moses need to have existed for us to entertain a thought about *this man in the picture*. The standard theory explains demonstratives no better than it explains non-demonstratives.

What about reference statements? If I say, pointing to a man, that the demonstrative "this" refers to *this* man, aren't I expressing a relation between language and the world? On the contrary, my *reference thesis* explains demonstrative statements also. According to the reference thesis, a reference statement is true if and only if the mentioned term co-refers with the term that is used. For example

This (pointing to picture) is Paul
The first word of the last sentence refers to *him* (pointing to picture again)

The reference statement is true because the mentioned term "this" in the first sentence co-refers with "him" used in the second sentence (the reference statement). We do not need object dependence to explain this. Semantic dependence will suffice. The images that supplement "this" and "him" provide the context, hence the meaning, and the meaning is that the two propositions, if true at all, must be true of a single thing. The theory of reference I have defended here can explain both demonstrative and non-demonstrative reference statements.

In summary, sense perception does not provide us with a more "intimate," more "direct" relation in which a subject may stand to an object, nor does it allow us to use singular terms to talk about the object in quite a different way. Demonstrative reference is simply another form of *co*-reference, where the context in which a singular term is used is set by sense data. When we point to an object, we make a particular kind of sign available, so that the hearer can determine whether two linguistic expressions co-refer or not.

SENSUS DIVINITATIS

The forms of reference and identity I have discussed so far involve perceptible signs or sense-images. For that reason, they cannot be *object* dependent in Evans' sense, although they may be semantically dependent on other signs. Can there be some other form of direct perception which allows identification of the kind envisaged by Evans, allowing us to entertain thoughts which would not be available if God did not exist? John Calvin thought there was a sense of Deity (*sensus divinitatis*) in all humans, not learned, but there "from the womb," which God has implanted to prevent anyone from pretending ignorance, and which nature does not allow us to forget. "There is, as the eminent pagan says, no nation so barbarous, no people so savage," says Calvin, "that they have not a deep seated conviction that there is a God."[17] Faith is not simply blind assent, which has "no dignity or value" (*Instit* 3. 11. 7), but rather knowledge by illumination. Thus, there is no reasonable non-belief in God, which Calvin claimed was the God of the *Christian* scriptures. Anyone who rejected them, namely the Turks, were "devils, for they do not keep themselves in the bounds of Holy Scripture."

Calvin's idea is the inspiration[18] behind the so-called reformed epistemology, the main proponents of which are William Alston, Alvin Plantinga, and Nicholas Wolterstorff. The target of reformed epistemology is classical foundationalism, which derives ultimately from Aristotle's view[19] that knowledge can be divided into truths, which are demonstrable from prior premises, and "immediate truths," which are indemonstrable, and which are required to avoid an infinite regress (otherwise every truth would require a prior truth, and demonstration would either be circular, or would require an infinite number of premises). Foundationalists maintain that some beliefs are "basic" and that all other beliefs inherit their knowledge or justification in virtue of receiving support from the properly basic beliefs. A properly basic belief is one that requires no justification or warrant from any other belief. Not all basic beliefs are *properly* basic. If a belief that is accepted in the basic way leads to a belief structure that is skewed (such as an admirer of Picasso believing that he didn't die and, like Elijah, "was directly transported to heaven in a peculiarly warped sort of chariot with a great misshapen eye in the middle of its side"), it is not properly basic.[20]

Plantinga does not proffer the *sensus divinitatis* as evidence for the existence of God. His claim is rather that if belief in God is the result of the sense, then this may result in knowledge, just as my belief that there is a book in front of me on the desk counts as knowledge if caused in the right way, that is, by the book reflecting light and striking my retina. "The *sensus divinitatis* resembles other belief-producing faculties or mechanisms" (p. 146). For example, upon beholding the sublime the night sky or a mountain view or the lonely desert, these divine beliefs just arise. "They are *occasioned* by the circumstances; they are not *conclusions* from them" (ibid, my emphasis). Alston contends[21] that some people have mystical experiences that may constitute such direct and non-sensory contact with God, supposedly involving a presentation of something, which the subject takes to be God, a form of perception that Alston considers to be analogous to, but different from sense perception. Beliefs formed as a result of such presentation he calls manifestation beliefs or M-beliefs.[22] Plantinga approvingly quotes the nineteenth-century Dutch theologian Hermann Bavinck, as saying that scripture "does not make God the conclusion of a syllogism, leaving it to us whether we think the argument holds or not," and that the certainty of our faith is not ultimately based on the proofs of natural theology, but rather by the "spontaneous testimony which forces itself upon us from every side." Unlike Calvin, Plantinga does not regard the sense of God as being something that "nature does not allow us to forget," but rather as a disposition that *may* (or may not) trigger belief in God. Nor is it his intention to demonstrate that the sense exists, or that it is actually the reason for belief in God. His thesis is that any beliefs that result from this faculty could be warranted, and we cannot claim that religious beliefs are irrational without showing that this account is false.

Reformed epistemology thus conflicts with the central thesis of classical foundationalism, whereby basic beliefs are restricted to those that are (i) self-evident, such as the proposition at two plus two equals four, (ii) incorrigible, or necessarily true simply by virtue of being believed, such as the belief that it *seems* to you that you see a tree, and (iii) evident to the senses, as in when you actually see a tree. Clearly belief in God cannot be based on the evidence of the senses (unless you are a prophet), nor is it self-evident or incorrigible.[23] Yet reformed epistemologists hold that belief in God can *properly* be taken as *basic*. It is entirely reasonable to believe in God, even if you have no argument for your belief, and even if you do not believe it on the basis of any other beliefs you hold. This also conflicts with the foundational assumptions of classical theism.

There is an extensive literature on reformed epistemology, but this is not a book on theory of knowledge, but the theory of meaning. In order for a divinely inspired belief to *about* God, it must be a singular belief, that is, a belief that has to be expressed by a singular proposition such as "God is speaking to me."[24] Likewise, in order to grasp that proposition, I must already know the meaning of the proper name "God," which will have been available to me *prior* to the revelation. Hence belief in God cannot be innate, for (as I argued in chapter 8) without the scriptures we cannot refer to God, or think about God, or identify any information or revelation as coming *from* God. The proper name "God," just like the proper names "Paul," "Moses," and so on, is semantically dependent on the Biblical texts. The *sensus divinitatis*, if it is to be a sense of *God*, that is, the being who revealed himself to Moses in the Torah, cannot possibly be inborn. Of course, it could be a sense of divinity in general, of some being who is omnipotent, omniscient, and so on, but then, as I argued in the previous chapter, how would that be a sense of *God*?

It follows that if the revelation expressed by "God is speaking to me" is not *itself* the reason for believing in the existence of God, the revelation is not properly basic with respect to my belief in his existence. For example, I might believe because I am convinced of the historical accuracy of the scriptures. When Josh McDowell was asked why he could not refute Christianity, he replied that he was not able to explain away the historical event of the resurrection. The revelation would then merely be that the being whose existence I have already accepted, is now speaking to me. It would not be a *sensus divinatis* in the required sense.[25]

What if a non-believer has a revelation that causes him or her to believe in the existence of God? Assume that he has read the scriptures, or has heard people using the proper name "God," but does not believe that there is a referent for the name, until he hears God saying "I forgive you," and as a direct result, believes that there really is someone speaking to him (and that he is not just hearing things), and that the speaker is the referent of "God." What precisely does he grasp as a result of this revelation? As Stewart Goetz points out, on various occasions his wife says to him "Stewart, I forgive you."[26] He knows that his wife is the referent of "I" because he knows other properties of her that enable him to individuate her. "She has a body which now is the only body two feet in front of my body, two feet to the left of the table which is on my right, etc." But if we hear God say "I forgive you," how do we understand that it is *God* forgiving us? If God is incorporeal, we cannot rely on a description of what God looks like, as with people that we are familiar with. If God has a corporeal voice, how do grasp that it is his voice, given the problem that Samuel, Gideon, and Saul had in the same situation? Goetz correctly points out that a voice in and of itself bears no self-authenticating marks of its owner. I have claimed the same about images: there is no feature of an image, in and of itself, that identifies the person it belongs to. Nor can there be anything specific to a perceptual revelation, such as an image or the sound of an utterance, that individuates the image or sound as belonging to God. Samuel heard God's voice and thought it belonged to Eli. Saul (Acts 9:4) heard a voice saying "Saul, Saul, why do you persecute *me*?" yet had to ask "who are *you*?" The reply came "*I* am Jesus, whom you are persecuting." Mary saw a man, that is, the image of a man, which she took to belong to the gardener. Gideon asked for a sign "that it is really *you* talking to me."

Moreover, this divine sense may explain how a *believer* is rational in believing as she does, or that the *belief* is rational, but it does not mean they are rational in trying to persuade others if, as Kant suggests, the belief lacks the sort of grounds that could be universally communicated.[27] Suppose you are working with a team of historians on the King Arthur narrative. Everyone on the team has access to primary sources on the story, such as manuscripts of varying ages and archeological evidence, and everyone agrees on what this evidence is (although not everyone may interpret the evidence in the same way). However, you claim to have a single piece of documentary evidence that trumps all this, and which conclusively proves the existence of Arthur, but you are unable to let the team see it. Only you have access to the document, but you say you cannot publish it: this is impossible for reasons you won't disclose. Now suppose this document really does exist, and suppose that it *does* provide strong support for the existence of Arthur. Then Plantinga would argue, and we should agree that it is reasonable or rational for *you* to believe in Arthur, where "being rational" is a property of you, or your belief. But this does not mean it is rational for you to try and persuade us on the strength of evidence that you are unable to disclose. The question is not whether *you* are rational, but whether *what you are doing* (arguing, persuading etc.) is rational. By analogy, even if there really is a "sense of the divine," and even if it is rational to believe on the basis of that sense, it is clearly not rational for anyone to try and persuade others merely on the strength of your own conviction, and your own basis for belief. For the basis itself cannot be disclosed. Typically, when someone is clearly utterly convinced of something, but is unable or unwilling to justify their conviction except by appealing to the conviction itself, we regard them as deranged. It is not that they are deranged for having the conviction, but rather, for the belief that they can somehow transmit or communicate or share the conviction to others, *qua* conviction. Nor, in such an event, is it rational for other people to believe on the strength of the conviction alone. As Kant notes, even if a judge believes in miracles or in diabolical temptation, he must ignore the accused man who pleads temptation, for he cannot summon the devil and have the two confront each other: "he can make absolutely *nothing rational* out of the case."[28]

You may object that hearing the voice of God is a form of sense perception, and that may that God could be revealed to us in such a way that his identity could be *signified* to us. Spinoza mentions a belief among some Jews that the words of the Ten Commandments were not *spoken* by God, that the Israelites merely heard inarticulate noises, and that the meaning was communicated directly to them, without the mediation of spoken language.[29] This would explain why the words of the Ten Commandments in Exodus differ from those in Deuteronomy.[30] The Commandments were therefore communicated by a form of telepathy. Likewise, the medieval philosophers, following Aristotle, believed that whereas written and spoken language signify objects by convention, and so differ between people, mental language is the same for all people, and signifies naturally. The concept of a dog is the same for all people, and naturally represents a dog. Augustine mentions something similar in *De Trinitate* XV, saying that a word that makes a sound outwardly is the sign of a word that gives light inwardly. The real word is inside us, made manifest by physical utterance, just as the Word of God was made flesh in Christ.[31] Alston[32] argues that mystical experiences are objective in the sense that they represent or refer to some objective state of affairs, such as *God being present*. "He fell under no one of my senses, yet my consciousness perceived him." This would be the sort of intimate revelation that Evans has in mind, where we are *en rapport* with a demonstrative referent of a thought. It is not that we have an image of *some* thing, and we think that *this* thing is F, via back reference, but where *"This* is God" signifies directly.

Perhaps such direct revelation is possible. The problem is how anyone could *communicate* this singular conception of God. It is the same problem as faced by Kant's judge. Even if he believes in the devil, he cannot summon him and have him confront the accused. Perhaps you and I have the same singular conception of God. How do we communicate this to *each other*? It is different from where we mutually confront some image. If an angel appears to us both, so I see you next to the angel, I see your gaze upon him, that is, see your eyes staring in that direction, and you see me doing the same. This common perceptual framework allows us to recognize what the other is recognizing. But if we are confronted internally, so that neither of us has the means of perceiving what the other is perceiving, we will be unable to identify. Both of us know that *this* (i.e., the internal referent) is God. But if you tell me "God is speaking to me" I must either take you on trust, or disbelieve you. There is nothing in the signification of "God" beyond its everyday signification, as was argued earlier.[33]

In any case, there is no clear evidence in scripture for such an incommunicable or singular conception of God, given the frequency with which (at least in the Christian and Hebrew Bibles)[34] the protagonists are given *signs* and *wonders*, either to confirm that God is sending the message, or that the message has been correctly understood or received. Gideon asked for a sign "that it is really *you* talking to me." When the people saw the miracle of the 5,000 (John 6:14), they said "Surely this is the Prophet who is to come into the world." Peter said (Acts 2:22) that the divine authority of Jesus was *clearly proved* (ἀποδεδειγμένον) by all the works (δυνάμεσι) and wonders (τέρασι) and signs (σημείοις), which God performed through him. "Sign" translates the Greek *semeion*, or the Hebrew, *owt* meaning "mark" or "token." "Marvel," or "wonder" or "portent" translate the Greek τέρατα and the Hebrew *mopheth*. The English world "miracle" comes from the Latin *miraculum*, namely object of wonder. Signs and wonders go together: a sign cannot be so unless it is evidently a sign, and so logically demands a miraculous or *wondrous* character to distinguish it from what is everyday and mundane. A cause for wonder, because it contrasts with the usual course of things, and so the result of the power of God, as though God is inactive or even powerless when nature follows its usual course. As Spinoza disapprovingly remarks, it is as though there are two powers at work in the world, the power of God, which is a sort of authority, and the power of natural things, which is a sort of impetus.[35] The signs may sometimes be private, as when God spoke to Gideon and Samuel. But they are often public, for example when God appeared to Moses and Aaron, Nadab, and Abihu, and the seventy elders of Israel, who "saw the God of Israel," Exodus 24:10); when the people traveling with Saul heard the sound of Jesus' voice, "speechless," for they heard the sound but did not see anyone (Acts 9:7); when Jesus appears to doubting Thomas and the others through a locked door, showing Thomas the wounds from the crucifixion ("Stop doubting and believe" John 20:27). The purpose of a publicly observable sign is not just to signify to those present, but also to those who are reading about them in the scriptures. John says, "these [signs] are *written* that you may believe that Jesus is the Messiah, the Son of God, and that by believing you may have life in his name."[36]

SUMMARY

The availability of sense perception and the possibility of demonstrative reference is no objection in principle to the thesis that all reference is coreference. Non-demonstrative reference is where the meaning of a singular term is determined wholly by a linguistic context, so that words determine the meaning of words. Demonstrative reference is where the meaning of a singular term is determined by non-linguistic items: by pictures, the sound of a voice, dress, facial appearance, and so on. Such items have a purely *indefinite content*, and in no case is the content determined directly by the *identity* of the object referred to.

Thus, demonstrative reference is not essentially different from reference involving names and definite descriptions and non-demonstrative pronouns. In both cases, singular terms require some narrative background. With propositional reference, the background is given by a text known to both the writer and their audience. With demonstrative reference, by information from visual or auditory images. Reference is not a relation between linguistic items and objects, but rather between linguistic items and *informational items*, which can be words or images. When God manifested himself through an avatar, Abraham could have pointed to the image of the man who approached the tent, and truly said "that is God," just as we can point to the coastline of a country we are approaching by air, and say "that is England." Just as the visible surface is not the whole surface, nor the whole object, why should this man be the whole of God? We may concede that God is revealed by some kind of mental proposition ("He fell under no one of my senses, yet my consciousness perceived him"), but such identification without re-identification is hard to conceptualize, moreover it could not be communicated to others except in the conventional way. The proper name in "God is speaking to me" either has its usual reference, or none at all.

This concludes the main arguments of the book. I began, as Strawson began, with story relative reference. Strawson's purpose was to seek some form of absolute or fixed point of reference—which he found in demonstrative perception—to which the different frames of relative reference could be anchored. I have rejected his conclusion. All reference and identification is relative to a body—indeed a physical body such as a text—of information. Such information can be in an identified or formally cited series of texts, or in a collection of texts by different authors who are aware of each other's work, of the texts their readers are aware of, and who use rules of reference consistent with that textual framework. Verbal discourse follows essentially the same rules, with perceptual information being a framework of signs to assist the written or verbal information.

Although reference appears to involve some form of absolute or fixed point of reference in reality, there is no such fixed point in reality. Reference is therefore an illusion. In the next and final chapter, I shall conclude with a discussion of a similar illusion that has captured the imagination of philosophers: *intentionality*.

NOTES

1. 1 Samuel 3:4.
2. Judges 6:17. *Oddly*, if "you" refers to the person he is addressing in the dialogue. Clearly Gideon means "that it is really *God* talking to me."
3. John 10:27, see also John 10: 3–5: "The gatekeeper opens the gate for him, and the sheep listen to his voice. He calls his own sheep by name and leads them

out. When he has brought out all his own, he goes on ahead of them, and his sheep follow him because they know his voice. But they will never follow a stranger; in fact, they will run away from him because they do not recognize a stranger's voice." Occasionally God speaks through animals. In Numbers 22, God (*Yahweh*) "opened a donkey's mouth," that is, caused the donkey to say "What have I done to you to make you beat me these three times?" (22:28).

4. Quran 10:94.
5. Strawson, *Individuals*, 18.
6. Ibid., 21.
7. Castañeda, "The semiotic profile of indexical (experiential) reference," 285–6.
8. Almost certainly an allusion to Frege: "It is surely clear that when anyone uses the sentence 'all men are mortal' he does not want to say something about some Chief Akpanya, of whom perhaps he has never heard"—review of Husserl's *Philosophie der Arithmetik* in *Zeitschrift für Philosophie und phil. Kritik*, vol. 103 (1894), 313–332, reprinted in Geach and Black *Translations from the Philosophical writings of Gottlob Frege*, 83. See also Frege's review of Schroeder, reprinted in Geach and Black *Translations from the Philosophical Writings of Gottlob Frege*, 105.
9. Evans, *The Varieties of Reference*, 64, my emphasis, see also p. 71. Likewise, Armstrong and Stanley ("Singular thoughts and singular propositions," 205) say that a singular thought is one that is *directly about* an object, such that the thought is "ontologically dependent" on it.
10. Chapter 7 on existence.
11. *Salome* (1923 dir. Charles Bryant).
12. Characters have no sense of embarrassment, because they have no sense of being observed by the camera.
13. *Treatise* I. iii. 2, Selby Bigge, 74.
14. The idea that numerical difference cannot be captured by difference of properties is an old idea. Black ("The identity of indiscernibles," 156) considers a universe that contains nothing but two spheres each made of chemically pure iron, and the same size, temperature, colour, and so on. "Then every quality and relational characteristic of the one would also be a property of the other." Yet they would be *two* spheres, for all that. Scotus (Ordinatio II.d3.n21, Vatican, 399) claims that our senses cannot distinguish this ray of the sun as being numerically different from another ray. Richard Rufus (Bauder, "A thirteenth-century debate on whether individuals have proper names," 23, citing *De ideis* 16, ad q. 1, Erfurt, Bibl. univ., Amploniana, Q.312, f.81va–85ra, 84va/Prague, Archiv Prazskeho Hradu, Ms. 80, fol. 33ra–36vb, 35rb ff) claims that we cannot name individuals because we do not have the ability to truly distinguish them from one another in this life.
15. Kaplan, by contrast, argues that demonstratives are directly referential expressions ("Demonstratives," 512–13). David points to Paul on his right, saying (A) "he lives in New Jersey." Kaplan argues that this cannot mean (B) "The person on David's right (at t) lives in New Jersey," for in the counterfactual circumstance where David is pointing to someone other than Paul, the description in (B) does not denote Paul, whereas the pronoun in (A) refers rigidly to him. Kaplan takes this to support the idea that sentences express Russellian propositions: Platonic, timeless mind-independent

entities that contain items in reality. A simpler explanation is that "he" simply refers back to the (visual) proposition entertained by everyone who can see David and the man next to him: "*someone* is standing to Paul's right." This is antecedent to the anaphor "*he* lives in New Jersey." Since pronouns rigidly designate, the modal proposition "he might have lived in Illinois" refers to the man *actually* standing next to David. By contrast, the proposition "it might have that the man standing next to David was from Illinois" is talking about whoever might, in the counterfactual circumstance, have been standing next to David.

16. As Richard Cartwright notes ("On the logical problems of the Trinity," 198), we can say "that is Descartes" (pointing to a picture), "that is the Sonesta Hotel" (pointing to a reflection in the water), or "that is the Fuller Brush man" (pointing to a foot in the doorway). Evans (*The Varieties of Reference*, 144) cites Moore's remark (Moore, "Some judgements of perception") that someone pointing in the direction of a beach from offshore, saying "this island is uninhabited" would have to be understood as referring to the island of which the beach was a part.

17. Calvin (*Institutes of the Christian Religion*, ed., 1960) Book I, Chapter iii, section 1.

18. But not the ultimate basis, for the tenets of reformed epistemology do not depend on it.

19. *Posterior Analytics*, I. 3, 72b18.

20. Plantinga, *Warranted Christian Belief*, 83.

21. Alston, 1991, chapter 1.

22. Alston, 1991, 13.

23. Plantinga, *Warranted Christian Belief*, 73.

24. For a similar argument see Goetz, "Belief in God is not properly basic."

25. Plantinga says (*Faith and Rationality: Reason and Belief in God*, 82) that it is not belief in God that is properly basic but rather beliefs, such as "God is speaking to me now" and "God has created all of this." But this amounts to belief in God. If I believe that God is speaking to me, then I believe that someone is speaking to me, that is, believe in the existence of someone speaking to me, moreover I believe that this someone is God. This amounts to, or involves, belief in God.

26. Goetz, "Belief in God is not properly basic," 479.

27. A821/B849 "the touchstone whereby we decide whether our holding a thing to be true is conviction (Überzeugung) or mere persuasion (Überredung) is therefore external, namely the possibility of communicating it and of finding it to be valid for all human reason."

28. *Religion within the Boundaries of Mere Reason and Other Writings*, 6:87, see also *Critique*, A821/B849. Kant also argues that there are no markers that can allow us to distinguish between authentic revelation and illusion (*Religion within the Boundaries of Mere Reason and Other Writings*, 6:109, 114), and that no doctrines that come from revelation alone are essential to our religious calling, for if they were not equally accessible to everyone there would be a violation of "ought implies can" (*Religion within the Boundaries of Mere Reason and Other Writings*, 6:103, 154–55).

29. Spinoza, *Theological-Political Treatise*, 2007, ed., 16.

30. For example, Deuteronomy adds, "Remember that you were a servant in the land of Egypt, and that the Lord your God brought you out from there with a mighty hand and by an outstretched arm; therefore your God commanded you to keep the Sabbath day." However, for the most part the differences consist in different words with the same or similar meanings, and that is Spinoza's point.

31. Augustine, *On the Trinity*, 15.11.20.

32. Alston, *Perceiving God*, 13.

33. For the same reason, I reject Castañeda's claim ("Self-consciousness, I-structures, and physiology," 127) that first-person reference is irreducible because it supposedly conveys an encounter or rapport with the referent that a non-indexical cannot convey, and that it is essentially subjective in that it expresses what is private to the speaker's perspective, so that other people cannot get a "cognitive fix" on the very same item in precisely the same way. This is similar to the idea, discussed in Strawson (*Individuals*, 102ff) that when I use "I" it has a reference or meaning for me that it has for no one else. For other people, it refers to my person, an object with certain bodily characteristics, location in space and time, and so on. For me, it refers to the subject of my experience, a "pure individual consciousness." The contents of my consciousness are accessible to me in a form that is not accessible to others, and I am also aware of myself in a way that is privileged and private. Now this may be true, and it is a complex and difficult metaphysical question. But I am not concerned with how we signify things that are inaccessible and that, in the sense intended, are seemingly impossible to signify. I am concerned with the outward and verifiable signs or symbols or other props by means of which we communicate co-reference. When we use the word "I," sometimes we signify co-reference, sometimes difference of reference. In no case is the reference subjective or "private." The silent film intertitle "Drink a little wine with *me*, Salome" is meaningless outside the visual context of Herod leaning forward to Salome and performing the actions of speaking. The purpose of attaching a speech bubble to the picture of a face in a cartoon is to make the reference public. Personal identity, that is, what constitutes one thing or set of things being the same person at a different time, is a difficult question for metaphysics, but I am not concerned with difficult questions of metaphysics, as opposed to simpler questions about how we *signify* personal identity.

34. Only a handful of verses in the Qur'an mention miracles in reference to Muhammad, including the splitting of the moon (Quran 54:2–1), and the assistance given to Muslims at the Battle of Badr (Quran 8:11–18). The Quran insists that its prophet does not work miracles, much for the same reasons as Jesus says "My sheep hear my voice, and I know them, and they follow me." For example 2:118, "Those who do not know say, 'Why does Allah not speak to us or there come to us a sign (āyatun)?' Thus spoke those before them like their words. Their hearts resemble each other. We have shown clearly the signs (l-āyāti) to a people who are certain [in faith]"; 6:37 "And they say, 'Why has a sign (āyatun) not been sent down to him from his Lord?' Say, "Indeed, Allah is Able to send down a sign (āyatan), but most of them do not know.'" See also 10:20, 13:7. For example, the Quran itself is the evidence, and isn't that enough (29:51)?

35. Spinoza complains (*Theological-Political Treatise*, ed., 2007, 84): "we cannot infer from miracles either the essence or the existence, or the providence, of God, but on the contrary that these are far better inferred from the fixed and and immutable order of nature. . . . Since the existence of God is not known of itself, it must necessarily be deduced from concepts whose truth is so firm and unquestionable that no power capable of changing them can exist, or be conceived."

36. On cases where the sign is not given to the prophet, because he is relying on earlier signs given to earlier prophets, or the *fulfillment* of a prophesy, see Spinoza, *Theological-Political Treatise*, ed., 2007, 29: "The prophecy of Jeremiah about the destruction of Jerusalem was confirmed by the prophecies of the other prophets and by the admonitions of the Law, and therefore did not need a sign" (Jer 28:9, "when the word of the prophet comes to pass, the prophet will be known as one whom the Lord has truly sent.") Kant slyly observes (*Religion within the Boundaries of Mere Reason and Other Writings* 6:84) that the introduction of a new and reformed religion (meaning Christianity) can be accompanied and "adorned" by miracles, to announce and provide authority for the end of the previous unreformed one. "For this reason wise governments have always granted that miracles did occur in ancient times, and have even received this opinion among the doctrines of official religion, but have not tolerated new miracles."

Chapter 11

Intentionality

At Innsbruck in the second decade of the seventeenth century, Christoph Scheiner settled a question that had remained undecided for at least a thousand years. He removed the eye of a recently dead ox, carefully cut away the sclera (the white covering) replacing it with translucent material from an eggshell. He placed the eye into a special aperture so that the front of the eye faced the outdoors, and the back was in a dark room. When he looked at the back of the eye, he saw an inverted image of all the objects in the scene outside.[1] He had proved for the first time the existence of the retinal image, and had finally decided the question of whether sight originates in the eye, or in the objects that we see.

Before that, there were two competing and opposite theories of vision. According to the *extramission* theory, sight is a power that originates in the eye, travels in a straight line to meet the object of sight, and takes on the form of the object, enabling us to see it at that instant. It was originally suggested by the Greek philosopher Empedocles, who suggested our eyes are like lanterns, blazing with a fire bestowed by the goddess Aphrodite, and the optics of Euclid and Ptolemy are based upon it. The Arab philosopher Al-Kindi (801–873) defended it in a popular textbook that influenced the theory of optics for many centuries in the Islamic world and the Latin West.

According to the *intromission* theory proposed by the Greek atomist Democritus, vision was enabled by images, thin replicas cast off by an object that strike the eye and cause us to see the object. The Persian philosopher Avicenna (980–1037) and his near-contemporary Al-Hazen (965–1040) argued cogently for the intromission theory, but Al-Kindi's theory proved more influential upon generations of Islamic scholars,[2] as well as later writers in the West. Roger Bacon and John Pecham argued for an amalgam of both theories, contending that rays issue from the eyes *and* from objects. It was not until 1604 that Johannes Kepler gave the correct explanation of how an image is formed on the retinal surface.[3] Scheiner's experiment with the ox eye was a neat practical demonstration of Kepler's theory. A few years later, Descartes made the theory the basis of practically his whole philosophy.

This story illustrates how scientific progress is often not so much about ideas that no one had thought of before, but rather about challenging old and deeply rooted ideas, moreover ideas that while wrong, are perfectly natural. Natural explanations of the world include the rising of the sun, the stationarity of the earth, the flatness and uprightness of the earth, the continuous nature of matter. They are natural because they are obvious, and they describe exactly how the world appears. The extramission theory is like that. Our visual field is mostly a blur, except for a small area in the middle, whose focus we can move to distant objects or near ones, with the effort of our eye. You are continually moving this focus as you read this very page. Al-Kindi argued that God made the eye spherical and mobile in order to move about and select the object to which it sends its ray. John Donne spoke of "The *light* that shines *comes* from thine eyes":

Our eye-beams twisted, and did thread
Our eyes upon one double string;
So to'intergraft our hands, as yet
Was all the means to make us one,
And pictures in our eyes to get
Was all our propagation.

The extramission theory captures perfectly how vision seems to be.

Eyebeams lingered in the folk consciousness long after Scheiner and Descartes. Winer showed quite recently[4] that many children and even adults believe in extramission, and argues that the illusion is a deeply ingrained misconception. It resists educational efforts: even college students who have been taught about the process of vision cannot overcome it. "Correct ideas about the process of vision can seemingly coexist with incorrect ones, *and the contradiction is not noticed.*" Biochemist and science historian Rupert Sheldrake has even constructed a purportedly *scientific* theory around it.

> The sense of being stared at implies that looking at a person or animal can affect that person or animal at a distance. An influence seems to pass from the observer to the observed. The sense of being stared at does not seem to fit in with theories that locate all perceptual activity inside the head. It seems more compatible with theories of vision that involve both inward and outward movements of influence.[5]

He concludes that the sense of being stared at "depends on perceptual fields that link the perceiver to that which is perceived. These fields are rooted in the brain, but extend far beyond it," and he suggests that these fields may be implied by quantum theory. Four hundred years after Scheiner's experiment, extramission has a powerful hold on our imagination.

INTENTIONALITY

I conclude this book with a discussion of a similar illusion that has captured the imagination of philosophers for at least a hundred years: *intentionality*,[6] sometimes called object-dependence, a supposed unmediated relationship between thought and reality, the cognitive correlate of the visual ray or eyebeam, which meets its object in external reality. The modern conception of intentionality was first suggested by Brentano in 1874:

> Every mental phenomenon is characterized by what the Scholastics of the Middle Ages called the intentional (or mental) inexistence of an object and what we might call, though not wholly unambiguously, reference to a content, direction toward an object (which is not to be understood here as meaning a thing [*Realität*]), or immanent objectivity. Every mental phenomenon includes something as object within itself, although they do not all do so in the same way. In presentation something is presented, in judgment something is affirmed or denied, in love loved, in hate hated, in desire desired and so on.[7]

He added that the characteristic of every mental activity is reference to *something* as an object, and that, in this respect, "every mental activity seems to be *something relational*."[8] This is not an accurate representation of the thought of the medieval scholastics, who spoke of *esse intentionale*, mental being, but not *inesse intentionale*. Nor is entirely clear what Brentano was talking about.[9] Why is the object of a mental phenomenon not a thing or a reality (*Realität*) even though it is an *object*? What is this object? Does it exist in the mind, or somewhere else?

There are many forms of Brentano's intentionality thesis, that is, the thesis that every mental phenomenon has *something* as an object. I have already discussed *direct reference*, the thesis that the *existence* and the *identity* of some thoughts depend on their having some individual as object. But the thesis is not restricted to direct reference. John Searle, no advocate of direct reference, characterizes intentionality as "that property of many mental states and events by which they are *directed at* or *about* or *of* objects and states of affairs in the world" (my emphasis).[10] Barry Smith characterizes it as a relation "linking subjects *to* objects in the world."[11] It seems like an extra-mental relation because it is natural to think of it as such. The proposition "a thinks about b" is of the same form as "a speaks to b," so it seems natural that it should have the same logical properties. Yet the relation, if such, is problematic. As Prior puts it,[12] the problem is that we have (a) X's thinking of Y cannot be a relation between X and Y when Y does not exist, yet (b) X's thinking of Y is the *same sort of thing* whether Y exists or not. "Something [either (a) or (b)] has to be given up here; what will it be?"

The relational hypothesis is an old and deeply rooted idea for the same reason as the folk belief that eyebeams are emitted from the eye, that the universe rotates around the earth, that the earth is flat, and so on. I have already argued there is no such *semantic* relation between language and the world (other forms of relation clearly exist), I shall now extend this argument to the relation between *thought* and the world.

THOUGHT

Thought is not belief, for belief is dispositional, that is, taking something to be the case without necessarily actively reflecting on it, whereas thought is occurrent, that is, requiring active reflection or formulation. One can believe in the existence of God or in the irrationality of the square root of 2, without reflecting on these facts at every waking moment. A thought, by contrast, is "at the forefront" of one's mind, something we have at a particular time, and is in some sense like an event in that it has a beginning and an end, at least if it is very complex. Many philosophers have characterized it as a form of inner speech,[13] including the scholastic philosophers who, following Aristotle, imagined there could be mental propositions, as well as the spoken and written propositions, which we use to express the mental ones. Aristotle speaks of affections (παθήματα) in the soul (ἐν τῇ ψυχῇ), New Testament Greek uses the term διαλογισμός, meaning calculation, consideration, speculation ("out of the heart of men proceed evil *thoughts*," Mark 7:21), or ἐνθύμησις ("Jesus, knowing their *thoughts*," Matt. 9:4). It is sometimes compared to a sort of speech in the heart. Anselm quotes Psalm 14:1 "the fool hath said in his heart, there is no God" (*dixit insipiens in corde suo non est deus*), see also Matt. 9:4, and so on.[14] For such reasons, it has been characterized as private and inaccessible.

Yet there is a sense of "thought" that is not private at all, and is accessible to everyone. The word which Aristotle uses for the sense of both an individual term and a proposition composed from such terms[15] is νόημα, which Boethius and the scholastics translate as *intellectus* or "understanding," a Latin word also used for the meaning, sense, or signification of a word. Some verbs may have different meanings (*intellectus*) says Quintilian (*Institutio Oratoria* 7,

9, 2).[16] When we disagree with the thoughts, views, or opinions expressed by other people, we surely disagree with what they are saying, for we rarely know what they are *thinking*. "The view from Brussels" is not about the view of any single individual, but rather the content of some official pronouncement. "The opinions expressed in this article are those of the authors" is a common disclaimer of legal liability, that is, liability for what is stated or expressed, rather than anything that might have been in the authors' minds, hardly a matter for litigation. We talk of a "balanced yet sincere view," yet there can be no *insincerely* held views, only the expression of views which are *not* held by the person expressing them. When we reject the "notion" or "idea" that the Forms lie outside the intellect, we are not usually rejecting what some philosopher was thinking in his mind or heart, but rather the corresponding doctrine that has been expressed many times in speech or writing. Frege points out[17] that if the thought corresponding to the statement of the Pythagorean theorem differs from person to person, then we should not say "the Pythagorean theorem" but "my Pythagorean theorem," "his Pythagorean theorem," and so on. If every thought is peculiar to a particular person, belonging only to the content of his heart or mind, there would be no body of science or knowledge that is common to all of us. He suggests that thoughts are a kind of third realm of things which are like ideas in that they cannot be perceived by sense, but akin to objects in that they do not belong to the contents of the consciousness of some bearer. Thus, thinking is the "apprehension" of thought, as if it were the perception of something objective and eternal, momentarily revealed to the subject. Similarly judgment is the acknowledgment of the truth of the thought, and assertion the manifestation or expression of that judgment.[18]

Frege's conception of a third realm of things, separate from ideas and objects, is implausible, yet we can easily make sense of such "public" thoughts through the supposition that a meaning or sense is a formal property of inscriptions, just like being an instance of the letter "a," or being square shaped or circular, but a relational rather than monadic property. "Moses" has no meaning on its own: Bosanquet suggests[19] that in unfamiliar material such as an ancient chronicle (or a genealogical table), we might identify the unknown possessor of a name without being sure what he, she or it might be. In this sense, the name is merely particular, that is, indefinite. To acquire meaning, a name must have a context. The tokens of the name "Omri" in the different fragments of the Mesha stele only acquire a meaning when the pieces have been cemented together. Meaning is a *formal* property of *physical* objects. Imagine the numbered pages scattered to the winds, in which case the meaning disappears, then collected and collated in the correct ordering, whereupon the meaning returns. *Pace* Frege, meaning or thought is not some Platonic entity existing in some third realm.[20]

Chapter 11

MENTAL STATES

We do not have to be too concerned about unexpressed thoughts if they remain unexpressed, as we will likely never know what they were. Suppose a person expresses the thought that snow is white, by uttering "snow is white." Under what conditions do we say that this is the verbal expression of a thought, which had been entertained at some previous time? We will never know, but we can assume that if that person has the unexpressed thought (e.g.) that Moses led the Israelites out of Egypt, then he or she is entertaining the thought that *would* be expressed by uttering the English sentence "Moses led the Israelites out of Egypt." Note the "would." There is no requirement that the person actually understand English, only that if he did understand English, and if he expressed the thought, *that* is what he would say.

On this assumption, the question of whether we are expressing a thought about *Moses* has an easy answer in our resolution of Kripke's puzzle.[21] For you to express the thought that Moses led the Israelites out of Egypt is simply for you to *state* that Moses led the Israelites out of Egypt, which will be the case so long as the word "Moses" that I am using here co-refers with the word you are using, which will, in turn, be true so long as you and I have identified the appropriate text, or context. Probably the mention of "Old Testament" or "Hebrew Bible" is enough.[22] Of course, you may have someone different in mind, but I argued earlier that this does not matter, just as it does not matter if in uttering "Baal was worshipped by the Christians" you inwardly mean or say to yourself "God the Father was worshipped by the Christians." The inward utterance is irrelevant, for the thought (or view, or opinion) you have expressed is that *Baal*, not God the Father, was worshipped, and so forth. Perhaps you wanted to express a different thought, but your intention is irrelevant, just as "the opinions expressed in this article" refers to what is said in the article itself, rather than anything the authors *really* had in mind.

There are separate questions about the neurological grounding of a thought in a brain state or mental state or whatever. If I entertain a thought without expressing it (or even if I do express it), there may be some event in the brain or the soul—a neurological or psychical basis or grounding—which corresponds to the thought or which is even identical with it. Explaining this would require expert understanding of neurology or brain science or psychology or clairvoyance, which would be very difficult if not impossible. But I do not think such an explanation is necessary to resolve the problem of intentionality, for the problem of explaining how a mental phenomenon, that is, a thought, could include "something as object within itself" has already been unraveled. The problem was to explain how thinking about, say, Asmodeus the demon, who does not exist, could be like thinking about Donald Trump, who clearly does exist. If it can't be a relation in the one case, it can't be a relation in the other, yet the phenomenon seems exactly the same in both cases.

I resolved the problem by arguing that there is no relation in either case. The inference to there being a relation between a name and an extra-mental object is based not on the fact that "John is thinking about Trump" is true, but on the *extraneous* fact that Trump is an existing person. The semantics of "is thinking about" do not require that it express a relation.[23] The "relation" is an illusion generated by the grammatical form of "Jake *has expressed a thought about* Asmodeus" or "Jake *is talking about* Asmodeus" (see chapter 7 on existence). The grammatical form is equivalent to the form of "Jake is touching Asmodeus" or "Jenny is married to Asmodeus," but as I argued in chapter 7, it has a different logical form. "Jake is talking about Asmodeus" implies that Jake is talking about someone, but does not imply that there is someone *such that* Jake is talking about him. The grammatical form is illusory in the same way that extramission is illusory, but while the extramission hypothesis was exploded in the early modern period, the intentionality illusion remains with us.[24]

Could we express a thought about Moses in a possible world where he was never mentioned in the Hebrew Bible, or where God had never given mankind the Bible? No, because propositions including with the name "Moses," or "Abraham" are semantically dependent on the Hebrew Bible, and if the semantics of the terms "God" and "Allah" are the same, then those terms are also semantically dependent on the Hebrew Bible. Propositions in the Quran containing "Allah" and propositions in the Christian Bible containing "God" cannot express what they are intended to express if the *text* they are dependent upon fails to exist. It would be the same as when the Mesha Stele was broken into fragments, and part of the meaning, namely the co-reference between the singular terms, was also lost. Imagine we only possessed a fragment of the final part reading "And *I* took it, for Chemosh restored it in my days," where "I" is meant to co-refer with "Mesha." With no understanding of which text the pronoun co-refers with, there would be no knowledge of what it co-refers with at all. Likewise (if I am right) we could not express a thought about God if scriptures had not come down to us. We could not express a thought, in the sense of "express" that I defined earlier, for the expression itself, the verbal proposition, would not have the required meaning.

Demonstrative reference, such as when we say "this apple"—pointing to the apple to which we wish to refer—also fosters the illusion of object-dependency. You cannot understand which apple I mean unless you see which apple I point to (imagine there are several apples on the table), and so apparently you cannot grasp the thought I have expressed without that apple, as though the thought depended for its existence and identity on the apple, and as though, while our brain sits protected by the cranium, hidden from the world, the power of our thought reaches out to any individual object in the universe we care to think about. As if, when you think about Mont Blanc, the mountain with all its snowfields is in some way trapped in our thought.

INTENTIONAL IDENTITY

The problem of "intentional identity" was first raised by Geach in respect of propositions where we report the thoughts of one or more people, and where *in some sense* they are reported to be thinking about the same object. For example:

> Hob thinks a witch has blighted Bob's mare, and Nob wonders whether she (i.e. the same witch) killed Cob's sow.

As Geach notes, we cannot construe the report as stating *of* some witch, or *of* some person, that Hob thinks that she has blighted some mare, and Nob wonders whether she killed some sow, for this would commit the reporter to the real existence of a witch, and the real identity of the objects of thought. The report could be true even if there were no such person. Nor can we replace the "she" or "the same witch" by a definite description like "the witch who blighted Bob's mare," given that Nob may not have any beliefs about Bob's mare. Perhaps Hob says (to Nob) that there is a witch in the village, without expressing his thought that the witch has blighted Bob's mare. Nob then wonders whether that witch, that is, the witch just mentioned by Hob, is the one the killed the sow. Geach considers and rejects various attempts at solution, concluding that it brings out how much is obscure about simple constructions of ordinary language, and how much ordinary language is less like a formal maze in a gentleman's garden and more like a jungle "whose paths are only kept free if logicians work hard with the machete, and where he who does not hesitate may none the less be lost."[25] The problem of "intentional identity" has generated a considerable literature, without any apparent resolution.

We can approach the problem, first, by considering thoughts that are expressed, on the assumption that a report of what was expressed must accurately report the thoughts themselves. After all, if an utterance really does express a thought, and if we report what was expressed, then we have reported the thought. If Peter expresses his thought by uttering "grass is green," and if he correctly understands what he has uttered, then I correctly report this by saying "Peter has expressed the thought that grass is green." The problem is then how to analyze reports such as the following.

(1) Hob says that a witch has blighted Bob's mare, and that she killed Cob's sow.
(2) Hob says that a witch has blighted Bob's mare, and Nob questions whether she killed Cob's sow.

The first report could be true simply because Hob has uttered the complex predication[26] "a witch has blighted Bob's mare and killed Cob's sow," which we could also report by placing the whole proposition in a "that" clause, thus "Hob says that a witch has blighted Bob's mare and killed Cob's sow." There can be co-reference in indirect as well as direct speech. A complex predication inside a "that" clause is the same as two simple propositions in "that" clauses, with the same predicates, and with tokens that co-refer.

Then, we ask when two tokens in a "that" clause co-refer. For this, we require only the assumption that when a complex predication is in a "that" clause, for example, "that a witch has blighted Bob's mare and killed Cob's sow," then the clause has the same meaning as a clause containing the corresponding conjunction of "that" clauses, that is, "that a witch has blighted Bob's mare, and *that* she has killed Cob's sow." Thus, "that a witch has blighted Bob's mare, and she has killed Cob's sow" is equivalent to "that *a witch* has blighted Bob's mare, and *that* she has killed Cob's sow." It follows that tokens in different "that" clauses can have co-reference, such as "a witch" and "she" just mentioned. Hence, "Hob says that a witch has blighted Bob's mare, and that she killed Cob's sow" is true if Hob utters "a witch has blighted Bob's mare and killed Cob's sow," that is, so long as the co-reference in the *report* corresponds to co-reference in the speech that is *reported*. This will be generally true so long as some discourse exists where there is co-reference, and where it is reported by using the same mechanism. We report anaphora by means of anaphora. Thus, discourse (2) could report a discourse where Hob utters Hob utters "a witch has blighted Bob's mare," and Nob asks "did *she* kill Cob's sow?," for Hob asserts *that* a witch has blighted Bob's mare, and Nob asks if it is true *that* she killed Cob's sow. The "that" clauses have the same subject, corresponding to co-reference in both the assertion and the question.

Note that the co-reference must be signified. Lanier gives the example where Al and Bud share a theory that a witch is in town and is wreaking havoc.[27] They decide to warn the town from separate locations, giving bystanders their planned speech: "There's a witch in town! She's wreaking havoc!" Hob hears Al and Nob hears Bud, but know nothing about Al or Bud before hearing them. They both believe what they hear. Later a person who observes both Hob and Nob muttering about witches speculates "Hob thinks there is a witch in town, and Nob thinks she's wreaking havoc." Lanier argues that the speculation is true, but only because Al and Bud shared their theory beforehand. If they have never met, but happen to say exactly the same thing because Al is delusional and Bud is bored and wants to start a rumor about a witch, Lanier believes that the speculation will be false. This is incorrect. First of all, if a person hears Hob and Nob muttering separately, that is, hears Hob say "There's a witch in town" and Nob say "There's a witch in town wreaking havoc," that is, so that there is nothing in the meaning of the utterances to connect the subjects, then the speculation is unsupported. Nob may be thinking of the same witch, but the expression of his thought has no semantic connection to Hob's expression of his thought. This is true even if Al and Bud have shared their theory about witches. By contrast, even if they have not shared any theory, *and* a person overhears them talking about "the same" witch, then the speculation is correct. For example, if Hob says "There's a witch in town" and Nob adds "*She* is wreaking havoc," then it is correct to report this by saying "Hob says there is a witch in town, and Nob says she's wreaking havoc." And if what they say expresses what they *think*, then it is correct to replace "say" with "think."

The situation is essentially the same as discussed earlier[28] where we have one document mentioning a man called "Ioannes Duns" who was born in Maxton, and another mentioning a man called "Fr. Johannes Dons" who was ordained at Northampton. It would be incorrect to report these documents as saying that a man was born in Maxton and was ordained at Northampton, for they do not *signify* that it was the same man. Even in the unlikely event that the person who wrote the birth certificate also certified the ordination, and was aware of the identity, the identity is neither stated nor signified.

Similar reasoning applies to problem cases such as "A wolf might come through the door. It might eat you."[29] We can resolve this into the two "that" clauses "It might be the case that a wolf comes through the door" and "It might be the case that it eats you," which are, in turn, convertible by "that" elimination and complex predication to "it might be the case that a wolf comes through the door and eats you."[30] Likewise for an example due to Edelberg.[31] Person A kills himself, but detectives Oneski and Twoski think he was murdered. Person B kills himself, but Oneski thinks that that person also murdered A, whereas Twoski disagrees. Therefore, "Twoski thinks someone murdered B, and Oneski thinks he murdered A" is true, but "Oneski thinks someone murdered A, and Twoski thinks he murdered B" is false. Once again, if none of these thoughts is expressed, it is difficult to say what either of them thinks, so their thoughts need to be expressed, that is, we must change every occurrence of "thinks" in the example to "says," and then we have to suppose what was actually *uttered* (as opposed to "stated") in that case. Imagine the following dialogue:

1. Oneski: The person who murdered B also murdered A.
2. Twoski: He murdered B, but he didn't murder A.

So Twoski *said* that someone murdered B, and Oneski said that he murdered A (because Twoski's "he" co-refers with Oneski's "the person who ...." If what they say reflects what they think, then "Twoski thinks someone murdered B, and Oneski thinks he murdered A" is true. And while Oneski said that someone, that is, the murderer of B murdered A, Twoski specifically denied this, and so, assuming once again that they say what they think, "Oneski thinks someone murdered A, and Twoski thinks he murdered B" is false.[32] All such problems about thoughts can be resolved in this way, that is, on the supposition that no *relevant* thoughts can remain unexpressed, and that all *coherent* expression in written or spoken language can resolve questions about co-reference, because that is what coherent expression is meant to do. The problem is intractable only on the supposition of mental states, which somehow target themselves directly, like eyebeams, onto past, present, and future individuals in reality.

SUMMARY

This concludes the book. My purpose has been to develop a theory to answer the question of whether the Jewish, Christian, and Muslim scriptures *pray* to the same God, and hence, on the assumption that praying to is a form of address, whether they *refer* to the same God. I have answered in the affirmative. Even though they may have radically different and conflicting ideas, it is *about* God that Jews, Christians, and Muslims are disagreeing. And they are certainly *praying* to the same God, assuming that prayer is a form of address, and that the person or being addressed is the referent of the name used in so addressing them.

However, I have argued that reference statements have an illusory grammatical form, and that "Aashir is praying to God" should not be taken at face value. Such a statement appears to assert a relation between users of language and the world, but really asserts a relation between a statement and some information source such as the scriptures. If Aashir utters "I seek forgiveness from Allah for all my sins and turn to Him," then for Aashir truly to be praying to Allah, the name "Allah" must refer to Allah. Even if Aashir does not express the prayer in words, the object of his thought must be the same as the referent of the name he would use if he did so express it. In order to refer to Allah, his use of the name, as of any proper name, must relate to the same information source that *I* am relating to when I use the name *here*. Likewise, for Malih's utterance, "Aashir is praying to Allah" to be true, Malih's use of the proper name "Allah" must involve the same information source that Aashir's use co-refers with, namely the Quran. The Quran, in turn, co-refers with the Hebrew Bible, which is the same source that Christians use when the use the name "God" or "The Lord." Likewise, Hannah can truly say "Aashir is praying to *God*" if her use of "God" co-refers with the Hebrew Bible, and Aashir's use co-refers with the Quran. The relation suggested by the grammar of such statements has no more reality than eyebeams.

This does not mean that the information value of a proper name is in any sense subjective, an associated conceptual representation or Fregean sense, which can differ from person to person. The ability to understand a text like the Hebrew Bible presupposes the ability to keep track of which individual is which by assigning the right token of a singular term to the right subject, or "anaphoric chain," a mixture of proper names and other singular terms, requiring knowledge of how discourses are constructed, literary or other conventions, and so on. The ability to understand proper names in ordinary use requires an appropriate narrative, or *virtual* narrative. This is possible because we ourselves are coauthors of a vast multiply-authored narrative, few chapters of which are available to everyone, but having a common thread available to all. We can all refer to Donald Trump because the parts of the narrative which refer to Trump are available to all. We can refer to Moses, or to Charles II, or to D'Artagnan, or to *God* for the same reason. Demonstrative reference may seem to be an exception, and it has seemed to many philosophers to be the archetype of genuine reference. Yet it is not essentially different from propositional reference. Both require some informational background, which for demonstrative reference is the information available from visual or auditory images. Abraham thought he saw *a man* near the great trees of Mamre while he was sitting at the entrance to his tent in the heat of the day. The visual information in itself was indefinite: "*a* man is before me." Later, he realized that *the* man was an avatar of God. The noun phrase "the man" co-refers with "a man."

I have argued for no specific position concerning the existence or non-existence of God, or his nature, or the truth or falsity of any of the three scriptures. I have defended no substantive original thesis in Biblical hermeneutics or theology. My positive thesis has been in the core topics of philosophical logic, that is, of reference, identity, truth, and existence. But this leaves an important question. How do we reconcile "Hands that flung stars into space" with "To cruel nails surrendered"? The "classical" conception of God, namely, as uncaused, uncreated, unchanging, transcendent creator of the universe, and so on, can clearly be arrived at by some process of natural reason, unaided by revelation (except the "revelation" of pure reason), and independently of scriptural authority. Yet, such a conception is a mere indefinite description. I have argued that we cannot understand the name "God" and we cannot have a *singular* conception of God without reference to the Biblical texts. Reason on its own cannot reveal God to us. If God has revealed himself in the world, it is through the scriptures, and if he has spoken to us, it is through his prophets: Πολυμερῶς καὶ πολυτρόπως πάλαι ὁ θεὸς λαλήσας τοῖς πατράσιν ἐν τοῖς προφήταις (Hebrews 1:1).[33]

NOTES

1. Scheiner, *Oculus hoc est: Fundamentum opticum*, Innsbruck, 1619, see also the more well-known description by René Descartes, La Dioptrique, *Discourses on Method, Optics, Geometry, and Meteorology*, trans. P. J. Olscamp (Indianapolis: Bobbs-Merrill, 1965), 93.

2. Among those who explicitly defended the extramission theory were al-Farabi (d. 950), Ubaid Allah ibn Jibril ibn Bakhtyashu (d. 1058), Ibn Hazm (d. 1064), Nasir al-Din al-Tusi (d. 1274), al Qarifi (d. after 1285), and Ahmad ibn Abi Ya'qubi (14C). Another, Salah al-Din ibn Yusuf (fl. 1296), wrote a treatise entitled "The Light of the Eyes," in which he developed the extramission theory of vision at considerable length. See Lindberg, *Theories of Vision from Al-kindi to Kepler*, passim.

3. Kepler, *Ad Vitellionem paralipomena*. For an English translation see Crombie "Kepler: De Modo Visionis."

4. Winer et al., "Fundamentally misunderstanding visual perception."

5. Sheldrake, "The sense of being stared at," 32.

6. *Intentio*: a directing of the mind toward anything, attention. The Latin translates the Arabic words ma'na and ma'qul of philosophers, such as Alfarabi and Avicenna, themselves supposedly translating Aristotle's *noema* at the beginning of *De interpretatione*. See Lagerlund, *Representation and Objects of Thought in Medieval Philosophy*, 11.

7. Brentano, *Psychology from an Empirical Standpoint*, trans. Rancurello, .88.

8. From the Appendix to the 1911 edition of his 1874 book.

9. See e.g. Crane, "Brentano's concept of intentional inexistence," 20 and *passim*.

10. Searle, *Intentionality*, 1.

11. Mulligan and Smith, "A relational theory of the act," 118.

12. Prior, *Objects of Thought*, 130.

13. E.g. Augustine, *De trinitate* 15.10.19 *Formata quippe cogitatio ab ea re quam scimus verbum est quod in corde dicimus, quod nec graecum est nec latinum nec linguae alicuius alterius*. "For the thought formed by the thing that we know, is the word which we speak in the heart: which is neither Greek nor Latin, nor of any other language" (my trans.).

14. See also 1 Cor. 2:11 "For who knows a person's thoughts except their own spirit within them?"

15. Aristotle says, for example (16a13), that nouns and verbs on their own are akin to understanding (νοήματι) without the sort of combination or separation that lead to truth or falsity.

16. C.f. *Latini sermonis intellectum habere*, Gaius, *Institutes of Roman Law*, 3, 93, Poste, 331.

17. Frege, "The thought: A logical inquiry" Geach (trans.), 301.

18. The dispute about whether words signify ideas or things is old. Writing in the late thirteenth century, Scotus (*Ordinatio* I, d. 27, q. 3; ed. Vatican, vol. 6, p. 97, n83) refers to it as a *magna altercatio*. For a background to the medieval dispute, see Buckner and Zupko, 2014, 172:187. The literature on this is vast: Bauder cites Panaccio ("From mental word to mental language"), Perler ("Things in the mind: Fourteenth-century controversies over "Intelligible Species,'" 1996), and Pini ("Signification of names in Duns scotus and some of his contemporaries").

19. Bosanquet, *Logic*, I.209.

20. Bianchi, *On Reference*, 96: "wherever according to standard accounts my utterance of 'Giulia' referred to Giulia because I was somehow thinking of her, I would rather say that I was thinking of Giulia because *when thinking I was tokening an expression of some public language that referred to her*" (my emphasis).

21. Chapter 9.

22. See chapter 4 on citation.

23. For a similar argument, see Sainsbury, *Thinking about Things*, 27–28.

24. For this reason, it will be obvious that I reject accounts such as Crimmins', which has "objects" playing the right part in the causal origin of a "notion," so that "the content of an idea can depend on its external properties, like facts about its origin." ("The prince and the phone booth: Reporting puzzling beliefs," 690).

25. Geach, *Logic Matters*, 153.

26. That is, a conjunction of predicates applied to a single token.

27. Lanier, "Intentional identity and descriptions," 293.

28. Chapter 5.

29. Roberts ("Modal subordination and pronominal anaphora in discourse") calls this "modal subordination."

30. This excludes the exceptional case where the first "might" governs a different possible situation from the second, but it is not at all clear what this would actually mean, so I shall set it aside for now.

31. Edelberg, "A new puzzle about intentional identity."

32. For a resolution on somewhat similar lines, see Slater, "The grammar of the attributes," using Hilbert's epsilon symbol. It is not clear to me that this works, given that the epsilon symbol is essentially an *indefinite*, rather than a definite description, and so cannot have co-reference in the sense I have defended here.

33. "In many places and in many ways God once spoke to [our] fathers through the prophets," my translation.

Bibliography

Abgaryan, G. V. (ed.), *Patmut'iwn Sebēosi*, Yerevan, 1979.
Adkins, Lesley, *Empires of the Plain: Henry Rawlinson and the Lost Languages of Babylon*, London: Harper Collins, 2003.
Ali, Abdullah Yousuf, *The Glorious Qur'an*, translated to English. Wordsworth Editions, 2000.
Ali, Kecia, *The Lives of Muhammad*, Cambridge, MA: Harvard University Press, 2014.
Alston, William P., *Perceiving God: The Epistemology of Religious Experience*, Ithaca, NY: Cornell University Press, 1991.
Altman, Matthew C., *The Palgrave Kant Handbook*, London: Palgrave Macmillan UK, 2017.
Aristotle, *Metaphysics*, trans. Ross, W. D., *Aristotle's Metaphysics*, Oxford: Clarendon Press, 1924.
Armstrong, Joshua and Stanley, Jason, "Singular thoughts and singular propositions," *Philosophical Studies* 154, no. 2 (June 2011), 205–222.
Ashworth, E. J., "Do words signify ideas or things? The scholastic sources of Locke's theory of language E. J. Ashworth," *Journal of the History of Philosophy* 19, no. 3 (July 1981).
Ashworth, E. J., "Can I speak more clearly than I understand? A problem of religious language in Henry of Ghent, Duns Scotus and Ockham," *Historiographia Linguistica* 7 (1980), 29–48.
Ashworth, E. J., "Medieval theories of singular terms," *Stanford Encyclopedia of Philosophy* (October 2015).
Ashworth, E. J., "Singular terms and singular concepts, from Buridan to the early sixteenth century," in *John Buridan and Beyond: Topics in the Language Sciences, 1300–1700*, ed. R.L. Friedman and S. Ebbesen, 121–152, Copenhagen, 2004.
Augustine, *De trinitate*, *Corpus christianorum series latina* tom. L and tom. L-A. Aurelii Augustini opera pars xvi.i. Cura et studio W. J. Mountain auxiliante Fr. Glorie. Turnholt: Brepols, 1968.

Baker, David W. and Arnold, Bill T., (eds.), *The Face of Old Testament Studies: A Survey of Contemporary Approaches*, Leicester: Apollos, 1999.

Baldwin, T., "G.E. Moore and the Cambridge School of Analysis," in *The Oxford Handbook of The History of Analytic Philosophy*, ed. Michael Beaney, 430–450. Oxford: OUP 2005.

Basset, L., "Apollonius between Homeric and Hellenistic Greek: The case of the 'Prepositive Article,'" in *Ancient Scholarship and Grammar*, ed. Stephanos Matthaios, Franco Montanari, Antonios Rengakos, 251–267. De Gruyter, 2011.

Bauder, R., "A thirteenth-century debate on whether individuals have proper names," PhD Thesis, Graduate Department of the Centre for Medieval Studies, University of Toronto 2016.

Beckwith, Francis J., "Philosophical problems with the Mormon concept of God," in *The Mormon Concept of God*, ed. Beckwith and S.E. Parrish (Studies in American religion), 53–80. Edwin Mellen, 1991.

Bentzen, A., *Introduction to the Old Testament, Vol. 1, The Canon of the Old Testament: The Text of the Old Testament: The Forms of the Old Testament Literature*, Copenhagen: GEC Gads Forlag, 1948.

Bianchi, A. (ed.), *On Reference*, Oxford: Oxford University Press, 2015.

Bianchi, A., "Repetition and reference," in Bianchi (ed.), 2015, 93–107.

Blachère, R., *Extraits des principaux géographes arabes du moyen âge*, Paris: Klincksieck, 1957.

Black, Max, "The identity of indiscernibles," *Mind* LXI, no. 242 (April, 1952).

Boethius, *Anicii Manlii Severini Boetii Commentarii in Librum Aristotelis Peri Hermeneias, Pars prior*, recensuit Carolus Meiser, versionem continuam et primam editionem continens. Lipsiae: In aedibus B.G. Teubneri, 1877.

Boethius, *Anicii Manlii Severini Boetii, Commentaria in Librum Aristotelis Peri Hermenias. Pars posterior*, secundam editionem et indices continens. Recensuit Carolus Meiser, Lipsiae: Teubner, 1880.

Bosanquet, *Logic, or, The Morphology of Knowledge*, Oxford: Clarendon Press, 1888.

Bostock, D., "Kripke on identity and necessity," *The Philosophical Quarterly* 27, no. 109 (October 1977), 313–324.

Brandom, R. *Making it Explicit*, Harvard, 1994.

Brentano, F., *Psychology from an Empirical Standpoint*, trans. A.C. Rancurello, D.B. Terrell, and L. McAlister. London: Routledge, 1973, 2nd ed., 1995.

Buckner, E., *Duns Scotus On Time and Existence: The Questions on Aristotle's On Interpretation*, trans. with introduction and commentary by Edward Buckner and Jack Zupko, Washington: Catholic University of America Press, 2014.

Buckner, E., "On the authenticity of Scotus's logical works," in *Maimonides on God and Duns Scotus on Logic and Metaphysics: Volume 12: Proceedings of the Society for Medieval Logic and Metaphysics*. Newcastle: Cambridge Scholars Publishing, 2015.

Burgess, J., "On a derivation of the necessity of identity," *Synthese* 191, no. 7 (2014a), 1567–1585.

Burgess, J., "Madagascar revisited," *Analysis* 74, no. 2 (1 April 2014), 195–201.

Burgess, J., *Saul Kripke: Puzzles and Mysteries*, Cambridge: Polity Press, 2013.
Buridan, J., *The Treatise on Consequences*, trans. with introduction by Peter King, Dordrecht: D. Reidel, 1985.
Burkitt, F.C. *Speculum Religionis: Being Essays and Studies in Religion and Literature from Plato to Von Hügel*, Oxford: Clarendon Press, 1929.
Busse, A., (ed.), *Porphyrii Isagoge, Commentaria in Aristotelem Graeca* IV I, Berlin, 1887.
Callebaut, A., "A propos du Bx. Jean Duns Scot de Littledean: Notes et recherches historiques de 1265 à 1292," *Archivum Franciscanum Historicum* 24 (1931), 305–329.
Calvin, J., *Institutes of the Christian Religion*, ed. J. T. McNeill and trans. and indexed by Ford Lewis Battles, Philadelphia: The Westminster Press, 1960.
Cartwright, R., "On the logical problems of the Trinity," in *Philosophical Essays*, 187–200, Cambridge, MA, London: MIT Press, 1987.
Casey, Robert P., "Clement of Alexandria and the beginnings of Christian platonism," *The Harvard Theological Review* 18, no. 1 (January 1925), 3–101.
Castañeda, Hector-Neri, "The semiotic profile of indexical (experiential) reference," *Synthese* 49, no. 2, (1981), 275–316.
Castañeda, H-N., "Self-consciousness, I-structures, and physiology," in *Philosophy and Psychopathology*, ed. M. Spitzer and B. Maher, 118–145. Berlin: Springer-44 Verlag, 1990.
Chastain, Charles, "Reference and context," in *Language, Mind, and Knowledge: Minnesota Studies in the Philosophy of Science, Volume VII*, 194–269, ed. Keith Gunderson. Minneapolis, 1975.
Chisholm, R. (ed.), *Realism and the Background of Phenomenology*, Illinois: Free Press of Glencoe, 1960.
Christophersen, Paul. *The Articles: A Study of their Theory and Use in English*, Copenhagen: Munksgaard, 1939.
Cook, Edward M., *A Glossary of Targum Onkelos According to Alexander Sperber's Edition*, Leiden; Boston: Brill, 2008.
Crane, T., "Brentano's concept of intentional inexistence," in *The Austrian Contribution to Analytic Philosophy*, ed. Mark Textor, 20–35. London: Routledge 2006.
Crane, T., "The singularity of singular thought," in *Aristotelian Society Supplementary Volume 85*, 21–43. Oxford: Blackwell Publishing, 2011.
Crimmins, M. and Perry, J., "The prince and the phone booth: Reporting puzzling beliefs," *The Journal of Philosophy* 86, no. 12 (Dec., 1989), 685–711.
Crombie, A.C., "Kepler: De Modo Visionis: A translation from the Latin of Ad Vitellionem Paralipomena, V, 2, and related passages on the formation of the retinal image," in *Melanges Alexandre Koyré*, Vol. I, L'Aventure de la Science, ed. I. Bernard Cohen and ReneTaton, 135–172. Paris: Hermann, 1964.
Crombie, Frederick, and Origen, *De Principiis* (trans.), *Nicene Fathers*, Vol. 4, ed. Alexander Roberts, James Donaldson, and A. Cleveland Coxe. Buffalo, NY: Christian Literature Publishing Co., 1885.
Cross, F. M., *Canaanite Myth and Hebrew Epic: Essays in the History of the Religion of Israel*. Cambridge, MA; London: Harvard University Press, 1973.

Cumming, S., "The dilemma of indefinites," in Bianchi (ed.), 335–349.
Cyril of Alexandria, Κατα ανθρωπομορφιτων (*Adversus Anthropomorphitas*) *Patrologia Graeca* 76, 1859, cols. 1066–1132.
Davidson, Herbert, *Moses Maimonides: The Man and His Works*, Oxford: Oxford University Press, 2005.
Davies, B., *Philosophy of Religion: A Guide and Anthology*, Oxford: Oxford University Press, 2000.
Davies, Philip R. and Rogerson, John William, *The Old Testament World*, Westminster: John Knox Press, 2005.
Davis, Craig, *Dating the Old Testament*, New York: RJ Commmunications, 2007.
Descartes, R., *La Dioptrique*, in *Discourses on Method, Optics, Geometry, and Meteorology*, trans. P. J. Olscamp. Indianapolis: Bobbs-Merrill, 1965.
Dever, W., *Did God Have a Wife? Archaeology and Folk Religion in Ancient Israel.* Grand Rapids, MI: Eerdmans 2005.
Dever, W., "An overview of Biblical archaeology—history, aims & methods," presented at Bard College in 2008, https://www.youtube.com/watch?v=jYc3xA0fZxE.
Devitt, Michael, "Against direct reference," *Midwest Studies in Philosophy* XIV (1989), 206–240 (reprinted in *On Sense and Direct Reference: Readings in the Philosophy of Language*, McGraw-Hill, 2007, 462–495).
Devitt, Michael, "Still against direct reference," in *Prospects for Meaning*, ed. Richard Schantz, 61–84. Berlin: Walter de Gruyter, 2012.
Diogenes Laertius, *Lives of Eminent Philosophers*, trans. R.D. Hicks. Heinemann, 1925.
Docherty, Henry, "The Brockie Mss. and Duns Scotus," in *De Doctrina Ioannis Duns Scoti*, 327–360. Rome, 1968.
Donnellan, Keith, "The contingent a priori and rigid designators," *Midwest Studies in Philosophy* 2 (1977), 12–27.
Drazin, I. and Wagner, S.M., *Onkelos on the Torah: Understanding the Bible Text*, Jerusalem; New York: Gefen, 2006.
Durrant, M., *The Logical Status of "God,"* London: Macmillan, 1973.
Edelberg, W. "A new puzzle about intentional identity," *Journal of Philosophical Logic* 15 (1986), 1–25.
Elbourne, P., *Situations and Individuals*, Cambridge: MIT Press, 2005.
Esposito, John L. (ed.), *The Oxford Dictionary of Islam*, Oxford: Oxford University Press, 2003.
Evans, G. "Pronouns, quantifiers, and relative clauses (I),"*Canadian Journal of Philosophy* 7 (1977), 467–536.
Evans, G., *The Varieties of Reference*, Oxford: Oxford University Press, 1982.
Evans, G. and Altham, J. E. J., "The causal theory of names," *Proceedings of the Aristotelian Society, Supplementary Volumes* 47 (1973), 187–225.
Feinberg, B. and Kasrils, R., *Bertrand Russell's America: His Transatlantic Travels and Writings. Volume Two 1945–1970*, Abingdon (England): Routledge, 2013.
Findlay, J.N., *Meinong's Theory of Objects and Values*, Oxford: Oxford University Press, 1933.

Frege, G. "Letter to Jourdain," in *Meaning and Reference*, ed. Moore, Oxford, 1993.
Frege, G. "On sense and reference," originally published as "Über Sinn und Bedeutung," in *Zeitschrift für Philosophie und philosophische Kritik* 100 (1892), 25–50, trans. Geach and Black, 56–78.
Frege, G. "A critical elucidation of some points in E. Schroeder's Vorlesungen Über Die Algebra der Logik," *Archiv fur systematische Philosophie* (1895), 433–456, trans. Geach, in Geach and Black, 86–106.
Frege, G. *Grundgesetze der Arithmetik*, Jena: Verlag Hermann Pohle, Band I/II. Translated by P. Ebert and M. Rossberg (with C. Wright) as *Basic Laws of Arithmetic: Derived using Concept-Script*, Oxford: Oxford University Press, 2013.
Frege, G. (trans. Geach) "The thought: A logical inquiry," *Mind*, New Series 65, no. 259 (Jul., 1956), 289–311.
Frege, G. *Posthumous Writings*, ed. Hans Hermes, Friedrich Kambartel, Friedrich Kaulbach; trans. Peter Long and Roger White, John Wiley & Sons, 1981.
Frege, G. *Philosophical and Mathematical Correspondence*, ed. Gottfried Gabriel, Hans Hermes, Friedrich Kambartel, Christian Thiel, Albert Veraart, Brian McGuinness, and Hans Kaal. Oxford: Blackwell Publishers.
Frege, G. "Letter to Jourdain," in *Meaning and Reference*, ed. Moore. Oxford, 1993.
Gaius, *Institutes of Roman Law*, with a translation and commentary by Edward Poste. Oxford: Clarendon Press, 1904.
Geach, P. and Black, M., *Translations from the Philosophical Writings of Gottlob Frege*, 3rd edition, Oxford, 1980.
Geach, P., *Mental Acts*, London, 1957.
Geach, P., *Reference and Generality*, Ithaca: Cornell University Press, 1962.
Geach, P., "Logical procedures and the identity of expressions," *Ratio* 7, no. 2 (1965), 199–205, reprinted in *Logic Matters* (1972: 110–111).
Geach, P., "Assertion," *Logic Matters*, 254–269, originally published in *Philosophical Review* 74, no. 4 (1965).
Geach, P., "Intentional identity," *The Journal of Philosophy* 64, no. 20 (1967), 627–632, reprinted in *Logic Matters* (1972), 146–152.
Geach, P., "The identity of propositions," *Logic Matters*, 166–174. Oxford: Blackwell, 1972.
Geach, P., *Logic Matters*, Oxford: Blackwell, 1972.
Geach, P., "Back reference," in *Language in Focus: Foundations, Methods and Systems*, ed. Kasher, 25–39. Springer Netherlands, 1975, originally in P. T. Geach, Back-reference. *Philosophia* 5, no. 3 (1975), 193–206.
Genette, G., *Paratexts: Thresholds of Interpretation*, Cambridge: Cambridge University Press, 1997.
Génébrard, Gilbert, *Chronographiæ libri quatuor*, Parisiis: Apud Martinum Iuvenem, 1580.
Ginsburg, C.D., *Introduction of the Massoretico-Critical Edition of the Hebrew Bible*, Trinitarian Bible Society, London 1897.
Giovio, Paolo, *Elogia virorum litteris illustrium*, Venice, 1546.
Glaser, Linda B., "Quran figure Zayd is a literary construct, says scholar," *Cornell Chronicle* (May 27, 2014).

Goetz, S.C., "Belief in God is not properly basic," *Religious Studies* 19, no. 4 (1983), 475–484.
Goswell, G., "The order of the Books in the Hebrew," *The Journal of the Evangelical Theological Society* 51, no. 4 (December 2008), 673–688.
Gracia, Jorge J.E., *A Theory of Textuality: The Logic and Epistemology*, Albany, NY: State University of New York Press, 1995.
Gracia, Jorge J.E., *How Can We Know What God Means? The Interpretation of Revelation*. New York: Palgrave Press, 2001.
Gregory the Great, *Dialogues*, trans. Warner. London: Philip Lee Warner, 1911.
Gregory of Nyssa, *Against Eunomius*, trans. H.A. Wilson, *Nicene and Post-Nicene Fathers*, Second Series, Vol. 5, ed. Philip Schaff and Henry Wace, Buffalo, NY: Christian Literature Publishing Co., 1893.
Guillaume, Alfred, *The Life of Muhammad – A Translation of Ibn Ishaq's Sirat Rasul Allah*. Oxford University Press, 2004.
Hackett, J., *Dictionary of Literary Biography: Medieval Philosophers*. Detroit; London: Gale Research, c1992. (Humanities 1 Reading Room).
Harris, J., *Hermes*, Williams, 1773.
Heusinger, K. von, *Reference and Anaphoric Relations*, Kluwer Academic Publishers, 2000.
Heusinger, K. von, "The reference of indefinites," in Heusinger (ed.), 247–265.
Hobbs, Jerry R., "Resolving pronoun references," *Lingua* 44 (1978), 311–338.
Hoek, Annewies van den, "How Alexandrian was Clement of Alexandria? Reflections on Clement and his Alexandrian background," *Heythrop Journal* 31, no. 2 (1990), 179–194.
Hopkins, Richard R., *How Greek Philosophy Corrupted the Christian Concept of God*, Utah: Horizon, 2009.
Hoyland, Robert G., *Seeing Islam as Others Saw It: A Survey and Evaluation of Christian, Jewish and Zoroastrian Writings on Early Islam*, Princeton: The Darwin Press, 1997.
Hughes, Christopher, *Kripke: Names, Necessity, and Identity*, Oxford: Clarendon, 2004.
Hughes, T. P., *Dictionary of Islam*, London: W.H. Allen, 1895.
Hume, David, *Dialogues concerning Natural Religion*, ed. Richard Popkin, Indianapolis: Hackett, 1980.
Hume, David, *A Treatise of Human Nature*, ed. L.A. Selby Bigge, Oxford: Clarendon, 1888.
Inbody, T., *The Faith of the Christian Church: An Introduction to Theology*, Eerdmans Publishing, 2005.
Jeffery, Arthur, *The Foreign Vocabulary of the Qur'ān*, Leiden: Brill, 1938/2006.
John Duns Scotus, *Contingency and Freedom*, trans. A. Vos Jaczn et al. Dordrecht: Kluwer, 1994.
John Duns Scotus, *Ordinatio II*, Dist. 1–3, ed. C. Balic, C. Barbaric, S. Buselic, B. Hechich, L. Modric, S. Nanni, R. Rosini, S. Ruiz de Loizaga, and C. Saco Alarcón. Città del Vaticano: Typis Polyglottis Vaticanis, 1973.
John Duns Scotus, *Quaestiones super libros Metaphysicorum Aristotelis, Libri VI–IX*, ed. G. Etzkorn, R. Andrews, G. Gál, R. Green, F. Kelly, G. Marcil, T. Noone, and

R. Wood, *Opera Philosophica* 4. St. Bonaventure, NY: The Franciscan Institute Press, 1997.
Johnson, W.E., *Logic*, Part I, Cambridge: Cambridge University Press, 1921.
John of Damascus, *De Haeresibus*, in Migne, *Patrologia Graeca*, vol. 94, 1864, cols. 763–773.
Kant, I., *Religion within the Boundaries of Mere Reason and Other Writings*, trans. and ed. Allen Wood, George Di Giovanni; with an introduction by Robert Merrihew Adams, Cambridge: Cambridge University Press, 1998.
Kaplan, David. "Bob and Carol and Ted and Alice," in *Approaches to Natural Language: Proceedings of the 1970 Stanford Workshop on Grammar and Semantics*, ed. K. J. J. Hintikka, J. M. E. Moravcsik and P. Suppes, 490–518. Dordrecht, 1973.
Kaplan, David, "Dthat," in: *Demonstratives*, ed. P. Yourgrau, 11–33, *Oxford Readings in Philosophy*, New York: Oxford UP, 1990. Originally appeared in P. Cole (ed.), *Syntax and Semantics 9*, 221–243, New York: Academic Press, 1978.
Kaplan, David, "Demonstratives," in *Themes from Kaplan*, ed. J. Almog, J. Perry, and H. Wettstein, 481–504. New York: Oxford University Press, 1977/1989.
Ismail ibn Kathir, *Tafsir Ibn Kathir*, Riyadh: Darussalam, 2003.
Jones, J.M.B., "Ibn Ishaq and al-Waqidi: The dream of 'Atiqa and the Raid to Nakhla in Relation to the Charge of Plagiarism,'" *Bulletin of the School of Oriental and African Studies* 22 (1959), 41–51.
Kenny, A., *A New History of Western Philosophy*, Oxford: Clarendon Press, 2005.
Kepler, J., *Ad Vitellionem paralipomena*, Frankfurt: C. Marnius & Heirs of J. Aubrius, 1604.
King, James, *Moab's Patriarchal Stone: Being an Account of the Moabite Stone, its Story and Teaching*, London: Bickers and Son, 1878.
King, Jeffrey, *The Nature and Structure of Content*, OUP, 2007.
King, Jeffrey C. "Context dependent quantifiers and donkey Anaphora," *Canadian Journal of Philosophy* 34 (Supplement) (2004), 97–127.
King, Jeffrey C., Lewis, Karen S., and King, Jeffrey C., "Anaphora," *The Stanford Encyclopedia of Philosophy*, Summer 2016 Edition.
Klima, Gyula, *Ars Artium: Essays in Philosophical Semantics, Medieval and Modern*, Budapest: Institute of Philosophy, Hungarian Academy of Sciences, 1988.
Klima, Gyula (trans.), *John Buridan: 'Summulae de Dialectica'*, Yale Library of Medieval Philosophy, New Haven-London: Yale University Press, 2001.
Klima, Gyula, *John Buridan*, OUP, 2009.
Klima, Gyula, "The grammar of 'God' and 'Being,'" in *Whose God? Which Tradition?* ed. D.Z. Phillips.
Kohler, K., *The Jewish Encyclopedia*, Vol. I, New York: Funk & Wagnalls Co., 1906.
Kretzmann, N., *William of Sherwood's Introduction to Logic*, trans. (from the edition of Grabmann) by Norman Kretzmann, Minneapolis, MN: University of Minnesota Press, 1966.
Kripke, S., "Identity and necessity," in *Identity and Individuation*, ed. Milton K. Munitz, 135–164. New York University Press, 1971.

Kripke, S., "Speaker's reference and semantic reference," *Midwest Studies in Philosophy* 2, no. 1 (1977), 255–276, also in in French, P. A., Uehling, Jr., T. E. and Wettstein, H. (eds.), *Contemporary Perspectives in the Philosophy of Language*, Minneapolis: University of Minnesota Press, 1979.

Kripke, S., "A puzzle about belief," in *Meaning and Use*, ed. A. Margarita, 239–283. Dordrecht: Reidel, 1979, more recently published in *Philosophical Troubles, Collected Papers* 1, 125–161, Oxford University Press, 2011.

Kripke, S., *Naming and Necessity*, Cambridge: Harvard University Press, 1980.

Künne, W., Newen, A., and Anduschus, M., eds., *Direct Reference, Indexicality, and Propositional Attitudes*, CSLI Publications, 1997.

Lappin, S. and Leass, H. J., *Computational Linguistics* 20 (1994), 535–561.

Lagerlund, H., *Representation and Objects of Thought in Medieval Philosophy*, ed. Henrik Lagerlund, London: Routledge, 2007.

Lanier, W., "Intentional identity and descriptions," *Philosophical Studies* 170, no 2 (September 2014), 289–302.

Lemche, Niels Peter, *Biblical Studies and the Failure of History: Changing Perspectives 3*, Sheffield: Equinox Publishing, 2013.

Lewis, C. I., *A Survey of Symbolic Logic,* Berkeley: University of California Press, 1918.

Lewis, D., "Scorekeeping in a language game," *Journal of Philosophical Logic* 8, no. 1 (1979), 339–359 (reprinted in *Semantics from Different Points of View*, ed. R. Bäuerle, U. Egli and A. von Stechow, 172–187. Berlin: Springer, 1979.

Lindberg, David C., *Theories of Vision from Al-kindi to Kepler*, Chicago: University of Chicago Press, 1996.

Little, A. G., "Chronological notes on the life of Duns Scotus," *English Historical Review* 47 (1932), 568–582.

Little, A. G., *Franciscan Papers, Lists, and Documents*, Manchester University Press, 1943.

Little, Donald P., "Narrative themes and devices in al-Waqidi's Kitab al-maghazi," in *Reason and Inspiration in Islam*, ed. Hermann Landolt and Todd Lawson, 34–45. London: I. B. Tauris, 2005.

Locke, J., *An Essay Concerning Human Understanding,* ed. Pringle Pattison, London, 1924.

Lockwood, M., "On predicating proper names," *The Philosophical Review* 84 (1975), 471–519.

Longeway, John Lee, *Demonstration and Scientific Knowledge in William of Ockham: A Translation of Summa Logicae III–II: De Syllogismo Demonstrativo, and Selections from the Prologue to the Ordinatio*, Notre Dame: University of Notre Dame Press, 2007.

Luxenberg, Christoph, *The Syro-Aramaic Reading of the Koran: A Contribution to the Decoding of the Language of the Koran*, Berlin: H. Schiler, 2007.

McCabe, Herbert, "Creation," *New Blackfriars* 61 (1980).

McDonald, L. and Sanders, J. "The canon debate," *Theological Studies* 65, Part 1 (2004), 181–182.

McDowell, J., *Theaetetus/Plato; Translated [From the Greek] With Notes*, Oxford: Clarendon Press, 1973.

Macler, F., *Histoire d'Héraclius: par l'évêque Sebêos; traduite de l'arménien et annotée par Frédéric Macler*, Paris: Imprimerie Nationale, 1904.
Maimonides, Moses, *The Guide for the Perplexed*, trans. from the Arabic by M. Friedlander, 2nd ed., London: George Routledge & Sons, 1904.
Marcus, Ruth Barcan, "Does the principle of substitutivity rest on a mistake?" in *The Logical Enterprise*, ed. Alan Ross Anderson, Ruth Barcan Marcus, R. M. Martin & Frederic B. Fitch. Yale University Press, 1975.
Marcus, Ruth Barcan, "Identity of individuals in a strict functional Calculus of second order," *Journal of Symbolic Logic* Vol. 12, No. 1 (Mar., 1947), pp. 12–15.
Marcus, Ruth Barcan, "Modalities and intensional languages," *Synthese* 13, no. 4 (1961), 303–322.
Marcus, Ruth Barcan, Quine, W. V., Kripke, Saul, and Føllesdal, Dagfinn, "Discussion on the paper of Ruth B. Marcus," *Synthese* 14 (1962), 132–143.
Meinong, Alexius, "Über Gegenstandstheorie," in *Untersuchung zur Gegenstandstheorie und Psychologie*, Leipzig: Johann Ambrosius Barth, 1904.
Metcalfe, Philip, *Whispering Wires: The Tragic Tale of an American Bootlegger*, Portland: Inkwater Press, 2007.
Mill, J. S., *A System of Logic*, 8th ed., London, 1904.
Mill, J. S., *An Examination of Sir William Hamilton's Philosophy*, 1865, Toronto 1979.
Miller, Barry, "Future individuals and Haecceitism," *Review of Metaphysics* 45 (September 1991), 3–28, esp. 10–11.
Moore, G. E., "Some judgements of perception," *Proceedings of the Aristotelian Society* xix (1918–19), 1–29.
Moore, A.W. (ed.), *Meaning and Reference*, Oxford, 1993.
Mulligan, Kevin and Smith, Barry, "A relational theory of the act," *Topoi* 5, no. 2 (1986), 115–130.
Napoli, E., "Names, indexicals and identity statements," in Künne et al. (eds), 1997, 185–212.
Nash, R., "Was the New Testament influenced by Pagan philosophy?" *Christian Research Journal* 16 (1993) 16–19, 35–38.
Nash, R., *The Gospel and the Greeks: Did the New Testament Borrow from Pagan Thought?* P & R Pub, 2003.
Neale, S., *Descriptions*, London/Cambridge, MA: MIT Press, 1990.
Niketas Byzantios (Niketas of Byzantium), *Confutatio dogmatum Mahomedis*, in Migne, *Patrologia Graeca* 105:670–848.
Nöldeke, Theodor, *Geschichte des Qorâns*, Gottingen, 1860.
Oppy, G., "Salmon on the contingent a priori and the necessary a posteriori," *Philosophical Studies*, 73 (1994), 5–33.
Owen, O. F., *The Organon, or Logical Treatises of Aristotle*, London: Bell and Sons, 1889.
Panaccio, Claude, "From mental word to mental language," *Philosophical Topics* 2, no. 2 1992, 125–147.
Parkes, Malcolm Beckwith, *Their Hands Before Our Eyes: A Closer Look at Scribes: the Lyell Lectures Delivered in the University of Oxford*, 1999, Aldershot: Ashgate, 2008.

Patterson, Paul A., *Visions of Christ: The Anthropomorphite Controversy of 399 CE*, Tübingen: Mohr Siebeck, 2012.
Paulsen, David L. "Early Christian belief in a corporeal deity: Origen and Augustine as reluctant witnesses," *The Harvard Theological Review* 83, no. 2 (April 1990).
Perler, Dominik, "Things in the mind: Fourteenth-century controversies over 'Intelligible Species,'" *Vivarium* 34, no. 2 (1996), 231–253.
Peter Abelard, *Dialectica*, ed. L.M. De Rijk, Assen: Van Gorcum, 1956.
Peters, F. E., *A Reader on Classical Islam*, Princeton: Princeton University Press, 1993.
Peter the Venerable, *Writings Against the Saracens: Peter the Venerable*, trans. Irven M. Resnick, Washington, DC: Catholic University of America Press, 2016.
Pickthall, M., *The Meaning of the Glorious Qur'an*, Hyderabad-Deccan, India: Government Central Press, 1938. Reissued as Al-Quran Al-Karim with English Translation by Pickthall (Islamabad, Pakistan, Islamic Research Institute, 1988).
Pini, Giorgio, "Signification of names in Duns Scotus and some of his contemporaries," *Vivarium* 39, no. 1 (2001), 20–51.
Pini, Giorgio, "Species, concept, and thing: Theories of signification in the second half of the thirteenth century," *Medieval Philosophy and Theology* 8 (1999), 21–52.
Pitcher, L., *Writing Ancient History: An Introduction to Classical Historiography*, London: Palgrave Macmillan, 2009.
Plantinga, Alvin, *The Nature of Necessity*, Oxford: Oxford University Press 1974.
Plantinga, Alvin, "A Boethian compromise," *American Philosophical Quarterly* 15, no. 2 (April 1978), 129–138.
Plantinga, Alvin, *Does God Have a Nature?* Milwaukee, WI: Marquette University Press, 1980.
Plantinga, Alvin and Nicholas Wolterstorff (eds.), *Faith and Rationality: Reason and Belief in God*, Notre Dame: University of Notre Dame Press, 1983.
Plantinga, Alvin, *Warranted Christian Belief*, Oxford: Oxford University Press 2000.
Plotinus, *The Enneads,* trans. Stephen MacKenna, London: Medici Society, 1917–1930.
Powers, David S., *Zayd,* Philadelphia: University of Pennsylvania Press, 2014.
Prior, A. N., *Objects of Thought*, Oxford: Clarendon Press, 1971.
Prior, A. N., *Papers in Logic and Ethics*, London: Duckworth 1976.
Provan, *A Biblical History of Israel*, Iain William Provan, V. Philips Long, Tremper Longman, Westminster: John Knox Press, 2003.
Quine, W. V. O., "Three grades of modal involvement," *Journal of Symbolic Logic* 20, Issue 2 (1955), 168–169.
Quine, Willard van Orman, *Word and Object*, Cambridge, MA: MIT Press, 1960.
Quine, Willard van Orman, *Methods of Logic*, London: Routledge, 1962.
Read, S., "Modality in Medieval Philosophy," (preprint), in *Routledge Handbook of Modality*, ed. Otavio Bueno and Scott Shalkowski. London: Routledge 2018.
Reeve, Michael D. ed., *Epitoma rei militaris*, Oxford: Oxford Medieval Texts, 2004.
Reid, T. *The Works of Thomas Reid*, ed. Hamilton, Edinburgh: Maclachlan and Stewart, 1863.

Reid, T. *A Brief Account of Aristotle's Logic*, in *The Works of Thomas Reid*, 681–707. Bristol, England: Thoemmes Press, 1994.

Rendtorff, Rolf, *The Problem of the Process of Transmission in the Pentateuch*, JSOT, 1990.

Resnick, I. M. (trans.), *Peter the Venerable Writings Against the Saracens*, Washington, DC: The Catholic University of America Press, 2016.

Richard, M., "Direct reference and ascriptions of belief," *Journal of Philosophical Logic* 12, no. 4 (1983), 425–452.

Richard, M., *Context and the Attitudes: Meaning in Context*, Oxford: OUP, 2013.

Rickless, S. "The semantic function of Chained pronouns," *Analysis* 58 (1998), 297–304.

Roberts, C., "Modal subordination and pronominal anaphora in discourse," *Linguistics and Philosophy* 12 (1989), 683–721.

Robinson, T. H., and Oesterley, W.O.E., *A History of Israel,* Oxford: Clarendon Press, 1948.

Runia, David T., *Philo and the Church Fathers: A Collection of Papers*, New York: Brill, 1995.

Ridolfi, Pietro (ed.), *Opera Quae Extant Omnia: vti eorum omnium Elenchus indicabit. Quadragesimale, Seraphin nuncupatum*. Vol. 4 *Sermones Extraordinarii*, Venice, 1591.

Rippin, A., "Syriac in the Qur'ān: Classical Muslim theories," in *The Qur'an in its Historical Context*, ed. G. S. Reynolds, 249–261, London: Routledge, 2008.

Russell, *On Denoting*, in Martinich.

Russell, B., *The Philosophy of Logical Atomism*, ed. J.G. Slater, London: George Allen & Unwin, 1986.

Ryle, G., "The theory of meaning," in *British Philosophy in the Mid-Century*, ed. J. H. Muirhead, 239–264. George Allen and Unwin, 1957.

Saeed, A., *The Qur'an: An Introduction*, London: Routledge, 2008.

Sainsbury, Mark, *Reference without Referents*, Oxford University Press, 2005.

Sainsbury, Mark, *Departing from Frege*, London: Routledge, 2002.

Sainsbury, Mark, "Fregean sense," in *Departing from Frege*, 125–136, London: Routledge, 2002.

Sainsbury, Mark, *Thinking about Things*, Oxford: Oxford University Press, 2018.

Sale, George, Savery, Claude Etienne, and Davenport, Richard Alfred, *The Koran, Commonly Called the Alcoran of Mohammed*, Translated into English Volume 1, London: Thomas Tegg, 1825.

Salmon, N., *Frege's Puzzle,* Cambridge, MA, 1986.

Salmon, N., "How to measure the standard metre," *Proceedings of the Aristotelian Society*, 88 (1987), 193–217.

Salmon, N., "Nonexistence," *Nous* 32 (1998), 277–319.

Salmon, N., "Mythical objects," in *Meaning and truth*, ed. J. Campbell, M. O'Rourke, and D. Shier, 105–123. New York: Seven Bridges Press, 2002.

Salmon, N., "A Millian heir rejects the wages of *Sinn*," in *Content, Cognition, and Communication: Philosophical Papers II*, 3–31, Oxford: Clarendon 2007.

Schantz, Richard, *Prospects for Meaning*, Berlin: Walter de Gruyter, 2012.

Scheiner, C., *Oculus hoc est: Fundamentum opticum*, Innsbruck, 1619.
Schiffer, Stephen, "A problem for a direct-reference theory of belief reports," *Nous* 40, no. 2 (June 2006), 361–368.
Schmitt, F. S. (ed.), "Proslogion," in *S. Anselmi Cantuariensis Archepiscopi opera Omnia*, Vol. 1, 93–122. Edinburgh, 1946.
Schumann, O., *Jesus the Messiah in Muslim Thought*, ISPCK/HMI, 2002.
Searle, John R., "Proper names," *Mind* 67 (1958), 166–173.
Searle, John R., "The logical status of fictional discourse," *New Literary History* 6, no. 2 (Winter, 1975), 319–332.
Searle, John R., *Intentionality: An Essay in the Philosophy of Mind*, Cambridge: Cambridge University Press, 1983.
Sheldrake, R., "The sense of being stared at," *Journal of Consciousness Studies* 12, no. 6 (2005), 32–49.
Siddiqi, Abdul Hamid (trans.), *Sahih Muslim (Al-Musnadu Al-Sahihu bi Naklil Adli)*, I–IV, New Delhi: Kitab Bhavan, 2000.
Silverman, E.K., *From Abraham to America: A History of Jewish Circumcision*, Lanham, MD: Rowman & Littlefield, 2006.
Ska, Jean Louis, *Introduction to Reading the Pentateuch*, Indiana: Eisenbrauns, 2006.
Slater, H., "The grammar of the attributes," in Heusinger, (ed.), 2000, 183–190.
Smith, A. (trans.) *Boethius on Aristotle on Interpretation, 1–3*, London: Duckworth, 2010.
Soames, S., "Why incomplete definite descriptions do not defeat Russell's theory of descriptions," *Teorema* XXIV, no. 3 (2005), 7–30.
Soames, S., "Direct reference, propositional attitudes, and semantic content," *Philosophical Topics* 15, 47–87, reprinted in *Philosophical Essays, Volume 2: The Philosophical Significance of Language*, Essay One, 2009, 33–71.
Sommer, Benjamin D., *The Bodies of God and the World of Ancient Israel*, Cambridge: Cambridge University Press, 2009.
Sommers, Fred, *The Logic of Natural Language*, Oxford: Clarendon, 1982.
Spinoza, B., *Theological-Political Treatise*, trans. Michael Silverthorne, Jonathan Israel, Cambridge: Cambridge University Press, 2007.
Stein, Robert H., "Luke," in *The New American Commentary*, Vol. 24, Nashville: B&H Publishing Group, 1992.
Leo Strauss on Maimonides: The Complete Writings, edited with an introduction by Kenneth Hart Green, Chicago; London: The University of Chicago Press, 2013.
Strawson, P. F., *Individuals*, London: Methuen, 1959.
Strawson, P. F., "On referring," *Mind*, New Series, Vol. 59, No. 235 (July 1950), pp. 320–344, also in *Logico-Linguistic Papers*, London: Methuen, 1971.
Stump, Eleonore, *The God of the Bible and the God of the philosophers*, Milwaukee: Marquette University Press, 2016.
Sudduth, M., *The Reformed Objection to Natural Theology*, London: Routledge, 2009.
Swinburne, R., *The Christian God*, Oxford, 1994.
al-Tabari, Muhammad Ibn Jarir, *Jami 'al-bayan 'an ta'wil al-Qur'an*. Edited by Mahmud Muhammad Shakir. 30 vols. Cairo, 1968.

Tabarroni, A., "The Tenth Thesis in Logic Condemned at Oxford in 1277," in Braakhuis and Kneepkens (eds.), 2003, 339–361.
Tarski, A., "The semantic conception of truth and the foundations of semantics," in *Readings in Philosophical Analysis*, ed. H. Feigl and W. Sellars. New York: Appleton-Century-Crofts, 1949.
Thomson, Robert W., and Howard-Johnston, James (eds.), *The Armenian History Attributed to Sebeos*, Liverpool: Liverpool University Press, 1999.
Vallicella, W. F., *A Paradigm Theory of Existence*, Dordrecht/Boston/London: Kluwer Academic Publishers, 2002.
Van Inwagen, P. V., "Existence, ontological commitment, and fictional entities," in *Existence: Essays in Ontology*, CUP, 2014.
Van Inwagen, Peter Van, "Creatures of fiction," *American Philosophical Quarterly* 14, no. 4 (October, 1977), 299–308.
Vos, Antonie, *The Philosophy of John Duns Scotus*, Edinburgh: Edinburgh University Press, 2006.
Wadding, Luke (ed.), *Opera omnia, quae hucusque reperiri potuerunt*, Lyon, 1639.
Warraq, Ibn, *The Quest for the Historical Muhammad*, Amherst: Prometheus Books, 2000.
Wenham, G.J., "Pondering the Pentateuch: The search for a new paradigm," in Baker et al. 1999, 116–144.
Wettstein, H., "On referents and reference fixing," in Schantz (ed.), 2012, 107–118.
Whybray, R.N., *The Making of the Pentateuch: A Methodological Study*, Sheffield: JSOT, 1987.
Wiggins, David, *Identity and Spatio-Temporal Continuity*, Oxford: Basil Blackwell, 1967.
William of Ockham, *Opera Philosophica* I-*Summa Logicae,* ed. Philotheus Boehner, Gedeon Gál, Stephen Brown, 899 p. St. Bonaventure, NY: Editiones Instituti Franciscani Universitatis S. Bonaventurae, 1974.
Williams, T. (ed.), *The Cambridge Companion to Duns Scotus*, Cambridge: Cambridge University Press, 2003.
Wilson, Neil L. "Substances without substrata," *The Review of Metaphysics* 12, no. 4 (1959), 521–539.
Winer, G. A., Cottrell, J. E., Gregg, V., Fournier, J. S., and Bica, L. A. "Fundamentally misunderstanding visual perception: Adults' beliefs in visual emissions," *American Psychologist* 57 (2002), 417–424.
Wiseman, N. P., *Essays on Various Subjects*, London: Charles Dolman, 1853.
Wittgenstein, L., *Notebooks 1914–1916*, trans. G.E.M. Anscombe. Oxford: Blackwell, 1969.
Wittgenstein, L., *Tractatus Logico-Philosophicus*, 1921, trans. D.F. Pears and B.F. McGuiness. London, 1961.
Wurthwein, E., *Text of the Old Testament*, Oxford: Blackwell, 1957.
Yonge, C. D., *Works of Philo Judaeus,* trans, 1854, reprinted. Peabody, MA: Hendrickson Publishers, 1993.

Index

Adam's sin, 59ff
Alston, William, xviin17, 181, 182, 185, 189nn21, 22, 190n32
ambiguity, 25, 28, 35n16, 64, 67, 80, 89, 122, 125, 161, 169n34; indefinite descriptions, 49; proper names, 19–20, 43, 152; resolution, 14, 23–24, 26, 29, 46, 56n9, 59, 153–58, 179
anthropomorphism. *See* corporealism
Aquinas, Thomas, 66–67, 74n24, 136–37, 139, 143, 147n57, 149, 166, 167, 170n47
Arabic, 15n6, 25, 67, 69–70, 135, 155–56, 166, 205n6
Aramaic, 22, 63, 67, 75nn28, 35, 95n31, 134, 146n12
Aristotle, xviin14, 17n18, 18, 64, 74n20, 122, 124, 128n10, 135, 138, 181, 185; semantics, 5–6, 17n21, 48, 99, 118, 122–23, 126; singular terms, 5, 31, 37; thought, 196, 205nn6, 15; truth, 121, 127n5
Ashworth, Jennifer, xviin15, 147n57
Augustine, 66, 82, 139, 185, 190n31, 205n13

baptism, xiv, 159
Beckwith, Francis, xiii, 145n7, 146n34
belief, xii–xiii, 7, 14, 30, 35n16, 61, 68, 72, 73n9, 93n10, 112n8, 113n10, 133, 140, 145n7, 150ff; folk, 194ff; properly basic, 182ff
Bianchi, Andrea, 99, 112n6, 127n6, 160, 164, 169n29, 206n20
Boethius, 53, 196
Bostock, David, 114n26
Brandom, Robert, ix, 16n16, 17n26
Burgess, John, 106, 112n8, 113n21, 114nn23, 31, 162, 169n35, 170n36

Calvin, John, 181, 182, 189n17; *sensus divinitatis*, 181, 182, 189n17
canon (scriptural), 63, 71, 74n17, 85, 86, 158
Cartwright, Richard, 189n16
Castañeda, Hector-Neri, 172, 175, 188n7, 190n33
Chastain, Charles, ix, 17n26, 20, 22, 34nn2, 3, 49, 52, 57n14
Christ, xi–xii, xiv, 26, 61, 65, 73n7, 77, 86, 136, 145n4, 172, 176–79, 185
common name, 4, 5, 10, 31, 33, 35n13, 52, 122, 168; term, 2, 5, 10
co-reference: across scriptures, 131; causal theory, 159ff; co-reference

thesis, 2, 5, 7–9, 11, 13–14, 19ff, 46, 59–60, 62, 97; identity, 107ff; implied, 81ff; intentionality, 201ff; perception, 175ff; puzzle of belief, 151ff; resolution, 20–23, 28, 35nn6, 8; semantic dependence, 140–41, 144; standard view of proposition, 118, 121, 123, 126
corporealism, 132ff
Crane, Tim, 74n21, 205n9

demonstratives, viii, 14, 27, 36n28, 41, 55, 113n18, 172ff, 199, 204
Descartes, René, 194, 205n1
descriptions, xiii, 26, 31, 121, 131; definite, 14, 17, 19, 23, 27ff, 32, 36, 39, 44, 46, 57n11, 65, 126, 154, 187, 200, 206n32; descriptive sense of, xiv–xv, 52, 53, 93, 173; disguised, 13, 150; of God, 132ff, 149, 164ff, 183; identifying, 81–84, 88–89, 92, 178; in identity statements, 98–99, 105; incomplete, 57n11; indefinite, 11, 27, 29, 40, 41, 42, 50, 51, 102, 111, 161, 204; initial description, 159; nondescription assumption, 3–4, 102
Devitt, Michael, 3, 16n7, 52, 58n32, 102, 112n4, 113n20, 115n36, 168n11
direct reference, xv, 3, 13, 16n7, 33, 47, 58n32, 74n21, 98–100, 106, 113n10, 115n36, 97ff, 168n11, 195
documentary hypothesis, 85, 86ff

epistemic context, 58n29, 106, 112n8, 114n26, 127
Evans, Gareth, 3–4, 16nn9, 10, 17n17, 41, 49–50, 58n20, 74n21, 120, 161–62, 169nn30, 32, 34, 35, 172, 175, 181, 185, 188n9, 189n16
existence, 31, 117ff; asserted *vs.* presupposed, 4–5, 117ff; copula and, 125; existential quantifier and, 124; historical, 7, 32, 50–51, 80, 83, 99, 109, 118, 160, 184; semantic dependency, 52–53

fiction. *See* proper name, empty
Franciscans, 88ff
Frege, Gottlob, xiv, 3–5, 15n4, 16n8, 17nn17, 21, 24, 18n27, 47, 56n8, 83, 95n29, 118, 123, 128n14, 188n8, 197, 206n17

Geach, Peter, ix, 4, 15, 16n11, 34n2, 49–52, 57nn17, 19, 58nn24, 28, 30, 115, 122, 128, 129n19, 188n8, 200, 206n17
God: anthromorphic conception, 132–34; causal conception, 158–64; classical theism, 136; direct conception, 171ff; everyday conception of, 149ff; existence of, 7, 13, 117ff, 138, 140, 182–83, 196; incorporeal conception of, 134; names, 85–86, 87, 131, 164–67; philosophers and, 131ff; reference to, xiv, 2, 5, 8, 9, 15, 47, 66–68, 71–73, 83; semantic conception of, 139–43; *sensus divinatis* and revelation of, 172, 181–86; simplicity of, 137–39; thinking about, 198 and *passim*
Goetz, Stewart, 183, 184, 189nn24, 26
grammar, 21, 48; grammatical form, vii–viii, 9–13, 16n15, 123–26, 129n20, 140, 199, 203–4, 206n32
Greek, xi, 18n31, 22, 32, 35n10, 36n27, 60, 62, 67, 69, 70, 81, 86, 95n31, 118, 132, 135, 145n10, 156, 186, 196, 205n13

Hawkins, Larycia, xi, xiii
Hebrew, xi, xvin1, 35nn10, 11, 63, 67, 69, 70, 75n28, 79, 85, 87, 95n31, 155, 156, 186
Hebrew Bible, 1, 10–12, 15, 29, 33, 36n32, 41, 51, 52, 59ff, 78, 92, 108, 119, 131ff, 155, 161, 162, 185, 198, 199, 204
heresy *vs.* idolatry, xii, 133
hermeneutics, xvi, 25, 46, 66, 72, 134, 204

Heusinger, Klaus, 49, 57n16
Hoyland, Robert, 94n12
Hume, David, 14, 43, 139, 147n49, 173, 177

identifying a text, 59ff, 149ff; Mesha stele, 84, 95n26, 140, 197, 199; physical binding, 62, 86, 153–54; virtual binding, 14, 153ff. *See also* documentary hypothesis
identity, 97ff and *passim*
image: God's, 87, 133, 136, 145; perceived, 173ff; retinal, 193–94, 204; and sense data, 173
individuation, xv, 31, 33, 41, 142, 183, 184
intentionality, 15, 129n19, 168n20, 187, 193ff

Jeffery, Arthur, 67, 70, 155, 168nn14, 15
John of Damascus, xii, xiii, xvin2, 24, 35
Johnson, William, 34n2, 55n3

Kant, Immanuel, 94n23, 142, 184–85, 189n28, 191
Kaplan, David, 99, 112n4, 113n9, 188n15
Kepler, Johannes, 4, 194, 205n3
Kripke, Saul, xiv, 3, 13, 14, 31, 32, 36n30, 37nn33, 39–40, 94n22, 100, 170n39; belief puzzle, 30, 150ff, 198; identity statements, 98, 99, 104ff

Lanier, William, 201–2, 206n27
Latin, 18n31, 22, 35n10, 43, 62, 70, 75n32, 91, 92, 114, 125, 129n19, 166, 186, 196, 205n6
Little, Andrew, 89, 95nn36, 39, 40, 96n52
Locke, John, vii, 10–12, 18n28, 52, 149, 167n1
logical intransivity, 124–26, 174–75

Maimonides, Moses, 20, 66, 67, 74n24, 134–36, 138, 143, 146nn12, 14, 18
Marcus, Ruth Barcan, 13, 104, 110, 113n21, 115nn41, 42, 168n16
Meinong, Alexius, 123, 126
mentioning, 59ff and *passim*
Mill, John S., xiv, 6, 16n5, 17n25, 18, 31–32, 37nn38, 41, 42, 46, 99, 112n3; Millianism. (*See* direct reference)
Mormon belief. *See* corporealism
Moses: baptism, viii, xiv; commentaries on, 66–67; existence of, 7, 31–32, 50–51, 121–22, 140; Imran, 24–25, 46; meaning of name, 9, 19, 20, 23, 26, 29, 44, 69, 105, 152, 158–64, 197–98; in New Testament, 78, 93; in the presence of God, 132, 136; in Quran, 71, 73, 78, 92
Muhammad, 24, 35n15, 69–70, 74n15, 78ff, 94n14, 160, 163, 168n14, 172, 190n34

New Testament, xv, 1, 12, 15, 35n15, 36n32, 40, 60, 61, 62, 64, 65, 67, 69–73, 73n7, 78, 80, 81, 85, 86, 92, 93, 131, 146n25, 156, 196
Niketas Byzantios, xii–xiii, 24, 67–68, 160, 163, 164
Nöldeke, Theodor, 70, 74n14, 75n35

ordinary language, 14, 113, 119, 141, 167, 200
Origen, 136, 145n5

Panaccio, Claude, 206n18
perception, 14, 115, 171ff
Peter Abelard, xv, xviin15, 3
Pini, Giorgio, 206n18
Plantinga, Alvin, 31, 37nn35, 36, 52, 139, 147nn50, 58, 181, 182, 184, 189nn20, 23, 25
Plato, 128n15; Platonism, xvii, 17n21, 133, 135, 138, 146n26, 148, 188, 197
Plotinus, 138

224 Index

Pontius Pilate: limestone inscription, 1, 94n16; New Testament, 24, 67, 78, 80, 81, 93, 153; Philo, 12, 81, 93; reference to, 175; Tacitus, 40
Porphyry, xv, xviin14, 58n35
Prior, Arthur, 16n5, 34n2, 196, 205n12
proper name: anaphoric co-reference, 8–9, 13–14, 19–20, 22, 23ff, 29, 32–33, 34nn2, 3, 48, 72, 84, 89, 126, 162; Aristotelian account, 5, 37; causal theory of, 158ff; dictionaries, 58n36; directly refers, xiv, xv, 3–4, 6–7, 16nn5, 15, 18n18, 32, 117, 168n16; empty, xii, 3–7, 16n10, 19–20, 68, 115, 117ff, 126, 127n3, 144, 160; express no property, 53, 126, 131ff; of God, xvin1, 1, 15n1, 149, 131ff, 183, 187, 203; identity statements, 97ff, 122; Niketas' theory, 68; objective meaning, 204; in Quran, 155; semantic dependency of, 10, 11, 42ff, 49, 118ff, 139, 156–57, 161; sense and reference of, 16n8; singular thought, 31, 47; standard meaning, 150ff
proposition, 3, 30; anaphoric account, 32–33, 120ff; Aristotelian account, 5, 17nn21, 22, 122–23, 126; constituents, 117ff; identity, 98ff; indefinite, 50; mental, 22, 148, 162, 185, 187, 196; Russellian, xvii, 13, 52, 58n31, 173, 188n15; self-evident, 143; semantically dependent, 144; specifying content, 53–54; standard theory of, 4, 47, 118

quantification, 49, 57nn11, 19, 119; domain of, 125; expresses existence, 124; "something," 128n16
Quine, Willard van Orman, 17nn19, 27, 104, 113n21, 124, 129n17
Quran, xv, xvi, 1, 2, 5, 8, 15, 15n2, 24, 25, 30, 35n16, 46, 60ff, 78, 80, 83, 92, 93n9, 131, 137, 143, 144n1, 155–56, 160, 164–65, 170n44, 172, 188n4, 190n34, 199, 204

reference thesis, 8, 9, 12, 13, 45ff, 107, 111, 112, 123, 180
Reid, Thomas, 10, 18n29, 32, 37n42
representation, 39, 101, 113n18, 173–74, 177–78, 185, 204, 205n6
Russell, Bertrand, xiv; and Earl Russell, 154–55, 156, 168n11; Russellian propositions, xviin17, 13, 17n22, 98, 100, 111, 167, 173, 188; theory of descriptions, 44–45, 50, 57n11, 144
Ryle, Gilbert, 112n5

Sainsbury, Mark, ix, 18n30, 47, 51, 56n8, 57n13, 58nn23, 26, 30, 128n16, 206n23
Salmon, Nathan, xiv, 55, 99, 100, 113nn11, 13, 14, 16, 18, 114n22, 147n58
Schiffer, Stephen, 113n10
Scotus, Johannes Duns, 18, 66, 88–91, 95nn35–37, 43, 129n20, 139, 178, 188n14, 206n18; haecceity (thisness), xv, 31, 37
Searle, John, xiv, 34n1, 37n37, 195, 205n10
semantic dependence, 14, 17n26, 121, 140, 141, 143, 144, 148n60, 154, 166, 173, 180, 183; dependency thesis, 10–12, 52ff; object dependence, 127n6, 181, 188, 199
semantic independence, 12, 40, 53, 54, 66, 87, 93, 97, 98, 141–43, 144, 157, 167
sense data, 173, 180, 181
singular: conception, xv, 11, 15, 185, 205; term, xiv, xvii, 2, 4–6, 11–12, 17n19, 20, 32, 40, 42–49, 52, 66, 98, 100, 111, 113nn10, 18, 119, 141, 144, 152, 160, 173, 175, 179, 181, 186, 187, 199, 204
Soames, Scott, 99

Sommer, Benjamin, 132–33, 144n2, 145n8

Sommers, Fred, 9, 34n2, 49, 50, 52, 56n10, 57nn14, 15, 58nn21, 29, 30, 122, 127n3, 128nn9, 11

Spinoza, Benedict, 24, 25, 36nn21, 25, 66, 133, 164, 170n42, 185, 186, 189n29, 190n30, 191nn35, 36

"standard" theory of reference. *See* direct reference

story-relative reference, xv, 14, 26, 34, 39ff, 77, 83, 84, 92, 187

Strawson, Peter, 14, 16n5, 18n32, 34n2, 36nn27, 31, 40, 55, 55n3, 56nn4, 5, 77, 83, 94n25, 142, 147n53, 172, 187, 188n5, 190n33

Swinburne, Richard, 145n11

thought, 4, 6, 10, 15, 16n8, 17nn22, 24, 32, 135, 139; intentional, 115, 124, 125, 164, 195, 196ff, 200ff; singular, 74, 147, 173, 175, 179–81, 185, 188; unexpressed, 198–200

transportability, 11–14, 42ff, 101, 118, 119, 141, 182

the Trinity, xii, 59, 61, 149, 189, 190

truth, 8, 16n8, 150, 151; Aristotle's account of, 126, 127n5, 205n15; contingent, 52, 103–4, 110–11, 114n26, 142–44, 145n7, 147n58; necessary, 97ff; of reference statement (see reference thesis); Tarski, A., 121, 127n5; truth bearer, 13, 17nn21, 22, 99, 148; truth condition, viii, 3, 47–48, 117, 119–21, 128n7, 179

Vallicella, William, viii, xiii, 37n36

Van Inwagen, Peter, 129

Warraq, Ibn, 74

Wellhausen, Julius. *See* documentary hypothesis

Wettstein, Howard, 31, 37n39, 99, 169n22

Wheaton College, xi

Wiggins, David, 108, 109, 115n37

William of Ockham, 114n26, 123, 170n37

Williams, Christopher, vii

About the Author

D. E. Buckner is a graduate of Bristol University, where he later taught philosophy. He has published in the areas of philosophy of language, logic, and medieval philosophy. Earlier publications include (with Jack Zupko) a translation, with commentary, of Duns Scotus's *Questions* on Aristotle's *Peri Hermenias*. Now retired from teaching, he lives with his family in Wandsworth, London. He is curator of the website *The Logic Museum*, a repository of primary sources in logic and metaphysics.

www.ingramcontent.com/pod-product-compliance
Lightning Source LLC
Chambersburg PA
CBHW050902300426
44111CB00010B/1350